The Reconstruction
of Patriotism

The Reconstruction of Patriotism

Education for Civic Consciousness

Morris Janowitz

The University of Chicago Press
Chicago & London

The University of Chicago Press, Chicago 60637
The University of Chicago Press, Ltd., London

© 1983 by The University of Chicago
All rights reserved. Published 1983
Paperback edition 1985
Printed in the United States of America
94 93 92 91 90 89 88 87 86 85   6 5 4 3 2

Library of Congress Cataloging in Publication Data

Janowitz, Morris.
    The reconstruction of patriotism.

    Includes index.
    1. Civics—Study and teaching—United States.
I. Title.
JA88.U6J36   1983   323.6'5'07073   83-14540
ISBN 0-226-39304-6 (cloth)
ISBN 0-226-39305-4 (paperback)

To Charles C. Moskos, Jr.

Contents

Prologue

*Is it oversimplifying? too much to say [...] while A-[...] rights [...] obligation??
emphasize rights
emphasize obligation*

A citizen is a person who owes allegiance to a specific government and is entitled to protection from that government and to the enjoyment of certain rights. It is widely recognized that effective citizenship rests on a rigorous and viable system of civic education which informs the individual of his civic rights and obligations. The long-term trend, however, has been to enhance citizen rights without effective articulation of citizen obligations. To restore a meaningful balance between the two is, in my view, the core issue in citizenship and civic education.

In Western political democracies, especially in the United States, there has emerged in recent decades widespread criticism of organized civic education—public and private. The scope and quality of civic education are matters of deep concern to public leaders, educators, and parents.

The first goal of this study is to explore origins and long-term trends in civic education in the United States. The second is to probe the dilemmas facing contemporary civic education. While my focus is on the United States, the issues discussed are common to all Western political democracies. I share the viewpoint that vastly improved civic education is required if democracies are to function with greater effectiveness.

I contend that there has been a decline in the vitality and clarity of civic education in the United States. It is not my purpose to glorify past achievements, since wide segments of the population were previously excluded from active citizenship. They were relatively untouched as well by organized civic education—public or private. Nevertheless, in the past, civic education operated to strengthen the political system and to deal with crucial problems of "nation building." The United States was born in an armed political revolution, but the American Revolution was more than a military battle; it served as a powerful agency of civic education. It was one of those rare cases of the armed seizure of political power which resulted in strengthening democratic institutions. During the nineteenth century the public school system, in acculturating the continuous flow of European immigrants, operated as a significant institution of civic education appropriate for a society struggling to develop mass citizenship. The Great Depression weakened the system of civic education. Tension and strains of economic collapse undermined social and political consensus. Fragmentation in civic education started to develop during the New Deal and became the norm after 1945.

The main thrust of my analysis is that the decline in civic education after 1945 was fashioned to a considerable extent by "intellectuals" and teachers more concerned with immediate political issues than with an educational format for understanding the long-term trends in the American "experience." The result has been a decline in the vitality of the school system's contribution to the resolution of social and political conflict. Other agencies of civic education too have become fragmented. Indeed, the dilemmas faced by the United States as a political system reflect the well-recognized, fundamental cleavages of occupation, race, sex, and age groupings. The United States must recognize alternative definitions of citizenship that have been created by professional educators of differing persuasion. We need to reconstruct a sense of patriotism—not in the traditional sense of civic citizenship but in a sense relevant for today. There is little reason to feel that a return to old formats of civic education are required, feasible, or desirable. Yet much may be learned by an overview of the more than two hundred years of trial and experimentation.

Citizenship is not a formal and abstract conception. To the contrary, it is an idea loaded with concrete, specific meanings which reflect the changing content of political conflict. The content of citizenship, as evolved since the Greek city-state, is a set of enduring political, economic, and social problems which remain very much alive. In the last fifty years we have witnessed an expansion in the substance and procedure of citizen rights, including an elaboration of ideological justification. On the other hand, clarification of citizen obligations and their implementation have lagged extensively.

Civic education limited to inculcation of traditional patriotism or conventional nationalist ideology is obviously inadequate for an advanced industrial society and a highly interdependent world. I find the words *national* and *patriotic* limiting, and offer the term *civic consciousness*. It refers to positive and meaningful attachments a person develops to the nation-state. Civic consciousness is compatible with and required for both national and international responsibilities and obligations. It involves elements of reason and self-criticism as well as personal commitment. In particular, civic consciousness is the process by which national attachments and obligations are molded into the search for supranational citizenship.

I am concerned in this book especially with developments since the end of World War II, which produced immense proliferation of civic rights and welfare-state benefits. But one must start with an historical perspective which highlights the impact of the American Revolution on the content and meaning of citizenship.

My intellectual approach reflects the traditions of realism in political sociology in which I have been immersed for a lifetime and from which I cannot escape. However, it is not a paradox for a sociological realist to be concerned with humane meanings and political values. Such realists, schooled in philosophical pragmatism, have a long tradition of searching out and emphasizing human efforts—in their various fragile forms—to achieve a higher morality in regulating societal institutions. The political and social construction of the social entity called the "citizen" has clearly been one such profound historic effort. Citizenship remains an idea loaded and overloaded with a variety of humane meanings, a subject of continuous debate and, in turn, endless struggle and conflict. Such conflict attracts the student of sociological realism.

Unfortunately, it is fashionable to equate realism with narrow pursuit of self-interest, especially economic self-interest. The fundamental assumption of this study is that narrow economic self-interest does not account for the positive role citizenship played in the development of democratic political institutions and practices. Citizenship rests on some elements of group obligation.

I do not accept the thesis widely held by university scholars that the second half of the twentieth century represents the triumph in the United States of economic ideology—left, liberal, or right. The argument is that the advent of advanced industrial society has been accompanied by intellectual, moral, and political supremacy of material values. No doubt developers of machine technology and information processing systems have relied extensively on economic analysis. As a result, a materialist conception of society and rational economics dominate much contemporary intellectual inquiry and have deeply penetrated political discourse. Those who hold such a materialistic conception argue that the idea of citizenship, although widely diffused and rhetorically stressed, has lost much if not most of its moral effectiveness as a sociopolitical formula for the self-regulation of a democratic polity. They also urge that the material and economic realities of contemporary society be candidly acknowledged; all other realities are mainly derivative.

It is not from personal perversity or a distaste for hedonistic materialism that I reject this "global" perspective. I do not underestimate the extent to which complex economic calculations have fashioned our daily existence. Economics and economic analysis are indispensable tools of an industrial society, although thoughtful economists have come to emphasize their limitations. Nor does my objection to economic ideology have its origin in old-fashioned philosophical debate on idealism versus materialism. It is simply that I do not believe that materialist modes of thinking inherent in rational economic calculations sufficiently account for the collective problem solving, inadequate though it may be, that takes place in the United States. Economic determinism, though pervasive, fails to explain satisfactorily the perspectives and behavior either of elites or of popular electorates.

I also believe that economic ideology—left, liberal, or right—is incapable of supplying elites and democratic publics with the rationale for the values that men and women should hold. Collective problem solving, in a democratic society with all its inconsistencies and incompleteness, rests on voluntarism, motivated by a sense of moral responsibility for the collective well-being. In other words, the idea of citizenship with a concern for civic obligations, no matter how incomplete and distorted, still helps to maintain democratic polities. The idea of citizenship or its equivalent is still required to explain the dynamics of democratic political institutions.

The elaboration, enlargement, and refinement of material wants in the second half of the twentieth century are impressive, and the present capacity to meet these wants is even more remarkable, by the standards of world history. But the "essence" of "material gains" is hardly to be judged as historically unique. The basic change lies in the immensely increased proportion of the population that can be indulged, if not satisfied. No matter how one defines citizenship, to be a citizen implies that one is an effective consumer, anchored in the economic system. Even the recipient of the kind of social welfare designed to deal with the most deprived persons and families is paid in money and encouraged to behave like a rational consumer.

However, rational economic decisions or the simple and direct pursuit of material advantage invariably involve other values, implicit or explicit. I speak not only of prestige, glory, and vanity but include "higher values" of equality of opportunity, individual freedom, transcendental social forms, and a sense of collective obligation. As a result, I find it misleading and counterproductive to assert that the outcomes of competitive parliamentary systems are "merely" or "in the last analysis" economic or materialistic.

To reject the hegemony of rationalistic economics does not require one to accept without reservation the idea that the political system is dominated by competing myths, myths which seek deviously to legitimate political power. The dissection of political myths is an element in the study of societal change but, like economic analysis, hardly a comprehensive "theory of history."

Civic education cannot be achieved by some ad hoc fusion of economic rationality and political mythology. My approach is to recognize the wide range of competing belief systems in a political democracy. These belief systems are the result of voluntaristic effort or purposive calculation, but the outcome is by no means predetermined. Moreover, old belief systems can be modified and new ones constructed. The idea of citizenship is precisely one of these very important belief systems, still not fully developed.

I want to probe the all too apparent defects of contemporary civic education. The current emphasis on rights as against obligations is pervasive and, at points, grotesque. Yet the strains and conflicts generated do not imply that multiparty political systems are on the threshold of collapse or revolution.

The idea of citizenship continues to reflect consciously formulated belief systems. We are dealing not with a mechanical reflection of social stratification and class but with premeditated efforts by political elites and counterelites to produce societal change.

My assessment of civic education, including its consequences, can be described as "institutional" and historical. Educational institutions have always been thought of as central. But I start my analysis not with the school system but with military institutions and service. The American Revolution and the crucial consequences of that armed struggle on the definition and content of citizenship is the point of departure. A concern with the consequences of military service requires a historical overview of military conscription in the United States, including the current all-volunteer force in "peacetime." The expanded "peacetime" all-volunteer military introduced in June 1973 constituted a completely new development in the United States.

The rise and decline of conscription supplies the context for examining the school—primary, secondary, and collegiate—as an agency of citizen education. In particular, I seek to contrast the period 1890–1940 with that of the post–World War II era. An effort is made to examine experimental work and national service programs, such as the Civilian Conservation Corps and VISTA, as elements in the reconstruction of civic education. The role of the mass media and voluntary associations is taken up at various points in the analysis.

After 1945, social research, using the sample survey, tended to deemphasize the impact of the mass media on civic attitudes and on the meaning of citizenship. My review of this literature indicates that survey methodology failed to capture the extensive role of the mass media. More recent findings, especially since 1970, converge with the outlook and impressions of mass media practitioners, namely that the mass media have powerful cumulative effects, both directly on the audience and indirectly through the mediation of local "opinion leaders."

Since Alexis de Tocqueville, students of citizenship and civic education have stressed the centrality of voluntary associations. The orientation of Alexis de Tocqueville, however, requires reassessment. His perspective, if applied uncritically to the contemporary period, does not identify the conditions under which voluntary associations are disruptive of democratic self-regulation.

The institutional exploration of civic education rests on a discussion of alternative meanings and definitions of citizenship, including related ideas of patriotism, ideology, and civic consciousness. In the first chapter, I will approach this task as well as the closely related one of assessing trends in the relative balance of obligation versus rights of citizenship.

Citizenship and the Institutions of Civic Education

THE SOCIOPOLITICAL CONCEPTION OF CITIZENSHIP

For the purpose of studying civic education, how shall we describe citizenship? Of the wide range of institutions concerned with civic education, on which shall we concentrate?

Laws of citizenship and immigration have developed into an elaborate corpus, based on legislation, judicial decisions, and administrative rulings. Such legal analysis is concerned with formal definitions and procedures for identifying who is a citizen, how to become one, and the benefits a citizen derives. Important as such definitions are, my own analysis makes use of a broad sociopolitical definition of citizenship formulated by political philosophers. In this perspective, the study of citizenship is but an aspect of the political sociology of the democratic nation-state. I seek to trace the long, tortured process of societal transformation by which "subjects" become "citizens."

Citizenship is bound up with political freedom. It implies allegiance of the individual to the larger society, but rests on a particular set of supporting political institutions and values. Citizenship, in this sense, historically and at present, is itself a crucial element of political democracy. (Authoritarian states speak of their citizens, but such usage is irrelevant to the formulations I use.)

There was a time, as late as the end of the nineteenth century, when most human beings thought of themselves, or could be classified, as essentially subjects. Only a small minority could be classified as citizens. Long-term consequences of the age of "democratic revolutions" fundamentally altered this pattern. The impact of World War I accelerated the shift and World War II diffused the concept worldwide. Yet there are nations, highly industrialized ones such as Japan, without effective terms for *citizen* and *citizenship*. Many parts of the world, especially in Muslim regions, have experienced religious upheavals in which the term has little or no currency. Frequently, the shift from subject to citizen has been merely symbolic. Even in nations which stress political citizenship and have extensive common traditions, such as the United States and Great Britain, there are important different realities in citizenship.

For Aristotle, "a citizen is one who permanently shares in the administration of justice and the holding of office."[1] The term *permanently* is essential in principle for his definition of the democratic citizen. However, it is useful to modify his definition to read, "A citizen is one who shares for any period of time in judicial and deliberative office."[2] I shall make use of his definition of a democratic citizen and recognize that elements of citizenship are found in all nation-states, even in the most repressive, totalitarian ones. There is a crucial threshold, however, between democratic and nondemocratic citizenship: democratic citizens, in Aristotle's definition, "permanently" share in the exercise of power. "Citizens, in the common sense of that term, are all who share in the civic life of ruling and being ruled in turn."[3] To be permanently ruled is to be denied citizenship. To rule permanently destroys citizenship for the ruler.

The modern student of politics must determine the minimum requirement for an individual to participate in the process of ruling. What are the criteria for effective electoral participation? Is voting sufficient? If voting is sustained and has important consequences, it in effect contributes greatly to democratic citizenship; but citizenship requires more than voting.

The "classical" definition of citizen rests on the assertion that citizenship involves a balance or fusion between rights and obligations. By rights I mean the legal, political, and socioeconomic prerogatives that the person enjoys because of the collective action of the political system. By civic obligations I mean the contributions and sacrifices a citizen makes to keep the political system effective. Those obligations are designed to prevent or thwart autocratic rule. If a democratic society seeks to manage itself by self-regulation and by the reduction of coercive practices, it requires more precise formulation of and greater implementation of citizen obligation. This involves realistic inquiry into particular social institutions, including those involved in civic education. Are social institutions organized and articulated to make the practice of citizen obligation feasible? In particular, do they operate to help or to hinder the exercise of essential

1. Ernest Barker, *The Politics of Aristotle* (Oxford: At the Clarendon Press, 1946), p. 92.
2. Ibid., p. 92.
3. Ibid., p. 134.

obligations? There is a great deal of rhetoric about citizen obligation but manifest weakness in the institutional base from which such obligation may be implemented.

The rights-oriented conception of citizenship that has gained currency since 1945 can be dramatically seen in the *Oxford English Dictionary* definition of 1961, which describes citizenship as "the position or status of being a citizen, with its rights and privileges."

Legal antecedents of citizenship in the United States can be traced back to the English feudal conceptions of the subject and the gradual, centuries-long transformation into citizen.[4] The idealized notion of the subject was that once a man became a subject—by birth or other basis—he owed personal allegiance to the king and such allegiance was perpetual and immutable. In fact, in the Anglo-American tradition, the struggle against feudal forms and the search for elements of participation occurred repeatedly. In England, by the time of the founding of North American colonies, royal doctrine of the perpetual and immutable subject had been openly challenged and the struggle for greater political consent was long in process.

Political philosophers have been concerned with the rationale—that is, ideology—under which the agitation for rule by political consent is justified. Great stress is placed on the notion of a compact. The struggle to establish citizenship and rule by consent is described by many scholars as having been pursued and justified as a compact between men. It was a volitional contract, which rested on consent and sought to guarantee the perpetuation of political consent.

The theory of government "by contract" is in my view more a metaphor than an accurate account of the emergence of citizenship.[5] It is much too rationalistic and individualistic an account of the historical process which produced the idea of citizenship. Instead, powerful ideas of mutual obligation were at work in fashioning the Anglo-American conception of the democratic citizen. Particular religious doctrines emphasized group responsibility.

In the case of the United States, grim realities of the frontier meant that distinctions faded between those who thought of themselves as royal subjects and those who did not. Operation of colonial government by a strict hierarchical principle had to be tempered by elements of rule by

4. James H. Kittner, *The Development of American Citizenship, 1608–1870* (Chapel Hill, N.C.: University of North Carolina Press, 1970), passim.
5. For example, "All citizenship—and not just that which was created by naturalization or revolutionary election—seemed definable in terms of a legal contract between the individual and the community at large." Ibid., p. 350.

consent. More important, the distinction between subject and alien was weak, since aliens were promised and given the rights of subjects and had equal obligations in collective efforts required for survival. The American Revolution greatly weakened English feudal traditions, requiring a new basis for political allegiance. The common experience of participating in a successful armed struggle contributed to group cohesion, which in time made possible a national state and a de facto definition of who was a citizen.

The United States Constitution does not contain an explicit definition of citizenship, partly to avoid these issues. It was not until the Fourteenth Amendment after the close of the Civil War that a legal and constitutional definition was enunciated. It settled the issue of *who* was a citizen; *what* "citizenship" is requires continued clarification. In simplest language, "all persons born or naturalized in the United States and subject to the jurisdiction thereof, are citizens of the United States and the state wherein they reside." The Civil War no doubt established the principle that citizenship was a national affair and would be managed by the Executive, Congress, and the Supreme Court. More important, if citizenship in the Anglo-American tradition was based on a contract—a contract which itself rested on consent—the Civil War demonstrated that the contract could be enforced by military action in the name of collective obligation.

The incorporation into citizen status of particular minority groups was slow and painful. In 1790, as a result of an act of the first U.S. Congress, only "free white persons" were eligible for citizenship. Exclusionary criteria were gradually eliminated. The Civil War decided that blacks were fully eligible. Only by 1924 did Indians achieve effective citizenship by congressional action, and the issue was not completely settled for orientals until after World War II. For a long period the status of women was ambiguous, and the debate about full citizenship of women is still not resolved. Only in recent years has the age for voting been reduced to eighteen. The expansion of qualification for citizenship has been gradual but relentless.

Thus, the history of citizenship as Aristotle used the term has been the record of increase in the segment of United States society who are citizens. Aside from the massive number of illegal immigrants, U.S. citizenship and its substantive benefits and rights have become almost "universal." The resident alien suffers few limitations compared with the citizen, with the exception of the right and duty to vote. In this sense the United States has become a "mass society." I do not use the term "mass society" as a large-scale impersonal society subject to destructive sociopolitical movements. Instead, mass society is one in which most of the population

? Questionable

participates in the political process and institutions, thereby enabling citizens to have meaningful access to leaders and elites.[6] It is an imperfect mass society, but a mass society nevertheless.

Citizenship in American history has been a powerful and attractive idea for those who did not hold that status. Fortunately, to obtain citizenship in the United States was a simple step. The need to attract immigrants meant easy access to citizenship during the colonial period and through the nineteenth century. The introduction of increased formalities hardly slowed the expansion in the number of "naturalized" citizens.

Furthermore, substantive differences between citizen and alien have decreased. In that sense there has been an erosion in the significance of citizenship. Aliens, although they do not receive the protection of constitutional guarantees which apply only to "citizens," are still protected by those laws which refer to "persons." They therefore receive the protection of the Bill of Rights and the Fourteenth Amendment (due process and equal protection). The courts, especially the Supreme Court, have looked with intense suspicion at any restrictions based on alien status. Restrictions that would limit aliens' ownership of land and natural resources and their access to employment have been struck down. With specific and limited exceptions, application for federal employment is available to aliens. Of special importance has been the limiting of restriction in obtaining welfare benefits. One startling development weakening the distinction between citizen and alien came with the 1982 Supreme Court decision that entitled sons and daughters of illegal immigrants to free public school education. In the nineteenth century, aliens voted extensively, though voting was later limited to citizens.[7] Residence requirements have been curtailed and literacy standards in effect abandoned. In other words, civic education for preparation for the crucial act of citizenship—voting—is not obligatory but a matter of voluntary participation. Of course, there are citizens who believe that voting should be required, or at least that there should be a penalty for not voting.

T. H. Marshall's influential essay "Citizenship and Social Class" is often invoked as a historical overview of the expansion of citizen rights.[8] He asserts, first, that civil rights were institutionalized in the eighteenth century. Then, in the nineteenth century, civil rights supplied the basis for achieving political rights. In turn, in the twentieth century, on the basis

6. See Edward Shils, "The Theory of Mass Society," *Diogenes*, no. 39, 1962. Reprinted in Shils, *Center and Periphery* (Chicago: University of Chicago Press, 1975).

7. Gerald M. Rosberg, "Aliens and Equal Protection: Why Not the Right to Vote?" *Michigan Law Review* 75 (April–May 1977): 1092–1135.

8. References are to the 1977 edition, T. H. Marshall, *Class, Citizenship, and Social Development* (Chicago: University of Chicago Press, 1977).

of the exercise of political rights, social rights were developed.[9] This frequently cited sequence is not the core of Marshall's contribution. The sequence applies most directly to Great Britain; in any case, there are questions about its accuracy. Marshall's central contribution, I would assert, rests in the fact that, already by 1949 when he presented "Citizenship and Social Class" in the form of the Alfred Marshall Lectures at Cambridge University, he explicitly believed that in the industrial arena the balance between rights and obligations had moved too far toward rights. In particular, trade union leaders needed to demonstrate a strong sense of responsibility and obligation to the nation. It was indeed bold for a sociologist oriented toward British socialism to offer such an assessment in 1949 and to imply that a better balance was required for a democratic nation.

Marshall clearly believes that citizenship is a crucial political and moral goal. He argues that the long-term historical extension of citizenship rights has supplied the basis for overcoming or at least tempering the gross injustices of social inequality. "Citizenship is a status bestowed on those who are full members of a community. All who possess the status are equal with respect to rights and duties with which the status is endorsed."[10] For Marshall, the implications of citizenship for social stratification are plain. "The equality implicit in the concept of citizenship, even though limited in content, undermined the inequality of the class system, which was in principle a total inequality."[11]

Marshall offers a list of essential citizen obligations which conforms to the conventional wisdom about civic duties: paying taxes; educating one's family; military service; and "promoting the welfare of the community," which he sees as all too general and vague. But Marshall does not neglect the sense of community. He states explicitly that citizenship requires a "bond" which rests on a "direct sense of community membership based on loyalty to a civilization which is a common possession."[12] Strikingly, his list does not include political participation, either in community voluntary associations or in elections, nor does it include jury duty, which many writers point to as an essential obligation.

9. Marshall uses the following definitions. "The civil element is composed of the rights necessary for individual freedom, liberty of the person, freedom of speech, thought and faith, the right to own property and to conclude valid contract, and the right to justice." For political rights, he states, "By the political element I mean the right to participate in the exercise of political power, as a member of a body invested with political authority or as an elector of the members of such a body." Marshall, *Class*, p. 78.

10. Ibid., p. 93.

11. Ibid., p. 93.

12. Ibid., p. 101.

Instead, Marshall opts for "industrial democracy," a frequent theme of European writers. Increased employee participation in management of the work place and especially an expanded sense of responsibility in trade unions is what Marshall means by industrial democracy. He in effect anticipated forms of codetermination in labor-management relations which contributed, in the period 1960–80, to greater industrial growth and efficiency and lower rates of inflation in Germany and Sweden, but which never matured in Great Britain.

In retrospect, Marshall's four-item list of civic obligations, even if we add his concern with industrial "codetermination," seems incomplete. From the standpoint of the United States, we would add electoral participation, membership in voluntary associations, and jury duty. Thirty years later, we ought to be able to offer a more precisely developed and operational set of civic obligations. Elaboration in law and in popular expectations of rights—economic, social, and political—has been extensive. But it is clear that similar "progress" in the formulation of obligations for an advanced industrial society has not been made either by political leaders or by students of citizenship. The imbalance that Marshall observed has not been corrected but, rather, has increased.

One relevant set of indicators is the attitude of college students toward the relative importance of rights and obligations of citizenship. They will carry the burden of effective citizenship in years ahead and are being exposed to an important agency of civic education—undergraduate social science instruction. With the assistance of colleagues at other colleges and universities, more than 1,500 students were surveyed in 1979. They were mainly undergraduate students with one group of high school students and two groups of military academy cadets. Attitudes to nine rights and nine obligations were probed, yielding results surprising in the degree of imbalance. The four key citizen rights are accorded the greatest importance, higher than that given to any obligation. These four rights are freedom of speech, choice of religion, right to vote, and right to a trial by jury. These traditional rights contained in the Bill of Rights are familiar to most college students. Economic and social rights were rated as less important than traditional political rights. Of special interest was the students' relatively weak support for "codetermination" in the industrial setting (the right to help decide policy in the work place). Students reflected the limited public discussion of industrial relations in the United States and widespread belief that the adversary stance of U.S. industrial relations must be taken as relatively unalterable.

Not only was no civic obligation rated as important as any one of the four traditional political rights, but several obligations were rated as much less important than all other rights. The three citizenship obligations which received the greatest support were the duty to educate one's children to civic responsibility, the duty to vote, and the duty to pay taxes. The conclusion that emerges is that citizenship duties are regarded as less important than citizenship rights. The right to vote is rated higher than the duty to vote; the right to a speedy trial by jury is considered more important than the obligation to serve on a jury. Some anomalies in the survey were difficult to reconcile with democratic self-regulation. Attitudes of military cadets in contrast to civilian students were revealing. On civic obligation, military cadets, unexpectedly, differed only slightly from their civilian counterparts. They were, however, markedly less supportive of rights, especially economic ones.

Unfortunately, there is no systematic data on attitudes toward rights and obligations among political leaders, local grass roots activists, or teachers. The issues tend to be downplayed in survey research studies, although these groups are well aware of their importance.

PATRIOTISM, IDEOLOGY, AND CIVIC CONSCIOUSNESS

The sociopolitical conception of citizenship does not exist in isolation. It takes on fuller meaning by examining three related terms: patriotism, ideology, and civic consciousness. The idea of citizenship has been profoundly influenced by Western nationalist revolutions, particularly the American and French revolutions. The nation-state was offered by the leaders of these revolutions as an appropriate unit for organizing social, economic, and political reform. It is not surprising that citizenship has in the past been bound up with patriotism and nationalist ideology. But nationalism and patriotism have become battered ideas under constant intellectual attack.

Therefore, a third term is introduced: civic consciousness. My interest in this term is multiple. I wish to avoid the negative connotations of patriotism as well as the persistent ambiguities of ideology. I also wish to deal explicitly with the reconstruction of patriotism into a format relevant for citizenship and civic education in today's highly interdependent world. Citizenship, I contend, involves nationalism and patriotism but does not mean xenophobia or militarism. An ideology requires thoroughgoing affirmation and produces comprehensive observance. It offers adherents a compelling code of behavior for most or all life situations. Patriotism, by contrast, is not based on an elaborated or complex system of ideas and symbols. Patriotism is a primordial attachment to a territory and a society—a deeply felt and primitive sentiment of belonging; a sense of identification similar to religious, racial, or ethnic identifications. Of course, patriotism has been historically associated with the ethos of modern national societies. It involves an automatic, almost unthinking response and is in this sense analogous to an ideology. But it offers no detailed code of behavior—rather, a generalized orientation to action.

Both ideology and patriotism as concepts suffer from an overload of polemics and the difficulty of precise meaning. One cannot avoid the issues that these ideas raise. The comprehensive character of an ideology has been the source of much criticism. Ideology also implies rigidity, often viewed with suspicion, and is thus at variance with pragmatic philosophy and with learning by experience, which has been central in the expansion of citizenship. But there is a powerful attraction in ideology because of its emphasis on explicit principles. The principle-mindedness of an advocate with a developed ideology remains a desired component of democratic discourse. One can speculate about an optimum "amount" of ideology in pragmatic and incremental democratic politics. The proper input might be described as a very small number of ideological adherents and a wide diffusion of their ideas, without rigid commitments which would block collective problem solving.

Patriotism, precisely because of its unreflective response, has been subject to intellectual, analytic, and moral criticism. In a period of scientific and technological development, patriotism becomes strained. The attack on ultranationalism has produced considerable popular uneasiness about patriotism. Vocal critics argue that the interdependence of the world community makes nationalism and traditional patriotism outmoded, useless, and even counterproductive. The argument rests on the worldwide diffusion of the weapons of mass destruction, which makes nationalism vestigial at best.

In this view, nuclear weapons ended the relevance of the nation-state, just as the nation-state, in an earlier age, ended the relevance of the city-state. Not only nuclear holocaust but fundamental distortion of human society could result if the nuclear arms race continues uninhibited. Some form of world government would appear to be the alternative if survival of human values is to be achieved. Therefore, conventional notions of citizenship are obsolete; world allegiance needs to be substituted for national patriotism. Only a tiny minority of the electorate adheres to such a view. Nevertheless, this type of thinking has discernibly weakened traditional forms of patriotism.

I reject this "world citizenship" analysis and the confusion it causes in civic education. To reject such analysis does not mean accepting the status quo or failing to recognize the profound transformation of the world arena in the last half century. The world community has become more and more interdependent, and the component "parts" are not effectively integrated. Existing forms of national and international organization suffer from "cultural lag." Social and political values prevent the emergence of more appropriate institutions. However, merely to assert that the nation-state is outmoded is to engage in an oversimplified form of societal evolution. Societal change which produces more complex and more interdependent organizations does not eliminate earlier and more self-contained social forms. Instead, these organizations become more specialized internally as new, more comprehensive ones arise.[13]

This is the case for a wide range of social institutions: the family, the local community, and, in particular, the nation-state. Urbanization and industrialization did not eliminate the family but narrowed its functions and altered its internal relations. The same is true of the local community. Elimination of the residential community, anticipated by some social forecasters, has not taken place with the increased population concentration and new modes of urban transportation. The local community has become more specialized as new and larger units of organization have been superimposed on local institutions. Likewise, the nation-state does not disappear but continues to transform itself.

The growth of world-regional and supranational organizations has been impressive even if their accomplishments have failed to meet expectations. We have created the bare bones for worldwide institutions. Yet the nation-state, in my opinion, remains the essential unit in the search for a more viable world order. The nation-state becomes even more important as specific functions and tasks are transferred to more encompassing institutions.

Implications for citizenship are clear, although the means for attaining them remain depressingly elusive. Each citizen of a democratic polity has a set of rights and obligations to his nation-state. These are paramount. Likewise, each person has a set of international or rather "supranational" rights and obligations, which remain diffuse and unclarified. There is no absolute incompatibility between the rights and obligations of national and of supranational citizenship. In effect, however, particular aspects of national citizenship have to be adapted to the requirements of a highly interdependent world. Yet, national citizenship is not expected to dissolve. Regional integration, developed in the economic institutions of Western Europe, can become crucial. Such developments only serve to specialize the functions of the nation-state and in fact increase its importance in fashioning the political base in the struggle for world order.

Because of extensive economic strains and gross dysfunctions of the nuclear arms race, the world arena is better characterized as "world dis-

13. National patriotism can articulate well with service in an international peace-keeping force. See, especially, Charles C. Moskos, *Peace Soldiers* (Chicago: University of Chicago Press, 1977).

order" than as "world system." But the elements of a rudimentary world community operate. To strengthen it, one must deny in part the Kantian assumption that universal freedom within nations is required. I am prepared to abandon this requirement since I do not expect the world community to be without misery and without war. The goal of national and international citizenship is a world in which the struggle against human misery is carried on with considerable energy—more than present levels of nationalism have engendered. The goal is a world in which war is limited to conventional weapons, and in which even conventional war is subject to persistent international political inhibition. In other words, the deliberate use of nuclear weapons or even the expectation of their inevitable use renders my analysis useless. Realistic world citizenship does not require a military balance based on the elimination of national and regional systems of nuclear weapons. Instead, it requires reasonable bilateral and multilateral accords of mutual controls, which I believe are feasible among existing political systems. Mutual controls must be augmented by effective national and supranational monitoring systems.[14]

Therefore, it becomes necessary throughout this study to ponder the definition and redefinition of nationalism, national ideology, and patriotism in the present day. Is it possible to think of a delicate balance of vigorous national sentiments with ever strengthened supranational civic aspirations? In sociological analysis, the distinction between "locals" and "cosmopolitans" is too often overdrawn and rigidly applied. The United States is not made up exclusively of nationalists (locals) or internationalists (cosmopolitans). Those who think of themselves as internationalists constitute a tiny minority. The bulk of the population is nationalist of varying intensity, although some nationalists have already expanded their sociopolitical space to include in varying degree a supranational perspective. International identifications are not necessarily developed at the expense of more localistic or delimited affiliations.

Nor is patriotism necessarily a barrier to the search for world citizenship. Articulated, self-conscious patriotism can foster a supranational spirit. In the United States, the refashioning of public attitudes has already proceeded to that point where "global" international sentiments are not the only alternative to traditional nationalism and conventional patriotism. Selected elements of the population are expressing an enlightened self-interested nationalism and a self-critical patriotism.

Patriotism and nationalist ideology of the reconstructed variety still require strong emphasis on tradition, though which elements of tradition are relevant may be debated. Many endeavors of a reconstructed civic

14. I am not ignoring the fact that democratic polities should and will be judged by a higher standard of performance in this regard than one-party states.

education are hardly new, but require more pointed articulation with the social structure and existing social institutions. At this point, a fuller definition of civic education and some illustrative propositions about its decline in effectiveness are in order.

The Institutions of Civic Consciousness

The school system is the central agency of civic education. Educational leaders claim that civic education is an ambiguous term, difficult to translate into instructional programs. Richard C. Remy and Mary Jane Turner, two university commentators on the principles of citizenship education, report the remarks of a staff member of the U.S. Senate who, in 1979, complained that "we'd like to draft legislation to promote citizenship education but we can't figure out what it is. Everyone we ask gives us a different definition."[15]

We cannot escape the problem by asserting that civic education is education designed to promote the type of citizen performance which Aristotle sought. Such a definition would be thought of by policymakers and administrators of mass education as a mere formalism without effective content. Instead, we would do well to start with a commonsense substantive definition and to recognize that it is only a first approximation. By civic education we mean (a) exposing students to central and enduring political traditions of the nation, (b) teaching essential knowledge about the organization and operation of contemporary governmental institutions, and (c) fashioning essential identifications and moral sentiments required for performance as effective citizens. Effective civic education would result in increased understanding and meaningful national identifications. It would strengthen civic consciousness.

To cynical critics, such a formulation means that, even in a democratic society, elected officials and government employees are largely concerned with perpetuating the political system and their own power. Such a critique of civic education is essentially useless. Not only are contemporary multiparty regimes worth perpetuating, but I assume that civic education contributes to institution building required to make a democratic polity more effective. The real issue concerning my definition of civic education is whether the use of the term will be relatively narrow or broad. Many practical issues about civic education rest on a difference of viewpoint between narrow and broad perspectives.

15. Richard C. Remy and Mary Jane Turner, "Basic Citizenship Competencies, Guidelines for Educators, Policymakers, and Citizens," *Quarterly Report, Mershon Center*, Ohio State University, 5 (Autumn 1979): 1.

A pointed debate about civic education has emerged since the 1930s. Considerable energy is expended in this debate, detracting from the actual performance of civic education.

In its narrow form, civic education focuses mainly on the relations of the student to central agencies of government. It draws on a broad basis of knowledge and background about governmental systems, and is concerned with the citizen's relations to political parties and central agencies of government. This kind of civic education is carried out by means of the school and selected voluntary associations concerned with national and patriotic meanings. Its methods are pedagogical and instructional, with the classroom as the learning center. Most educational leaders concerned with civic education prefer the narrow approach, for it makes civic education a distinct, structured part of the curriculum and a manageable task. Civic education becomes at least something that can be identified and taught.

Support for civic education of a wider sort rests with university professors. Interested in broad ends and means, they believe that civic education cannot be limited to the study of political institutions. The goals of civic education involve an overview of fundamental values, practices, and interpersonal relations in a democratic society. A democratic society rests on civility. Civility must be studied as it operates, or as it fails to operate, in the society as a whole. Teachers who hold this broad view of civic education argue that the classroom, even the school itself, is much too narrow a base; civic education requires the teacher not only to make use of the educational resources of the system but also to expose students to youth groups and community associations in the outside world.

It is easy to anticipate controversy between these two approaches. Adherents to the narrow approach see a broad strategy as vague and unstructured—not as civic education but as a subtle form of political indoctrination and agitation. Advocates of the broad approach, on the other hand, view a specialized curriculum as mechanical and failing to impart a sense of reality. Debate has been continuous over the last quarter of a century because of the inability of alternative strategies to generate an effective synthesis, creative solutions, or effective teaching procedures.

To what extent has civic education deteriorated since 1945 precisely because it has failed to develop a clarity about its scope and content? To what extent does civic education remain unclear as to its academic content, and to what extent has it become involved in various forms of diffuse political action—tasks more appropriately performed by independent voluntary associations and community groups? For my purpose, a narrow definition of ends and a broad one of means best serve civic education. I believe that civic education should employ academic instruction of the individual in his national political setting; this is a narrow conception of ends. But to circumscribe civic education to formal instruction in the school system—even the full curriculum of the school—is too limited to deal with the imbalance of citizen rights and obligations. I shall use a broad institutional approach, which, under advanced industrialism, does not deny the centrality of the school. I shall make the school system the core of my interest, but I shall range broadly over other institutions, including military service and experimental work and community service programs.

To distinguish between indoctrination and education is essential. In the interest of the widest agreement, I have pursued my study on the basis of the common understanding of indoctrination as the process of fashioning attitudes and behavior of a partisan or sectarian nature by emphasizing a preconceived—and unified—symbolic content. It amounts to a one-sided inculcation of basic principles. Although any democratic society rests on some essential elements of political indoctrination, hopefully of a circumscribed content, democratic societies are inherently suspicious of indoctrination. Therefore, techniques of civic education must blend with the work of the school in general. This means that teaching should develop critical skills and a sense of self-criticism as well as areas of common consensus.

I shall not start with the school system. It is my view that the forms and content of citizenship are deeply, in fact fundamentally, conditioned by the different forms of social organization of military service. To explore this issue in present-day society means starting with the role of the citizen soldier in the colonial period and in the American Revolution. The American Revolution was a powerful experience in civic education.

Military Service and the Citizen Soldier

The strongest test of citizen obligation is performance of military service in defense of the nation-state. Such an assertion is fully compatible with conscientious objection to military service based on religious, ethical, or even political grounds. Extensive or ad hoc exemptions can undermine the legitimacy of compulsory military service, but such an outcome is hardly predetermined. A democratic polity does not require a tyranny of the majority. To state the issue alternatively, military obligation may be highly distasteful, but it cannot be without pervasive legitimacy as an expression of democratic citizenship.

The argument of military service and citizenship can be pressed even further. I plan to examine the observation that particular forms of military service can serve and have served as a form of effective civic education.

14

Such an assertion has its paradoxes. Military institutions, even in peacetime but especially in wartime, are authoritarian structures, which operate at variance with the procedures of a democratic polity. I offer that observation, although my years of research on military organization indicate the decline of authoritarian sanctions and the growth of managerial authority in the armed forces.

The bulk of the armed forces are not fighters. Nevertheless, participants in military formations are subject in varying degree to the "management of violence." My reading of politicomilitary history and my specific analysis of the experiences of the United States lead me to the conclusion that military experience, although it may in the generality of world history be destructive of democratic values, is not universally so. The case of the United States and selected Western democracies has been at least a partial exception.

I make no claim fully to understand the paradox. Mass armed forces, with effective discipline and technologically advanced weapons, developed first in the West. Yet democratic political institutions were able to emerge and persist in the West despite the growth of these military institutions, which increased in their organizational weight and potential political power.

Military dictatorship was not the outcome. No one would deny the current role of military leaders as a powerful pressure group in Western democratic states. But Harold D. Lasswell's provocative image of the "garrison state" (in an article published in 1941), with greatly enhanced political power of the professional military, has not come into being in the twentieth century in the countries he describes.[16] The military remains under the control of the civilian elites. In Western nation-states, advanced industrialism has been accompanied by a decline in the threat of direct political intervention by the military. Even in the historically troublesome case of Germany, we have the emergence of civilian control of the armies of the Federal Republic of Germany.

In modern history, military elites of the West have had the resources and organizational power to effect far greater military intervention into the political process than has actually taken place. In other regions, however, weaker armies have exerted greater political power. The very limited military forces of "developing" nations have since 1945 revealed extensive capacity of their military elites to dominate political life in their nation-states. Obviously we are dealing not only with the relative resources and potential power of the military, but with the weakness of civil-political institutions in the third world.

16. Harold D. Lasswell, "The Garrison State," *American Journal of Sociology* 46, no. 4 (January 1941): 455–68.

In Western parliamentary polities, can one discern the conditions under which military service has operated as a positive and effective form of civic education? It is clear that, for fighters and nonfighters alike, military service does fashion, for better or for worse, group sentiments and affiliations. The historical record does not permit one to offer the conclusion that conscript armies with widespread participation serve as effective agencies of citizen education. Conscription per se is not the relevant variable. There are too many cases of authoritarian regimes which have perpetuated centralized and arbitrary power by the use of conscription. These regimes have used conscription as a system of police and coercive control over the population both in and outside of military experience. Many of these regimes were gradually weakened by the mass mobilization that conscription generated.

It is, rather, the development and acceptance of the concept of the citizen soldier—as both a political symbol and military reality—that has been operative in civic education and civilian supremacy. The citizen soldier has a long history, back to the Greek city-states. But the American and French Revolutions have come to serve as the historic moments in the emergence of the modern military and political version of this classic formula. (I would not overlook the equivalent experience of Great Britain, where local militia had important implications for citizen participation in the political control of the central armed forces.)

There are, of course, a variety of forms of service for the citizen soldier in the United States: service in the local militia (later the National Guard); membership in volunteer military units; and, most extensive, participation in conscripted forces with large reserve components. The idea of the citizen soldier is as much a political and ideological formula as it is a system of organizing military manpower. Regardless of the type of service, however, military service rests on the obligation of the citizen to the nation-state.[17] Although cadres of career professionals are required, the citizenry supplies the bulk of personnel.

The person who serves as a citizen soldier need not lose his civilian political rights, though they may be temporarily constricted. In fact, military service demonstrates one's citizenship and in turn one's citizenship is enhanced by military service. There is a strong element of symbolic myth in the citizen soldier, but the symbolic content has its political importance along with the actual military realities.

I suggest the following hypothesis for the United States, which can be adapted to other Western political democracies. From the American Rev-

17. Morris Janowitz, "Military Institutions and Citizenship in Western Societies," *Armed Forces and Society*, Winter 1976, 185–204.

olution to the end of World War II, military service, expressed by the duties and obligations of various forms of the citizen soldier, was compatible with parliamentary democracy. Military experience during the American Revolution operated as a form of civic education in support of the democratic polity. This is not to justify the moral worth of any particular military action, to imply that results were uniformly beneficial, or to overlook the hyperpatriotism that the agitation of veteran groups generated. It is to prepare the basis for assessing the overall civilian control and citizen soldier format in comparison with other forms of military service.

It is necessary to include limiting conditions. In June 1973, conscription was terminated and the consequences of military service as an agency of civic education became problematic. For the first time in U.S. history, the nation created in "peacetime" an "expanded" military establishment manned by volunteers. Both the short-term and long-term consequences of this institutional development are not predetermined. The impact of service in the all-volunteer force, with extensively self-selected personnel, needs to be closely examined. After almost a decade of the all-volunteer system there are complex organization and recruitment problems—problems of numbers, quality, social representativeness, and sociopolitical orientation of its personnel. These problems impinge on both the short-term volunteer and the long-term career military. By the early 1980s, the system of recruitment and compensation clearly needed modification, if only because of the decline in the size of cohorts coming of age for military service.

It is also clear that if the armed forces are to be militarily effective and responsible to civilian authority and serve as an agency of civic education, basic structural changes in the all-volunteer force will be required. But from our point of view of citizen education and citizenship, the passage of one decade has indicated that civilian intervention is, over the long run, required to maintain an all-volunteer force compatible with a democratic polity. The United States hardly faces the dangers of an organized military intrusion into the political system, although the military continually demonstrates its effectiveness as a pressure group. The personnel of the all-volunteer force should be prevented from developing a unified and explicit radical conservative outlook, thereby losing its political neutrality. In other words, the political task is to make life in the military compatible with the traditions of a nonpartisan but politically informed military. A nonpartisan military can be and must be committed to the rules and procedures of a democratic polity.

The all-volunteer force requires careful oversight by elected political leaders because it is an institution with which the nation has had no

17

previous experience. Leaders need to keep alive important elements of the citizen soldier concept.[18]

With the introduction of nuclear weapons, the historical cycle from war to peace and from peace to war gives way to a chronic tension among superpowers, flanked by their client states. The resulting "siege mentality" has the potential to undermine traditional values of personal freedom and individuality and threatens to narrow national values into rigid and mechanical patriotism.

The Mass School System

In 1931, Charles E. Merriam contended that "the school emerges in recent times as the major instrument in the shaping of civic education."[19] That statement supplies an important benchmark for subsequent criticism (in which I share) that the school system has declined in its effectiveness as an agency of civic education. The causes are complex. I am particularly interested in comparing the period 1890–1940 with the post–World War II era, 1945–80.

By 1890, the United States had emerged from the Civil War and was experiencing massive immigration from Europe. The teaching of history, now firmly rooted in the common school curriculum, became an essential ingredient in civic education. Although routinized, it had some positive consequences in nation building. History teaching is effective in a national setting of social and cultural homogeneity, where there is considerable agreement about what is important to be transmitted. In the period 1890–1940 there was considerable ambiguity or variation in the definition of the "heritage" of American history. The appropriate treatment of European immigrants and, even more to the point, the position and role of American Indians and blacks profoundly complicated the teaching of history. It is also well to keep in mind that, for the post–Civil War period, civic education was directed not only to the waves of immigrants and their children, about whom social historians have been primarily concerned, but to native-born generations. The perspectives and civic attitudes of native-born Americans were of decisive importance in dealing with each wave of newcomers. Much of the key political leadership and many of the professional educators were drawn from earlier arrivals. After 1890 the flow of immigrants became even greater, and the ability of the school system to teach history was strained by the immense variation in student backgrounds.

18. Morris Janowitz, "The Citizen Soldier and National Service," *Air University Review* 31 (November–December 1979): 2–16.

19. Charles E. Merriam, *The Making of Citizens: A Comparative Study of Methods of Civic Training* (Chicago: University of Chicago Press, 1931), p. 273.

Between 1890 and 1940, the public school nevertheless played an important role in civic education, despite limitations in the teaching of history. Instead of focusing on a segment of the curriculum, I am concerned with the educational experience as a whole. In particular, I am interested in the effectiveness or lack of effectiveness of the school as a bridging institution from the local residential neighborhood to the larger metropolis, to the larger society, and to the nation-state. No doubt, I risk historical oversimplification when I seek to compare and contrast the periods 1890–1945 and 1945–80. But there is a discernible difference in the school as an institution of civic education between one period and the next.

Before 1945, young people were socialized into the larger society mainly through work, though education obviously helped and gradually became crucial.[20] The long-term trend has been one of widespread economic advance with longer residence in metropolitan centers. The economist Thomas Sowell argues that "there are, apparently, traits that do and traits that do not produce economic advance, and there are historical conditions that do and do not produce these traits in various groups. However, all ethnic groups have adapted to American conditions to some extent, and virtually all have risen significantly as a result."[21]

Such a formulation supplies the context for assessing the performance of the public school system. In a parallel fashion, I am strongly attracted to and shall explore the proposition that, during the period 1890–1940, the school system used local and primordial attachments as active ingredients in fashioning national identifications.

The U.S. schools have never operated as a system of educational assimilation, in which youngsters are required to give up their familial cultural attachments. It has been a system of acculturation through which existing attachments were accepted in varying degree and new identifications simultaneously fostered. (*Assimilation* implies loss of older identity, while *acculturation* means the addition of new values while retaining crucial elements of one's older identity.)[22]

During this period of search for national citizenship, racial minorities were relatively untouched by the public education system. But for second-generation native-born children and for immigrants, in varying degrees, primary and secondary education taught basic English-language skills and presented a point of entrance into the larger society by means of access

20. Stanley Lieberson, *A Piece of the Pie: Black and White Immigrants since 1880* (Berkeley: University of California Press, 1980).

21. Thomas Sowell, *Race and Economics* (New York: Longman, 1975), p. 148.

22. For a converging point of view see Milton M. Gordon, *Assimilation in American Life: The Role of Race, Religion, and National Origins* (New York: Oxford University Press, 1964).

to the labor market and to increased opportunities for postsecondary education.

The primacy of English-language instruction was not interpreted by immigrants as a barrier to the preservation or even enhancement of their ethnic and linguistic heritage. The public school system operated as an acculturation mechanism and overtly used limited amounts of nationalist and patriotic symbolism. It is striking that this low-key process did make effective but incomplete contributions to a sense of national consciousness required for political participation.

There was a great deal of rhetoric about "Americanization," especially during World War I and the strained period thereafter. But the process of nation building was that of "old world traits transplanted."[23] Although the long-term trend was toward some form of the "melting pot," the fusion was rather indirect and variegated, and local political leaders made explicit appeals to ethnic "nationality." As described by the "Chicago school" of sociologists, the process was less Americanization than "hyphenated Americanization." Primordial attachments that were transplanted were not simply survivals of a former existence; they were cultural elements of considerable vitality, which played a positive role in linking the new immigrants to the larger society. Particularly in the years 1890–1910, the variety of Eastern and Southern European ethnic groups experienced freedom from "old world" political and economic restraints, which produced cultural and political enrichment in the United States.

All of this is well known. However, it needs to be stressed that ethnic identifications, except for some limited radical groups, did not serve as a basis for political separatism in America. To the contrary, ethnic attachments were compatible with and contributed to the dominant trend toward political acculturation, and the school was a vital element in this transformation.

By contrast, in the period after 1945 and especially after 1960, the strategy of balancing local primordial attachments with the goal of national affiliation was strained. New directions emerged. The long-term outcome can only be dimly perceived. An important trend, although hardly the only one, was a pattern which, for lack of a better term, I will call the "new communalism."

Under the new communalism, emphasis on ethnic and racial nationalism momentarily outweighed concern with national citizenship among particular social segments. One constituency for the new trend was the black community, some of whose members believed that they were excluded from economic and political advantages of the European—old and new—

23. W. I. Thomas with Robert E. Park and Herbert A. Miller, *Old World Traits Transplanted* (New York: Harper and Brothers, 1921).

immigrants. Among blacks, as well as other ethnic groups of higher status with longer experience of gradual acculturation, elements of a primordial revival were partly a response to black nationalism and partly a self-generated search for a new basis of group cohesion not supplied by the diffuse acculturation. Blacks were joined by other racial and ethnic groups, particularly the Spanish-speaking, who, because of the close proximity of their homelands, represented a very special type of immigrant.

Social scientists who have studied ethnicity have not systematically measured the scope and intensity of these new trends. Primordial solidarity among submerged groups has been powerful, but extensive intermarriage across ethnic lines has served to "mix the population" and weaken ethnic solidarity.[24] The ethnic revival observed among intellectuals and selected offspring of acculturated families, though real, has been overstated. Ethnic affiliation persists most visibly among the new, post-1945 immigrants, mainly Hispanics.

These issues need to be stated in alternative terms. In the post–World War II period, the school system's efforts in civic education were directed largely toward the acculturation of minority groups who felt themselves excluded from economic and political opportunity. In this same period, however, the bulk of students in the school system were not low-status "minority" group members. The indifference to national symbolism among these cohorts of young people represented narrow hedonism, at times a counterculture perspective, and, more often, loss of confidence in the governmental process, generated by the war in Vietnam, Watergate, and the increasing inability of elected officials to manage the socioeconomic dilemmas of an advanced industrial society. The decline in the school as an agency of civic education is not limited to ethnic or racial groupings but involves a wider range of intergenerational relations and tensions.

These ambiguities erupted during a period of immense expansion of the public school system. After World War II, the United States pushed closer and closer to the goal of universal high school education. By 1976, survey data demonstrated that parents universally aspired for their children to graduate from high school, and only about 5 percent thought that their children would not.[25] These expectations were realistic. Of the total age group 25–29 in 1977, 89.6 percent had completed high school. The percentage of blacks was lower—67.2 percent—but rising.[26] Yet the ca-

24. See Edward O. Laumann, *Bonds of Pluralism: The Form and Substance of Urban Social Networks* (New York: John Wiley, 1973).

25. Foundation for Child Development, National Survey of Children, unpublished data as reported in Mary A. Gollady and Jay Noell, eds., *The Conditions of Education*, 1978 edition, p. 22.

26. U.S. Department of Commerce, Bureau of the Census, *Educational Attainment in the United States: March 1977 and 1976*, series P-20, no. 314.

pacity of the mass education system to produce basic literacy and to increase academic levels of performance has been called into question. For example, the data indicate a decline in college entrance test scores. At this point, it suffices to emphasize that, while most of the decline is due to the changed social composition of students being tested, we are dealing with organizational limitations in the capacity of the system to educate. The limitations include the increased disarticulation—or separation—of the school system from work and narrowing opportunities for employment while attending school.

Likewise, the decline—or, if you wish, the limitations—in the capacity of the mass school system since 1945 to make a contribution to civic education had consequences for both low- and middle-strata children, although the implications for life chances were more visible for the lowest socioeconomic groups. By the 1960s, the inability of the educational system to perform effectively for the lowest strata of society resulted in strong attacks, initially by black ethnic nationalist movements and by other deprived and low-status groups. While the long-term trend toward acculturation continued, the immediate impact of ethnic nationalism was reinforced by the mass media. In particular quarters, the school was no longer thought of as a bridging institution to the larger society. Instead, it was viewed by local groups as an arena for developing ethnic nationalist identifications and for immediate mobilization for confrontation politics. This is dramatically shown by the slogan "Teaching English as a Second Language" (TESL). English was not thought to be primary. But TESL was and is more core American than bilingual education. Bilingual and, more recently, bicultural education reflects the new communalism. TESL is, in theory, antithetical to bilingual and bicultural education because it accepts the goal of acculturation to the English language. In practice, however, it frequently operates as a form of bilingualism.

The period of ethnic ultranationalism was destined to be short-lived in America, but important residues remain. In Spanish-speaking groups, ethnic nationalism appears more persistent than ever. As a result of these nationalist agitations, the capacity of the mass public school to provide basic literacy was disrupted and the limited civic education in the secondary schools weakened.

The simplistic patriotism and hyphenated ethnicity of the public school milieux came to be viewed by some educators as naive and too much oriented to the status quo. The delicate balance by which national identifications were built on local primordial attachments remained strained through the decade of the 1970s. The new communalism failed in part because its adherents were not content with the circumscribed life space and life chances it afforded. But it was a distorted form of "success," for it helped thwart an effective movement toward new forms of civic consciousness.

In these trends, the role of social studies and the behavioral sciences warrants careful assessment. I am struck by the fact that the impact of social science in both periods was initially and primarily on the teaching faculty. Social studies helped fashion the attitudes of the faculty, and, in turn, the faculty communicated their sentiments to students. I contend that during the first period of the search for national citizenship (1890–1940), social studies, despite their limitations, informed the faculty realistically of the meaning of cultural diversity and the variegated aspirations of its students. Social studies helped to bridge the gap between teacher and student and increased faculty effectiveness. During this early period, social studies also helped the school to bridge the gulf between local community and larger society, articulating with the strategy of hyphenated acculturation. After World War II, however, social studies changed in content and contributed to the delegitimization of social and political institutions. I believe that the teaching profession after 1945 performed its civic task less effectively than before the marked restriction of immigration in the 1920s. Elements of the teaching faculty encouraged student confrontation in the name of civil and economic rights, echoing the ethnic and racial nationalists' argument that the strategy of acculturation had failed to assist submerged minorities. During the period of communalism, social studies were used to support—but without lasting success—a separatist political ideology that was incompatible with civic education in a democratic polity.

Thus far, I may have given the impression that the development of basic literacy and the rudiments of civic education are distinct goals in mass education. Of course they are not. One cannot expect to increase basic literacy without concern for effective civic education. I shall use an underlying assumption to guide my analysis of literacy and civic education which reverses "common sense" wisdom. We have been operating on the assumption that the capacity of mass education to improve students' academic and technical skills would result in a stronger sense of citizenship. Such an assumption is too narrow. I will proceed on the broader and dual assumption that, under advanced industrialism, if mass education is to achieve basic skill and academic goals, it must simultaneously develop in its students meaningful national identifications and an operative sense of citizenship. I shall explore the proposition that, in the past, mass education proceeded on the principle that basic education was required for citizenship; today, a sense of national civic sentiment is required to assist basic education. Neither localistic territorial and/or community affiliations nor primordial ethnic attachments will suffice as the basis of civic education.

23

For the modern nation-state, civic education that is parochial or separatist and does not relate to the political and economic system of the nation is unlikely to contribute to the required level of academic achievement. To be literate—and that includes the motivation to be literate—one must believe that effective national citizenship is within one's grasp.

The sociopolitical meaning of citizenship is inextricably bound up with contemporary debates over equality. The societal definition that gives greater saliency to citizen rights than to citizen obligations is rapidly internalized by each new group of aliens who become citizens. Although "alien" is a general category of persons, it in effect has come to mean a position of inferiority based on race or specific national origin. To become a citizen is to eliminate an assumed basis of subservience. The citizen has developed the absolute right to a passport and to enter and leave the United States at will. The alien must meet a set of legal requirements to become a resident alien and in turn a citizen. These requirements are a reflection of the immense pressure of "foreigners" to become citizens. Yet if the alien meets these requirements, he has most of the benefits of citizenship even if he chooses to remain a resident alien. As the status of citizen and resident alien converge, the last twenty years have seen the development of a new distinction—between the citizen and resident alien, on the one hand, and the illegal alien, on the other. This trend produces a deep division in U.S. society. The granting of citizenship to a portion of illegal immigrants who have long resided in the United States will constitute another profound reduction in status differences between citizen and alien. The redefinition of citizenship is pressed as an extension of the classical struggle over civil, political, and social inequality. In the contemporary setting, the fundamental issue for a mass society is how broadly equality shall be defined and enforced by governmental sanctions and social norms. Shall the traditional equality of opportunity be redefined to include equality of result?

The combined drive for greater social and economic benefits, together with the corresponding pressure for the extension of citizenship, represent political forces that are hard to dissipate. But it is more rhetorical than clarifying when Ralf Dahrendorf asserts that "there are historical forces too powerful to be contained . . . Citizenship is one of them . . . There is, in other words, a suicidal strain in the citizen, a death drive which is very evident today (1974)."[27] I clearly prefer the formulation I have presented, namely, that the central issue is the long-term historical imbalance of rights versus obligations. The intellectual clarification of this imbalance is an essential and hopefully a restorative enterprise, especially for those concerned with civic education.

27. Ralf Dahrendorf, "Citizenship and Beyond: The Social Dynamics of an Idea," *Social Research* 41 (Winter 1974): 699.

It should be apparent that the emphasis on rights rather than obligations is not confined to any particular segment of the social structure. During the period of search for national citizenship, it made sense to expect that teaching of academic skills would strengthen the sense of citizenship and, in turn, foster effective citizenship. We start with the American Revolution and move to the present day. In the late twentieth century, an emergent sense of citizenship is a prerequisite for effective academic learning. Not only are we dealing with pressing educational disabilities—academic and civic—of deprived elements of society, but we must ensure that more privileged groups also make effective use of mass education. I shall highlight the parallel between the "citizen soldier" idea, which emphasized broad-scale citizen participation in the military, and the common school, which sought to spread the educational experience as widely as possible.

Two

The American Revolution and the Citizen Soldier Concept

THE POLITICS OF MILITARY OBLIGATION

The American Revolution destroyed the basis of the British political power in the thirteen colonies. It was an armed seizure of political power which broke the monarchical political rule. The result of the American Revolution was to create a new political system.

But the new political system was loose and fragile; it took more than two decades for the United States to develop a minimum of social cohesion and political solidarity so that it could act as a nation in its own defense. In this respect the American Revolution is a unique political achievement. The colonists fought a prolonged, although in many respects circumscribed, military campaign to achieve political victory. Their military campaign rested on mobilization of wide segments of the rank and file of the population. Military service was a form of citizen education.

The result was not only the formation of an independent nation-state. The military campaigns and conduct of the war contributed decisively to the building of postrevolutionary political democratic institutions. The war was, in fact, as important as the colonial education system in defining citizenship. As we shall see, civic obligation, enforced citizen obligation, was a root element in the revolutionary forces.

The number of cases in which armed revolutionary conflict has helped to build democratic nation-states is indeed limited. It is my goal to explore the American military experience not only in the Revolution but in subsequent periods of intensive military service, including the post–World War II draft and the introduction in 1973 of an expanded "peacetime" all-volunteer force for the first time in U.S. history. I shall assess how far, and under what conditions, popular military service strengthened democratic commitments, both of the rank and file and of the political leadership.

Unresolved moral dilemmas are involved in judging the impact of force on the political process. My democratic frame of reference commits me to the logic that the less force is applied, the more likely it is that desired political goals will be achieved.

Goals and practices of armed movements and of organized military formations are hardly unified and integrated. Often they operate on a double standard or with varying standards, so that the consequences on citizenship can be mixed. The traditions created by the U.S. Continental army during the American Revolution were reasonable both by the standards of the day and in their own right. But the military force which emerged in "peacetime" to define and expand the borders of the new nation resulted in continuous military expeditions against Indians, which must be judged negatively. The mass armed forces which the U.S. created in the Civil War and in conflicts of the twentieth century were not built on the operational code of the Indian fighters but had more in common with U.S. Continental forces.

In my analysis of military service and civic education I have no alternative but to accept the converging conclusions of modern scholars which have become dominant and seem plausible. It is generally argued that the decline of feudalism in the West and the emergence in Western Europe of democratic political forms could not have been achieved without resort to armed insurrection. In the case of the American and French nation-states, this view is clearly supported. The case of Great Britain is more complex. The conduct and the relative success of these armed outbursts were subject to wide latitude by the leadership involved (see the analysis presented by writers such as R. R. Palmer in *The Age of Democratic Revolution*, and Barrington Moore, Jr., in *Social Origins of Dictatorship and Democracy*).[1]

The sociopolitical movements which strengthen democratic political institutions also need to be distinguished from those on which the imperialism of Western Europe and the United States were based. Joseph Schumpeter, in *Imperialism and Social Classes*,[2] rejects a narrow economic explanation of "modern" imperialism. Instead, he emphasizes the anti-imperialism perspective of the "free traders." He does not see imperialism based on immediate advantages derived from conquest. For him, the "belligerence and war policy of the autocratic state" rests on powerful residues

1. R. R. Palmer, *The Age of Democratic Revolution: A Political History of Europe and America, 1760–1800* (Princeton: Princeton University Press, 1964); Barrington Moore, Jr., *Social Origins of Dictatorship and Democracy* (Boston: Beacon, 1966).

2. Joseph Schumpeter, *Imperialism and Social Classes* (New York: Augustus M. Kelley, 1951).

and inheritance of an older feudal order.[3] Imperialist aspirations are to be explained by the necessities of an outdated internal and domestic social structure. In Schumpeter's view, imperialist expansions, launched from Western Europe, were efforts to accommodate archaic interests of landed elements and to perpetuate inherited dispositions of ruling groups and the ruler himself of autocratic states.

In this view, imperialism is not a result of the changing social order but, rather, an effort to maintain an older sociopolitical system. I would add that in the era from the American and French revolutions to the outbreak of World War I, these landed interests found for themselves enclaves in the national armies which were gradually being refashioned into "modern" bureaucratic and professional entities. It was not only in the elite monarchical military units but also in colonial contingents that personnel of a "feudal" type were concentrated and traditions were most strongly maintained. In essence, the development of a military establishment under effective civilian parliamentary control involved breaking, or at least weakening, the political and organizational power of these feudal elements. Although weakened by domestic revolution and insurrection as well as by military professionalism, the feudal spirit persisted, especially in the colonial units stationed overseas, until the start of World War II in 1939.

While there is hardly comprehensive agreement among writers on the decline of feudalism, they are strikingly explicit about the link between armed revolution and the possibility of an emerging democratic regime. The cases in which armed revolutions or insurrections actually assisted the institutionalization of parliamentary regimes is so small, however, that to generalize is hazardous. The experience of the Italian city-states as well as political developments in the Dutch struggle for independence are relevant. But for our purposes, the American Revolution is the starting point. The political outcome of the American Revolution was assisted by the relative material abundance of the colonies; this was not a revolution which took place in a setting of starvation and misery. Furthermore, the colonists had rudimentary institutions of self-government and some experience in handling these institutions.

In the research literature on the political consequences of the American revolutionary war, two general observations stand out. One deals with the limited destructiveness of the war, both in human and in material costs. The second focuses on the citizen soldier format of the military, or, more precisely, on the balance between citizen soldier and regular military. In essence, despite its long duration and extensive military operations and

3. Ibid., p. 76.

even elements of terror, the American Revolution was a relatively limited and contained armed struggle. Such a conclusion is based on broad observation, as well as detailed and delimited studies. It also involves the treatment of prisoners of war as well as of civilians on both sides during the actual revolution. It spills over to the handling of "loyalist" civilians after military engagements ceased. The conclusion rests on the assertion that we are dealing not with minor differences but, rather, with a decisive characterization. In other words, both for the British authorities and for the American revolutionaries, the potential for greater destruction was present. Deliberate decisions on both sides contained the level, scope, and amount of misery.

During the American Revolution, some activists argued that American leadership did not sufficiently exploit available revolutionary methods. Military figures such as Charles Lee pressed for a more aggressive strategy. They preferred a more thoroughgoing revolution. Retrospectively, their perspective is labeled "radical," since it is assumed that they were seeking more drastic and more equalitarian political goals. It is difficult to ascertain whether they were actually more radical or merely more ruthless. In any case, adherents of such a point of view were a small minority.

If the term *radical* seems inappropriate to the goals of American political leaders, their aspirations were clearly drastic and involved fundamental change. It required the outbreak of armed conflict to make American leadership fully conscious of these goals. They clearly wished to establish an independent state, governed by a legislative assembly and with an elected leader. In effect, their goals must be considered revolutionary and the achievement of these goals a monumental accomplishment.

The American Revolution had its brutish episodes, but the overall conduct of hostilities was remarkably restrained. Explaining the circumscribed level of violence has repeatedly emphasized the outlook—both military and political—of George Washington. This outlook led him to impose, to the extent that he could, controls over military operations that can be labeled pragmatic.

No doubt George Washington's restraint in the use of force is an expression of his personality and values. But the underlying explanation of the politicomilitary success of the colonists involves more than the "great man in history." It involves political goals of dominant civilian leaders and their ability to develop a military system under civilian control. The explanation rests on a balance in the military between the citizen soldier and the conventional regulars soldier. The citizen soldier format was concentrated in local militia and statewide volunteer units and in the irregular forces, while the Continental army recruited and was organized as an American equivalent of European standing armies. The dramatic separation from

29

England was achieved with a new mixture of regulars and citizen soldiers. This new type of military organization was revolutionary in terms of its basic legitimacy and the political assumptions it used and engendered.

THE CITIZEN SOLDIER IN THE AMERICAN REVOLUTION

National armies of the late eighteenth century, including the British regulars in North America, stood in sharp contrast to the military forces of the colonists, which in varying degrees incorporated the idea of political and citizen rights of men. Standing national armies of the period were instruments of the regime, especially of the monarch himself. These military institutions were repressive both in internal organization and in the role they played in their own societies. They were officered overwhelmingly by members of the upper strata, mainly the minor gentry. The rank and file were, in effect, nonpolitical mercenaries, engaged for long periods and often pressed into service. These armies were hardly popular institutions in the sense that they were broadly based, reflecting the values of the larger society, and receiving widespread political support. To the contrary, monarchical armies were extensive and highly visible appendages to an authoritarian elite.

By contrast, American revolutionaries, by creating the citizen soldier, broadened the base of recruitment of the officer corps, especially in the militia. The idea of the citizen soldier gave political legitimacy to the rank and file being transformed from subjects to citizens. They were, in effect, an army which more and more had the features of a popular force. Rulers of the national monarchical armies aimed to keep the rank and file inert. The citizen soldier, on the other hand, was thought of as a potential member of the nation-state. Entering military service made him more a member of the nation-state and less an appendage to the upper strata. Military service emerged as a hallmark of citizenship, and citizenship as the hallmark of political democracy. In essence, Aristotle's definition of the citizen was operative as the citizen performed his obligations in defending his political homeland.

The citizen soldier concept had its origins in the Greek city-state and in the early Roman military system. In European history, the concept had its institutional antecedents before the American and French revolutions in the militia and national guard units of England and France. These units were of particular importance as a political counterweight to the centralized standing armies of the postfeudal kings. In the colonies of North America, the citizen soldier concept was widespread in the local militia.

The citizen soldier is both a political and a military concept, a mixture of genuine utility and effective myth. There has been endless debate about the effectiveness of the citizen soldier in contrast to the performance of the "regular" soldier. Military historians have come to the conclusion that local militia and state volunteer units played an important role in supporting the Continental army in the ultimate defeat of British forces.[4] In reality, the citizen soldier fuses with the professional military in mixtures dictated by different military settings. As a result, the history of the U.S. military establishment is one of compromise between policies designed to strengthen the professional "standing" forces and policies emphasizing the citizen soldier concept.

The citizen soldier concept has traditionally been embodied in the colonial militia, state and national guard formations, federal conscription, and the reserves. But the citizen soldier is also a political idea with important goals because it served (a) to reinforce civilian control, (b) to balance local political interests against the power of the central establishment, and (c) to mobilize a wide range of relevant talents and skills from civilian society for use in the military. For long periods of time, the U.S. armed forces were so small that the idea of the citizen soldier applied mainly to the reserves and the national guard.

In varying degree, in the militia, the conscript military, and the associated reserve forces, the notion of the citizen soldier is characterized by three significant dimensions: obligatory service, universality or a pervasive element of universality, and essential legitimacy as judged by democratic standards. From my point of view, obligatory service is the key element. Obligatory service highlights the difference between eighteenth-century standing armies based on repressive authority and mercenary forms of incentive and armed forces created as a result, or under the influence of, the American and French revolutions.

Militia service and conscript service mean obligatory—compulsory—service, in contrast to the voluntary or mercenary service. Obligatory service of the citizen soldier variety is based on a concept of the individual's duty to the state. Obviously, authoritarian regimes have always made use of compulsion, but they are not based on forms of citizen soldier service. The basic element of consent, that is, popular support for the military, is missing. In theory, the original militia of the colonial period was based on obligatory service. Historians such as John Shy have emphasized the diversity and complexity of the colonial militia.[5] But the general element

4. For a balanced analysis of the militia, see Robert C. Pugh, "The Revolutionary Militia in the Southern Campaigns, 1780–1781," *William and Mary Quarterly*, 3d series, 14 (1957): 154–75; Don Higginbotham, "The American Militia: A Traditional Institution with Revolutionary Responsibilities," in Don Higginbotham, ed., *Reconsideration of the Revolutionary War* (Westport, Conn.: Greenwood Press, 1978), pp. 83–103.

5. John B. Shy, "A New Look at Colonial Militia," *William and Mary Quarterly* 20 (April 1963): 171–85.

was that all citizens were enrolled and subject to military service. Although particular groups were excluded, such as blacks, Indians, or indentured servants, it must be underlined that political leaders believed and acted on the assumption that all able-bodied adults, especially young men, could be armed if required. In effect, all able-bodied persons were required to register and were potential soldiers.

This is a very revolutionary assumption. In a monarchical system, the royal leadership wished to arm only those members of society who would remain inert or supportive of the regime. Monarchs avoided the practice and rhetoric of a nation in arms because they were uncertain of the consequence.

Obligatory systems always contain escape mechanisms for particular persons and groups. Nevertheless, the U.S. military depended on various systems of obligatory service and conscription during the American Revolution and the Civil War. They were very loose systems, and many people either did not serve or purchased substitutes. The institutionalization of conscription during World War I eliminated an important escape mechanism, that of hiring substitutes. But new exemptions were developed; for example, during World Wars I and II, exemptions were introduced for various skill groups, specific categories of family members, as well as conscientious objectors.

As applied to the militia and conscript force, the citizen soldier concept emphasizes universal service. Both the American Revolution and the French Revolution dramatized the theme of the "nation in arms."[6] Again this symbolism stands in opposition to feudal practices and the defense of the absolute monarchs. But the principles of universal service did not mean, originally, even as a political ideal, that every able-bodied man would actually serve. Universal service pertained to certain age groups: younger men, those able to fight most effectively. Interestingly enough, throughout U.S. history, the application of an age criterion has not been a point of controversy. In essence, the American Revolution did not achieve universal obligatory service, an unreal goal given the pragmatic needs of agriculture and manufacturing. But participation was extremely widespread, although often for a limited time period. The military force, because of the revolutionary goals of its political leaders, had in effect broken with the existing European format of limited mobilization. Service was based on obligation in a democratic framework and the morality of the cause rather than mercenary incentives. Participation in the American Revolution increased the participants' attachment to the larger collectivity—the seeds of na-

6. Orville T. Murphy, "The American Revolutionary Army and the Concept of 'Levée en Masse,' " *Military Affairs* 23 (Spring 1959): 13–20.

tionalism and patriotism were planted. The development of national patriotism is not assured. The results could well have been a strong regionalism
and factionalism. The colonists won a victory that achieved political separation from England, but it did not lead to glorification of the military.
In fact, among the civilian-based militia, participation in the war strengthened respect for civilian leaders and enhanced the willingness of both
leadership and the popular electorate to take part in political compromise.
The pattern of political control of the armed forces, the civil-military
relations which emerged during the American Revolution, had a powerful
influence, both for the immediate postwar period and for the long term,
on behalf of civilian control.

THE POLITICAL CONSEQUENCES OF MILITARY OPERATIONS

An assessment of the consequences of the American Revolution as a form
of civic education depends on one's view of the social, economic, and
political outcomes of the Revolution. J. Franklin Jameson's essay *The
American Revolution Considered as a Social Movement*, written more than a
half century ago, still makes a good point of departure.[8] It has been
followed by a mass of more refined historical scholarship and extensive
critical reviews. Recent studies have suggested that the American Revolution did not accomplish much fundamental change, except for the sev-
ering of political rule from the British. According to this view, the movement
toward political democracy was effectively in process when the American
Revolution broke out. It is argued that the abolition of legal privilege, the
"great goal of European revolutions of the late eighteenth century,"[9] and
the achieving of equality of status before the law were attained in the
American colonies at least by the early years of the eighteenth century.

I am inclined to accept the orientation of Jameson. He considers the
American Revolution a threshold of change, resulting in extensive transformation. The Revolution broadened the franchise and eliminated pri-
mogeniture, two basic elements in subsequent urbanization, economic
growth, and political democracy in the United States. Jameson also points
to the importance of political change as a stimulus to agricultural and
technological development. He emphasizes the contribution of the Amer-

7. Stanley Elkins and Eric McKittrick, "The Founding Fathers: Young Men of
the Revolution," *Political Science Quarterly* 76 (March 1961): 181–216.

8. J. Franklin Jameson, *The American Revolution Considered as a Social Movement*
(Princeton: Princeton University Press, 1926). See also Gordon Wood, *The Creation
of the American Republic* (Chapel Hill: University of North Carolina Press, 1969);
Richard B. Morris, "We the People of the United States: The Bicentennial of a
People's Revolution," *American Historical Review* 82 (February 1977): 1–19.

9. Bernard Bailyn, "Political Experience and Enlightenment Ideas in Eighteenth
Century America," *American Historical Review* 67 (1971): 348.

33

ican Revolution to democratic institutions during a period in which these institutions were still struggling for acceptance, stability, and effectiveness.

I would further assert that, without the armed conflict, there was no certainty that a confederation of colonies would have emerged. Territorial fragmentation was more likely, especially between northern and southern colonies. Moreover, although Jameson does not go deeply into military service and civil-military relations, the Revolution did not crush political democracy as it might have. The organization of the revolutionary armed forces and the manner in which the war was conducted turn out to be crucial in strengthening the democratic polity.

As Linda Grant DePauw points out, at the start of the Revolution the politically interested and involved segment of the population was limited to free adult white men who owned some property. The remaining 85 percent of the population was relatively inert politically.[10] By the close of the Revolution, that inert percentage was much reduced. Most Americans, especially the leadership groups, came to accept the main ideas of the Whig outlook. Short-term politicization was extensive. This overwhelming majority accepted the legitimacy of political institutions established during military hostilities. At the same time, the politicizing of the population also mobilized loyalist sentiment; at least 20 percent of the population remained committed to the loyalists.

When the war was over, the bulk of the formerly political inert reverted to their relative indifference, but an important segment remained politically alert. The long-term increase in political interest substantially strengthened democratic politics. I am impressed not only by the increased citizen political participation, but with the marked broadening of the social basis of elected representatives.[11]

The increased political involvement was in part a result of the skillful propaganda of revolutionary intellectuals, making widespread and effective use of the "mass media."[12] The propaganda was strongly ideological. In reaction to Charles Beard's economic determinist interpretation of the American Revolution, current historians have come to emphasize (and in fact overemphasize) ideological themes as the basis of political participation and support for the revolutionary cause. Bernard Bailyn, in *The Ideological*

10. Linda Grant DePauw, "Politicizing the Political Inert," in *The American Revolution: Changing Perspective*, eds., William M. Fowler, Jr., and Wallace Coyle (Boston: Northeastern University, 1979), p. 16.

11. Jackson Turner Main, "Government by the People: The American Revolution and the Democratization of the Legislature," *William and Mary Quarterly* 22 (1966): 391–407.

12. John C. Miller, *Sam Adams, Pioneer in Propaganda* (Boston: Little, Brown and Co., 1936); Philip Davidson, *Propaganda and the American Revolution, 1763–1783* (Chapel Hill: University of North Carolina Press, 1941).

Origins of the American Revolution, asserts that the "revolution was above all else an ideological, constitutional political struggle and not primarily a controversy between social groups undertaken to force changes in the organization of the society or economy."[13]

One can acknowledge the strong role of ideology, especially among select segments of higher social strata in the colonies, without overstating its consequence. It is revealing that "intellectuals" and the propaganda they generated made frequent references to the "ancient republics." They saw themselves as reviving and continuing a long-term historical process. They emphasized the dangers of a centralized national armed force, a theme which grew in popular consciousness.

Even more striking was the propagandists' emphasis, in their mass appeals, on the rightfulness of their cause. The ideological appeals to morality were phrased in religious language. They asserted that God and religion were on the revolutionaries' side. Such religious appeals emphasized group responsibility, a theme highly appropriate for an armed revolutionary movement. The invoking of religion articulated with the sentiments of an important segment of the colonial population.[14] Economic self-interest, however, was not absent as a motivating element.

Propaganda notwithstanding, I contend that politicization within the rank and file was mainly a result of military and paramilitary service.[15] Opposition grew, and, in time, hostility emerged among the politically inert section toward the presence and practices of British forces.

In examining the American Revolution as a form of civic education, we may start with the estimated number of adults involved. Females as well as males need to be considered, since revolutions produce a mobilization of the population which encompasses them in the military as opposed to their rejection during "normal" or "peace" time.[16] These estimates are hardly definitive although supported by internal evidence; and it is difficult to distinguish between militia, state troops, and members of the Continental army. From available research, the following picture emerges. During

13. Bernard Bailyn, *The Ideological Origins of the American Revolution* (Cambridge: Harvard University Press, 1967), p. 319.

14. Charles Royster, *A Revolutionary People at War: The Continental Army and American Character, 1775–1783* (Chapel Hill: University of North Carolina Press, 1979).

15. I have found the following sources most useful: Don Higginbotham, *The War of American Independence: Military Attitudes, Policies, and Practice, 1763–1789* (New York: Macmillan Publishing Co., 1971); John Shy, *A People Numerous and Armed: Reflections on the Military Struggle for American Independence* (New York: Oxford University Press, 1976); Richard H. Kohn, *Eagle and Sword: The Federalists and the Creation of the Military Establishment in America, 1783–1802* (New York: The Free Press, 1975).

16. Linda K. Kerber, *Women of the Republic: Intellect and Ideology in Revolutionary America* (Chapel Hill: University of North Carolina Press, 1980).

the course of the war, the British built up a larger force of regulars than all the soldiers who served in the Continental army. As a struggle between mainline forces of the day, the balance was decisively on the side of the British. In the spring of 1775, they had a force of 6,991 stationed in the American colonies, while the bulk of the British army was stationed in the British Isles.[17] By October 1778, British forces in the American colonies had been expanded to 52,561, about half the total of British military, which numbered 112,239. British military personnel stationed in the American colonies remained roughly at the same expanded level until the end of the war, with 42,223 troops stationed in the American colonies.

By contrast, the U.S. Continental forces never reached more than 20,000 at the high point of mobilization in 1780. The size of the Continental army varied from 17,517 in 1775 to 20,086 in 1779 and dropped to 9,278 in 1782. (These figures are average monthly totals.)[18] In short, the British had two to three times more "regular" troops than the colonists, leaving aside the question of training and weapons.

The numerical advantage of the British in regular army troops has to be balanced off against extensive deployment of the revolutionary militia. The total population of the colonies in 1775 was 2,500,000, of whom 20 percent were black. By 1781, despite the ravages of war, the population had risen to 2,781,000. Of the male population, Howard Peckham estimates that between 200,000 and 250,000 men were of military age.[19] He offers the suggestion that, at any given time, the colonists had in the field 30,000 men—both Continental and militia—although the number probably was larger during intense fighting. Moreover, the vital statistic was that, of 200,000–250,000 military age men, at least 100,000 saw service at one time or another. I have seen estimates as high as 200,000. The secretary of war in 1790 estimated that total enlistments, including the multiple enlistment of one person, reached 396,000. Nor should it be forgotten that an estimated 50,000 colonists served in the British forces at one time or another, a not inconsequential number.

As for female participation, Linda Grant DePauw estimated that there were 20,000 "women of the army" between 1775 and 1783.[20] By my estimate, this is a relatively higher figure than the proportion of women

17. Philip B. N. Katcher, *Encyclopedia of British, Provincial and German Army Units, 1775–1783*, quoting Lord North's reports.
18. Charles H. Lesser, ed., *The Sinews of Independence: Monthly Strength Reports of the Continental Army* (Chicago: University of Chicago Press, 1976).
19. Howard H. Peckham, *The War for Independence* (Chicago: University of Chicago Press, 1974), pp. 129–35.
20. Linda Grant DePauw, "Women in Combat: The Revolutionary Experience," *Armed Forces and Society* 7 (Winter 1980): 209–26. For a critique of Linda Grant DePauw see "Commentary" by Janice E. McKenney, *Armed Forces and Society* 8 (Summer 1982): 686–92.

(8 percent) in the all-volunteer ground force by 1980. Women of the revolutionary period were organized both for auxiliary military service and for direct combat support tasks, including servicing cannon during hostilities. A few hundred women served in uniform with the Continental forces. They were integrated by the simple procedure of issuing them regular male uniforms. The entire able-bodied adult population, both female and male, at some times and some places participated in local defense efforts.

The military effectiveness of the militia has been a subject of endless historical debate. George Washington had a low opinion of their fighting effectiveness. Some units fought British regulars with little success. On the other hand, leaders in, and spokesmen for, the militia in the post–revolutionary war period exaggerated the military importance of the militia as part of the political argument against a standing army. Present-day military historians present a more balanced picture: The militia engaged in local policing duties, patrolling and guarding installations and supplies, offensive irregular warfare, including endless raids and skirmishes, as well as mainline combat.

Militia forces, by their performance in battle, may not have been decisive in achieving final victory. But without the services of the militia as political organizer and educator by means of coercion, persuasion, and a combination of both, one can conclude that the revolutionaries would not have won. If one thinks of the American Revolution as a sociopolitical movement, contributions of the militia were indeed decisive.

One needs to probe continually why the colonists became unified and did not fragment into smaller political units. We are dealing with a triangular struggle, a pattern repeatedly encountered in the so-called wars of national liberation in the period after 1945.[21] The two contending regular armies fought each other directly and indirectly, but the core of the conflict was efforts of each side to win the support of the civilian population. Clearly, the colonists, mainly through their militia, had the organizational advantage over the British authorities in dealing with the civilians.

It should be emphasized that, until 1775, rank-and-file colonists accepted the presence of British regulars; British forces did not start their military actions in an unfavorable public opinion setting. The general outlook was that British regular forces were essential to contain the Indians and to defend American colonies against possible expansion by the French and Spanish. Until the outbreak of armed revolution, state legislatures played a central role in deciding when and how the British troops would be deployed.

21. Shy, *A People Numerous and Armed*, pp. 198–99.

Attitudes were transformed rapidly after Lexington and Concord, and not mainly on the basis of ideological arguments. Of course, new policies of the British toward the colonists, particularly in taxation, started the growth of anti-British sentiment which came to engulf the British military. But the hostility to British regulars was rooted in grass-roots contacts between the rank-and-file colonists and British soldiers. There was constant friction in the day-to-day administration and stationing of British troops. Soon after the start of hostilities they were seen no longer as defenders of the colonies but as occupiers with all the negative connotations the term implies. Hostility escalated with the destruction wrought by the British armed force. But personal contact was of major importance, centering on opposition to troop behavior such as flirting with local girls and fist fighting. This increased opposition and contributed directly to the politicization of the inert population.

British higher authorities were aware of the deteriorating relations between their military forces and local civilian populations. Individual commanders sought to correct or at least moderate the tensions and chronic outbursts. Their task was complicated by the inability of British forces to extend local security to the bulk of the loyalist population. Loyalist elements formed their own self-defense units to resist the pressures of the revolutionary militia. The deployment of armed British loyalists either failed or produced excessive use of force which, over the long run, was counterproductive. Historians have debated the question of why British authorities did not engage in harsher measures, especially against rebel members of the militia. The varied answers all have an element of plausibility. They include the traditions and moral basis of the British officer corps and the links of British forces to British society; the specific actions and attitudes of top generals, particularly Sir Henry Clinton. Most likely, the British rejected the use of extensive terrorism since they could not offer adequate security to their colonial loyalists. In more pointed terms, most British authorities in the American colonies recognized that if a lasting "victory" or even a face-saving settlement was to be achieved, political support from important segments of civilians was required. Terrorism would not work toward such goals. In any case, the American colonies were spared a "bitter end" conflict since excesses by the rebel militia also were not escalated. Thus the groundwork was laid for political compromises after hostilities.

On the side of the revolutionary forces, a popular and relatively effective militia system did not spring up overnight. Each state except Pennsylvania had its own militia. The militia came into being with the very founding of the colonies as a means of local defense against the Indians. But the indigenous military forces of the colonies developed rapidly into a dual system. Along with the recruitment of soldiers for local defense, there were pressures to send military personnel to join expeditionary forces to fight Indians on the frontier and to participate in operations against the French.

So the militia formally was an obligatory system, a form of conscription under which each able-bodied man was required to register. Service was not thought of as mercenary. Of course, even for local self-defense there were inequities and privileged exemptions. The rank and file of the militia, especially those engaged in frontier operations, were recruited heavily from the young and those without property. Officers tended to come from the better situated social strata.

When the revolutionary war broke out and a continental army was being organized, Washington preferred volunteers. But reliance on volunteers, even with meaningful bounties, did not produce sufficient numbers. Conscription, in the form of a rather loose system of "selective service," was introduced. The term of enlistment was generally twelve months, since longer terms would work grave economic hardship on families of those conscripted. Married men were exempt. Since only a portion of the eligibles were recruited, the necessary quota for each state was divided among the militia regiments, and in each regiment the appropriate number was selected by lot.

The system was not all-inclusive, and there was bias because a prospective conscript could hire a substitute. Despite these distortions, there was a marked degree of representativeness. Certainly, the colonial military was much more representative than the British regular forces. In effect, the revolutionary army represented a break with the format of monarchical armies of Europe, including the forces of Great Britain. In these armies, the ordinary soldiers were mainly mercenaries. They were seen as agents of the state without political rights. The officers had upper-strata self-conceptions, and were recruited heavily from minor gentry families.

The diverse social backgrounds in the various colonial forces meant that the military had broad connections to civilian society. Many segments of civilian society had relatives and friends in military service, so that the active duty forces had a strong base of civilian contact and support. I would also speculate, on the basis of research and observation, that the social diversity of the colonial forces broadened their military's perspectives. Homogeneous military units develop a uniform outlook about the outside world, while contact with differing social types can lead to toleration and a sense of the necessity for internal compromise.

The British forces not only were occupiers but had a social structure that separated them from the ordinary colonial citizen. Neither the self-defined aristocrats of the British nor their heavy concentration of "lumpen

39

proletariat" made effective contact with colonial society. Interestingly enough, some enlisted personnel in the British army and the hired Hessian troops, in particular, deserted once they saw that the Americans considered them as just another group of potential immigrants.

Many of the colonists had their own personal weapons. Broadening the social base of the revolutionary armed forces by means of an imperfect system of conscription was a remarkable step. It was even more remarkable that oppositionist colonial leaders believed and anticipated that wide segments of the armed citizenry would support colonial political leaders and state legislatures, and they did. They were, in effect, citizens with varying degrees of political, especially electoral, rights.

Equally remarkable was the broadening of the social base of recruitment of the colonial officer cadres. There were not a sufficient number of "upper class" from the minor gentry to perpetuate the European pattern. One study of the top elite of the Continental army—twenty-nine major generals—found that they were well situated but hardly reflected an aristocratic mold.[22] This group represented a limited amount of military experience and no military education. Many served in the state militia, but in the Revolution few distinguished themselves as military commanders in the field. They operated in a broad spectrum of tasks as administrators and were heavily involved in civil-military relations and in maintaining troop morale. With a strong concentration of prior civil and political experience, they easily readjusted to civilian life at the end of hostilities.

Although the colonial militia often elected their officers, their internal organization was less important politically than their societal context. A small but distinct minority of those who entered the militia and the state volunteer units were committed to the building of a democratic political system. At least, they fully accepted the emerging indigenous political institutions. In essence, the political overtones of the militia and the state volunteer units reflected the culture of civilian society with an increasingly democratic content. A minority of militia men became loyalist as individuals or as units. But the very fact that most members, both enlisted men and officers, had earlier been involved in local defense increased their commitment to the goals of an independent nation-state. By 1776, local militia and some state volunteer units were institutions that had existed as much as a century and had a reasonable amount of experience. In the decade before the outbreak of hostilities, various localities and states had strengthened their militia groups as a political counterweight to the presence of British regulars.

22. Don Higginbotham, "Military Leadership in the American Revolution," in *Leadership in the American Revolution* (Washington: Library of Congress, 1974), pp. 92–111.

The Revolution redefined the operational goals and political meaning of membership in the militia. As appropriately summarized by John Shy, "popular military service was as old as the colonies, but never before had its performance or avoidance defined political categories."[23] Immediately, the colonial militia became a political arm of the revolutionary civilian leaders. The militia enforced control over its members, by coercion if necessary, which spilled over to the civilian population. This was especially the case where British military authority was limited or even totally absent. The militia operated by a mixture of force and persuasion. The militia worked to prevent defectors and strengthened the morale of those who thought of themselves as rebels. Many apathetic men were swept into the militia, and even those in mild opposition were at times forced to serve. The militia acted as a mobilizer of sentiments drawing on its traditions which included civil supremacy and respect for democratic ideals.

Although the militia men were quick to use force, the fact that their ranks included some less than enthusiastic meant that it was an arena of "give and take" or political compromise. High turnover in personnel meant that the bulk were called on to make "reasonable" sacrifices in a setting of ever-present mortal danger. Few became embittered because of prolonged deployment, and few manifested extremist attitudes immediately after the war, a fact that is highly relevant for my concern with the Revolution as an experience in civil education.

Historians have debated the extent of repression immediately after the end of hostilities. Although many loyalists had to flee the colonies for Canada and elsewhere, reconciliation came rapidly and was more extensive, certainly, than after the French Revolution. The spirit of the militia was certainly not vengeful. War frenzy was strong in 1776 and 1777, but six years of persistent hostilities cooled the fighting ardor. As John Shy observes, "Bitter experience of fighting from weakness had all but obliterated the naive optimism of 1776, and had sensitized Americans to their own political peril."[24] The colonists won the war and achieved political separation, but the victory was not so decisive that political leadership could impose an arbitrary and extremist formula of government on those who had reservations about the war of independence. Moreover, the famine and widespread economic misery which often accompany successful revolution were absent. Relatively favorable material circumstances contributed to avoiding fragmentation of former colonies.

The civil-military relations that emerged in the American Revolution has had a profound influence on the nation. A democratic society rests

23. Shy, *A People Numerous and Armed*, p. 219.
24. Ibid., p. 17.

on a delicate but effective balance between a center of authority and local political initiative. If the political system of the nation-state rests on an overcentralized concentration of authority, the essential spirit of localism can be thwarted. By contrast, if there is too weak a central authority, the nation-state can easily fragment. The organization of authority of the revolutionary military forces represented a relatively effective balance between elements of centralization and localism.

In the decades after the Revolution, the militia continued to operate as a pressure group against a strong national army and to demand priority for itself. There was extensive support in the electorate for this arrangement. Richard H. Kohn has documented the long and difficult struggle to develop and institutionalize a workable federal military force.[25] The result was a politically acceptable balance which contributed to democratic institution building.

Certain officers tried to undermine or at least challenge the civilian political institutions and leadership. The highly publicized Newburgh "conspiracy" was an abortive effort to organize opposition to the Continental Congress because of its failure adequately to compensate the officer corps. George Washington helped control and divert this organization of discontent. The issue lasted until the 1780s, when officers received a lump-sum retirement settlement. Antidemocratic efforts by members of the officer corps were limited and gradually disappeared.

Civic consciousness, as I define the term, is hard to measure. The most that can be said is that political leadership had enough civic consciousness to create a viable national entity. But what were the enduring or long-term consequences of this form of civic education, as embodied in the citizen soldier concept? The expression of the citizen soldier in the face of the increased size and destructiveness of modern warfare was the extension of the draft in World War I and World War II and the striking continuity of the militia concept in the form of the national guard. In sketching out the civic education resulting from military service we are dealing not only with the rise but, in turn, with the fall of conscription in the United States. I believe that, with the fall of conscription, officially on 30 June 1973, and the establishment of an expanded "peacetime" all-volunteer military establishment, the contribution of military service to civic education becomes problematic. The next chapter investigates the proposition that military service in the federal forces, from the point of view of civic education and effective citizenship, has developed the potential to be counterproductive.

25. Kohn, *Eagle and Sword*.

Three

Military Service as Civic Education

THE RISE OF CONSCRIPTION

In the two hundred years since the American Revolution, the nation has had extensive military experience. What social and political consequences did performing one's military obligation have on the attitudes of those engaged in the major and minor wars the United States fought? The "citizen soldier" concept has certainly persisted. With the expanded all-volunteer force, however, the contribution of the armed forces to civic education of the rank-and-file soldier, and even of the short-term officer, has declined. Efforts to avoid conscription, and the ability of the military to avoid excessive militarization of its personnel, have characterized U.S. civil-military relations for two hundred years.

We must start with the American Revolution and the period immediately after the war. Two attitudes stand out. First, the framers of the Constitution found themselves under pressure not to create a "standing army" such as the British force which fought in the American Revolution. American revolutionary leaders did organize a continental military force, but relied heavily on militia recruitment. With the end of hostilities, large segments of those who served in the revolutionary forces, as well as many in the civilian population, expressed opposition to a centralized army. Instead, there was a great deal of support for a militia system under the control of local authorities. If there had to be a national military, it should be as small as possible.

In the years immediately after the Revolution, both military and political reasons were offered in support of a militia system. It was argued that the British regulars were defeated to an important extent by local, part-time forces. Moreover, the militia system, with its local affiliations, was considered more appropriate for the new society with its aspirations for democratic rule. It was argued that a local militia system strengthened democratic forms both during and after the Revolution, and would continue to serve as a useful counterweight to the central government.

Federal forces grew very slowly. The new government had to face strong opposition to establishing even a small "standing military." Instead, a dual system developed. The two segments of the military establishment would exist side by side—the local militia and the federal forces.

The militia was as much a political formula with localistic roots as it was a part of the military establishment. Almost explicitly, it was designed to reduce the threat of arbitrary government by a national military. The militia, therefore, had considerable local political support. Continuities with the militia system exist in the reserve units of the contemporary all-volunteer military.

In the postrevolutionary period, the Americans sought to build their military as a nonmercenary, citizen soldier force under partial direction of career officers. Federal regulation of the local forces grew as warmaking became more and more complicated, yet dualism was maintained and perpetuated for local political goals. While regular professional officers argued for a unified national system, political leaders voted to keep the dual system alive. The military professional component has increased, but the local militia, now the national guard, has exhibited remarkable staying power. This power extended from the reorganization and reconstitution of the military after the debacle of the War of 1812 up to the present day.

During the revolutionary war, the ideology of obligatory service was strong. When the framers of the Constitution sought to maintain the militia, they had to face the difficulties of keeping alive the obligatory requirement. With the end of the war, and with reduced threat from Indians, fewer and fewer were required to serve.

Our goal is to probe for generalizations about the social and political impact of military service on soldiers who served in various military engagements of the United States. We are concerned with the continuities and the differences from one war to the next.

Between the end of the revolutionary war and 1945, the United States, while struggling to perfect its democratic institutions, fought three major and three lesser wars. These hostilities did not create an ethos of militarism. This is not to underestimate the human costs or the social and political distrust that were generated, but merely to assert that the milieu of the U.S. military, even during wartime, had powerful civilian overtones. The citizen soldier was prepared to fight and to follow the career military. Yet the ethos created within the ranks of the military forces was strikingly civilian and indifferent to the ideology of militarism.

With the exception of the Civil War, military participation up to 1945 served to incorporate the citizen soldier into the larger society. Values of the men on active duty—in national guard units or in federal units—were essentially a reflection of their civilian education and experience. The civic education, mainly informal, that military service generated was not based on admiration of military tradition. Nor, as we shall see, did the American military create elaborate machinery to indoctrinate its personnel. Until Korea, the United States had won all its military engagements, and the various military campaigns had extensive popular support. The major and minor wars were seen as specific national engagements having readily attainable goals in a relatively limited time. The end of hostilities, after the revolutionary war and all subsequent wars, meant an end to the military organization created to fight and win each particular engagement. This pattern established in the American Revolution persisted to the period immediately following World War II, and was reversed only when the United States found itself in the international struggles of the post-1945 era. In essence, civilian control of the military was based on the drastic reduction of the size and resources of the military as soon as the United States achieved its military goals. Korea and Vietnam represented a new type of large-scale war for the United States.

The numbers of personnel involved in the major and minor wars of the United States should be recalled at this point:

Military Engagements	Personnel
Revolutionary war	184,000 to 250,000 (estimate)
War of 1812	286,730
Mexican War	78,718
Civil War	
Union forces only	2,213,000
Confederate forces	600,000 to 1,500,000 (estimate)
Spanish-American War	300,000
World War I	4,744,000
World War II	16,354,000
Korea	5,764,000
Vietnam	8,811,000

A more stable military system started to develop with military reforms of the turn of the century. While units of the national guard became better organized and more durable, the basic change was mobilization based on conscription, planned in peacetime and implemented in wartime. This occurred in part because the military did not see itself as a center for indoctrination.

Between the end of the American revolutionary war and the introduction of the expanded all-volunteer military force in 1973, the armed forces of the United States underwent drastic changes in personnel and military technology and considerable transformation in organization.[1] The growth in destructive capacity almost defies comprehension. The destructive potentials require military formations to disperse their manpower in order to survive an assault.[2] To accommodate such warmaking potentials, military organizations had to transform their systems of communication, authority, and discipline. Paradoxically, increase in firepower reduced the number of military personnel directly involved in purely military operations. The armed forces moved gradually and steadily to a format similar to large-scale civilian organizations. But the threat of war meant that armed forces maintained a special organizational climate required for combat operations. The classical question of how long the battle could be sustained now makes deterrence an ever more attractive goal to both political leaders and military commanders.

Until the outbreak of World War II, the growth in firepower per fighter was a discontinuous process—long periods of stagnation followed by intensive outbursts of research and development. For the United States, fluctuation in manpower levels between wartime and peacetime was extreme, reflecting the periodicity of military operations and the absence of continuing conscription. World War II and the resulting "permanent" tension between the United States and the Soviet Union, both armed with nuclear weapons, altered the traditional pattern of military ups and downs. Research and development were routinized, and increases in the destructive capacity of the military took the overtones of a "doomsday" machine. Likewise, after 1945, levels of personnel moved toward a relatively steady state. Indeed, World War II produced relatively less manpower mobilization than did World War I. In turn, the Korean conflict required

1. Most writings about U.S. military history do not serve the purposes of describing broad institutional developments. There are, however, bold and imaginative studies such as Russell F. Weigley, *History of the United States Army* (New York: Macmillan Publishing Co., 1967); Walter Millis, *Arms and Men: A Study of American Military History* (New York: G. P. Putnam's Sons, 1956).

2. Statistics on trends in the number of "fighters" deployed per kilometer of "front" dramatically represent the "revolution" in military organization. In the Civil War, there were approximately 7,650 men per kilometer of fighting front; by World War I, only 2,110; by World War II, 787. By 1976, military plans had dropped the figure to 74. These data take on even more pointed meaning when the firepower per forward man is charted over time. In the Civil War, a forward man carried 9.1 pounds of firepower; by World War II, the figure had reached 161; as of 1976, 1,162.

relatively less mobilization than World War II, and the expansion in military manpower during the Vietnam conflict produced a further decline in mobilization. The armed forces had essentially shifted from a mobilization cadre to that of a "force in being" when the expanded all-volunteer force was introduced in 1973.

The dual system of military manpower in the United States, like so many constitutional and governmental arrangements developed after the close of the American Revolution, was based on compromise. It was a compromise of the convictions of those political leaders opposed to a "standing force" and those who wished to see a strong professional federal force.

Historians have debated the military effectiveness of the system that operated from the period after the American Revolution until the termination of the Vietnam intervention. In retrospect, they have exposed a multitude of repeated minor and major, even fundamental, defects. Military organization is by its nature easy prey, and justifiably so, to such post hoc assessments. My own focus is upon the compatibility of the attitudes of military personnel with the long-term goals of a political democracy. Again and again I am struck by the absence of a strong militaristic ethos in the U.S. armed forces. Service has highlighted pragmatic efforts rather than military traditions. As Alfred Vagt puts it, the U.S. has emphasized the military way rather than militaristic patterns. Until the end of World War II, successful civil-military relations in the United States decisively increased popular acceptance of conscription and mass military service. The weakness of civil-military relations after 1945, I would argue, lay in the political imbalance between president and Congress in managing international affairs.

In the course of U.S. history, federal authority over the state-based militia and later over the national guard has grown. Yet the dual system has persisted, and locally based militia or national guard units have resisted efforts by the federal establishment to "take over" the reserves.[3] In the pluralistic format of the U.S. military, there are important elements of vitality and initiative.

Advocates of the national guard should not be viewed as simply pursuing narrow self-interest. Although organizational preservation and expansion are powerful drives, spokesmen for the citizen soldier format have contended that grass-roots attachment and sense of cohesion in the militia–

3. For a historical overview of the reserve system see Robert L. Goldich, "Historical Continuity in the U.S. Military Reserve System," *Armed Forces and Society* 7 (Fall 1980): 88–112.

national guard units are valuable military assets which should not be arbitrarily thrust aside in the name of national "efficiency." The dual system balances the strength of pluralist organization against useless rivalry.

The effectiveness of the national guard in mobilizing political support has received considerable attention. The persistence of the system has meant that numerous domestic "law and order" tasks—internal policing assignments, especially in connection with urban disorders and with public service strikes—fall heavily on the national guard. In turn, federal troops have been largely relieved of this irksome task. A democratic polity seeks, as far as possible, to separate its internal police function from the national defense mission. Such a separation helps to maintain and strengthen civil rights. The national guard has meant that the United States has been able to avoid a national police force. A form of civic education has been at work as the national guard has responded to reduce outbursts of local tension.[4]

But it is national defense that remains the core of the dual system. When the founding fathers turned their attention to the design of a peacetime army and navy, they were aware of strong support for a militia system which would embody the ideology of the citizen soldier. The organizational details proposed for well-regulated militia varied, and often had elements of unreality. Frequently, paper plans rather than military resources were the result.

Although he preferred volunteers, George Washington came to subscribe to a form of *levée en masse*—based on citizen obligation. As a priority, young men would be designated as the advance group, while a wide age spectrum served as a reserve force to support federal formations. The Militia Act of 1792 was passed to give renewed authority to state efforts. In effect, a system was created that continued the ideology of the citizen soldier but involved considerable personal voluntarism. If the militia was called to active duty, the tour of duty was sharply limited. Heavy reliance on rotation of personnel served to spread the burden. But it was the federal component that encountered the strongest opposition. The end of the revolutionary war saw the disbanding of the Continental army. In 1787, Congress affirmed the reestablishment of a federal force when it authorized a regiment of 700 men to police the frontier. Establishment of a naval force had an equally modest beginning. It took many years of agitation by "nationalist" political leaders to "institutionalize" the idea of a permanent

4. Specific policing tasks vary with the passage of time. In recent years they have involved the management of the strains generated by public service strikes. See James B. Jacobs, "The Role of Military Forces in Public Sector Labor Relations," *Industrial and Labor Relations Review* 35 (January 1982): 163–80.

army and navy—and it was indeed small until the outbreak of the War of 1812.[5]

The War of 1812 was the first real test of the U.S. dual ground force establishment. It was also a test of naval elements. The hasty expansion which resulted from the threat and actuality of war was carried out with considerable confusion. The United States "won" the War of 1812, but the dual system failed as a military format even in that small war. The system was continued mainly because of political opposition to an excessively centralized and federally dominated military structure. Moreover, the dual system had managed to thwart the British, so it seemed best to leave the system untouched.

After the War of 1812, the militia declined, especially as frontier warfare moved westward. In 1846, a congressional announcement described the militia system as "virtually dead." Moreover, the Mexican War enhanced the self-esteem and public reputation of federal forces—both West Point graduates and rank-and-file enlisted personnel. But the state-based militia system survived. Local political interests and social functions performed by a variety of elite state volunteers supplied the necessary political support to keep the system functioning or at least to maintain its formal structure. Militia units thought of themselves as representatives of the larger civil society or a personification of the nation. Format and relative size varied markedly from state to state, but the common element was an awareness of domestic political realities. That these militia and volunteer units resisted pressure to organize as ethnic enclaves was one of their main contributions to civic education.

With the trauma of the Civil War and its immense manpower requirements, the dual system was deeply strained; at times it actually broke down. When the war started, the North did not have enough federal troops to repress the insurrection. The Confederacy introduced a form of conscription, and the war settled down to a long and horrible confrontation. The state militia, and state volunteer system, served as important instruments of recruitment and military organization. The state volunteer system has been described by careful scholars as a quasi-levy or a form of draft. National and state quotas were established, and regiments were required to recruit and select the necessary manpower. Robert L. Goldich characterized it as "probably more analogous to the conscript forces raised by the United States during both world wars."[6]

Later, when Union leaders believed it necessary to pass a draft, it produced little additional manpower but generated considerable rioting and popular opposition. The draft riots were in part the result of outbursts

5. Kohn, *Eagle and Sword*, passim.
6. Robert L. Goldich, "Historical Continuity," p. 102.

by relatively recent immigrants who felt impressed or who had little knowledge of, or sympathy for, the Union's efforts. Under both state levies and the federal draft, the individual had the option of hiring substitutes. Yet the Civil War demonstrated the continued viability of the citizen soldier concept. The federal draft represented an important but partial step in nationalizing the recruitment base and supplied political support for future expansion in the recruitment of citizen soldiers. Neither during the Civil War nor during the two world wars, however, did conscription serve as an adequate substitute for local recruitment. By World War I, in addition to sheer local political support, state-based units had the historical record of their performance both in the Civil War and in the Spanish-American War, where their reasonable effectiveness was used to justify their continued existence. More important, parochial solidarity made their units "in being" more rapidly available than new federal units.

In World War I, conscription worked with considerable effectiveness; it triumphed during World War II. The draft not only operated with administrative dispatch but had sensitive local roots. Especially in World War II, immense numbers of draftees became the essential manpower recruits and "swamped" the national guard. The traditional debate about a completely unified system was intensified at the end of World War II but without real consequence. The dual system remained operative, not only for the ground forces, but also for the navy and air force. World War II was both the high point and the start of the decline of conscription in the United States. The national guard, on the other hand, remained an important repository of the citizen soldier concept as the nation moved toward a volunteer force.

The numbers enrolled in the state militia and later the national guard have generally been larger than in federal forces, but training has been less militarized. The state-based system, with its organizational and political diversity, inhibited the development of a unified and integrated military subculture. Such military culture that has existed in the United States was concentrated in the South, but the selection of military academy cadets on the basis of region, together with the geographical spread in the state-based systems, operated as counterweights to Southern military culture.

For some people, attracted to soldiering mainly because they were fond of military life, military and naval service were little related to civic education, either positive or negative. Still, most career officers and soldiers since the American Revolution have expressed a diffuse but powerful sense of nationalism.

By the middle of the nineteenth century, patriotism was often accompanied by primitive and hostile overtones—hardly responsible civic consciousness. During the nineteenth century, expansionism was widely accepted by the civilian population and especially by the military. The movement westward did not require lobbying by the national military establishment although federal troops were essential for security, policing, and fighting Indian wars. Both the Mexican and the Spanish-American wars demonstrated the depth of crude nationalist sentiments, which could be made use of by the military. These two wars reveal a negative dimension in the nation's civic values—powerful xenophobia.

The wars against Mexico and the Spanish were startling in their popularity and in their aggressiveness. Some leaders believed that the success of these military engagements would produce benefits both for the United States and for the populations who would become subject to U.S. influence. Others saw expansion as both a profound error and a moral injustice. But one cannot overlook the fact that many participating Americans demonstrated satisfaction that they were able to join in a small, relatively short and manageable military engagement which tested their personal military capacities. As in Great Britain during the nineteenth century, these wars demonstrated that it was possible to organize imperialist military campaigns "abroad" while pressing forward with democratic institution building "at home."

But should not the Civil War be attracting our main attention as an experience in civic education? Was the Civil War a military event comparable to the American Revolution in forging the United States into an independent nation-state?

It is hard to think of fratricide as the setting for building effective citizenship. I speak not mainly of creating national loyalty, which may be the result of a civil war for segments of the victorious side. By citizenship, I refer to the popular attitudes and institutions required for building consent and the exercising of power in a democratic polity.

If the question is posed in this fashion, then at least a negative answer about the Civil War is possible. The nation-state survived as a political entity; indivisibility of the political union was affirmed. The Constitution was no mere piece of paper but a franchise for government. The nation did not merely survive; it endured with enough vitality to reconstruct its central political institutions in a democratic format.

Unfortunately, I cannot point to a body of data about changes in attitudes as a result of military participation in a civil war which seemed to have no end and whose political boundaries were almost all-encompassing. There is less research to assist in making assertions that there is about the American Revolution. Obviously, the basis of morale and the aftermath of the military experience was markedly different in the North and in the South. Northern troops fought mainly out of loyalty to their comrades and to the military system constructed by political and military authorities. But loyalty also included acceptance of an idea about the sanctity of the Union and the nation-state. Slavery was at best a secondary issue, though it grew more important with the passage of time and the increased loss of human life. This is not to say that the Northern armies were ideologically motivated. Many were made nationalists or stronger nationalists by the course of the war. There were Northerners opposed to the war on principle. They and their political leaders were a limited constituency. Much more important were those who were opposed because they did not wish to risk their lives for the preservation of an idea they accepted only mildly. In the end, Northern troops, despite personal hardship, did not develop extensive alienated cadres in opposition to federal political leadership. They soon returned home, and their main political interest was demands for veterans' benefits. They found a relatively intact local community system with strong elements of continuity which helped to integrate them into civilian society and the larger political system. The capacity of the United States quickly to absorb its former citizen soldiers has been conspicuous, except for the Vietnam engagement.

By contrast, Southern troops and their officers, because of the intensity of their defeat and the agonies of reconstruction, were more profoundly influenced by their participation in the Civil War. Confederate officers and enlisted men returned to their homes only to find that military defeat in the field had not effectively ended the Civil War. An important minority was prepared, or persuaded or coerced, to carry on armed opposition to the Union victory and political goals in the South. With the subtle use of force as well as outright intimidation they succeeded in implanting a new form of "slavery" which, despite gradual erosion, took almost a century to eliminate. If military defeat and occupation were designed to "improve" popular attitudes, the aftermath of the Civil War in the South was a complete failure in civic education. (The defeat of National Socialism and the military occupation of West Germany demonstrate that positive results have been realized in at least one major historical case.)

If, before the Civil War, the South was a region with a distinct culture, the war only served to emphasize its separateness from the rest of the nation. Southern politics rested on its own limited definition of citizenry and, in effect, maintained that definition after military defeat. The South was unaltered by the Fourteenth Amendment, which after the Civil War nominally gave legal citizenship to "all persons born or naturalized in the United States." In fact, the limited citizenry brought into power once again a political oligarchy which stressed its own version of the accomplishments of the Confederate army. This historical interpretation had immense political consequence. Members of the Southern oligarchy not only ruled the postbellum South but, because of the seniority system of Congress, ironically came to exercise disproportionate political power at the national level.

The Civil War strengthened regional patriotism in the South, which later could be linked to the patriotism extant in the larger society. It is not strange that, given the traditions of the South in military matters, military defeat served to strengthen martial attitudes and interests. Southerners became extensively involved once again in the management of the U.S. military establishment and contributed to fashioning its sociopolitical perspectives.

It is not unusual in Western nations for less industrialized regions with hereditary landed interests to be the locus of military and expansionist attitudes. In the United States, the Civil War did not disrupt traditional, rural values but strengthened them to a degree. Thus not only in the immediate postbellum years but, as John S. Reed has so penetratingly observed, into the 1960s and beyond, the South has maintained much greater continuity in culture and attitudes than the rest of U.S. society.[7]

More than twenty years separated the participation of the U.S. military in World Wars I and II. However, from the point of view of citizenship, we can think of the military developments and impact as one prolonged engagement, with a major interruption. In both wars, reservists were called to active duty, but the important development was institutionalization of the draft. While in both wars there were imperfections in the system of conscription, the procedure worked with reasonable effectiveness. The relative equality of treatment legitimated the draft system and contributed to the popular acceptance of the war aims. The conscription system had a positive impact on the troops and on important elements in their civic education. The rank and file of the military were further integrated into the larger society because conscription had a strong element of equality. Despite extensive distortions in their treatment, minority groups and their leaders did serve in the military.

United States authorities in World War I immediately faced the "alien" problem. Wave after wave of immigrants had increased the number of aliens. The tradition of the United States was not to make a sharp distinction between citizens and aliens in recruitment to the armed services, especially in time of war. Security and loyalty, of course, were paramount. Therefore, aliens were classified as either cobelligerents, neutrals, or enemies, and the first two categories were acceptable for induction, if otherwise qualified. James Jacobs estimates that approximately 9 percent of

7. John S. Reed, *The Enduring South: Subcultural Persistence in Mass Society* (Chapel Hill: University of North Carolina Press, 1972).

World War I military personnel were not citizens; aliens were thus an important source of personnel.[8] The United States has continued its efforts to recruit aliens for military service although the numbers have declined. Aliens who have served in the U.S. military are entitled to more liberal naturalization procedures and are exempt from the requirement of lawful admission for permanent residence. As of 1980, under the expanded all-volunteer force, the number of aliens serving is estimated at more than 35,000 or approximately 1.8 percent.

Once aliens were accepted as volunteers or drafted, the military made efforts to integrate them into the armed forces and facilitate their acculturation into American society. During World War I, certain ethnic leaders in the United States, inspired by the self-determination appeals of President Woodrow Wilson, sought, for political objectives, to have military units organized on nationality lines. As with earlier efforts to establish ethnic units, civilian and military leaders successfully resisted such proposals, which were clearly at odds with U.S. military tradition and with the political principles of the period.

Black personnel represented a disturbing exception, since they were essentially segregated. During World War I, particular black political leaders agitated to have blacks armed in segregated units for purposes of "race" pride and to establish the loyalty and citizen worth of black troops. They pressed that such troops should not be limited to supply and support duties, but armed for active combat. To be armed was the essential symbolism of equality and full citizenship. In World War II, hardly anyone advocated ethnically homogeneous military units. The principle of acculturation without necessary loss of personal ethnic attachments was the accepted organizational principle. Black leaders continued pressure during World War II to arm blacks, but added the motif of "armed and integrated," a condition that came during the Korean War and contributed to the integration of blacks in civilian society. By contrast, military personnel of German extraction could request assignment to the Pacific theater. An interesting strategy was followed by the Nisei—second-generation Japanese living in the United States—who were assigned at their request to Japanese-American special units to demonstrate their loyalty, which they did by their combat achievements.

World War I produced intense concern about morale and fighting effectiveness. Among objects of special concern were the morale of ground combat units who had to bear the burden of war casualties, and the extent to which recent immigrants had been "acculturated" and were in fact loyal

8. James B. Jacobs and Leslie Anne Hayes, "The Eligibility and Obligation of Aliens to Serve in the United States Armed Forces: A Historical-Legal Analysis," *Armed Forces and Society* 7 (Winter 1981): 188–90.

and committed to U.S. military policies. In World War I the United States launched extensive—no doubt excessive—propaganda efforts. These efforts were directed toward the domestic population as well as to allies, neutrals, and enemy nations overseas. It was therefore understandable that U.S. troops were to be designated as a "target audience" for indoctrination and education. The justification was that a democratic society required informed military personnel if they were to fight effectively.

The high command of the U.S. was opposed to such programs.[9] Army leaders believed that the training recruits had received from civilian society was adequate for acceptance into the army. The military were skeptical of their ability to launch indoctrination programs and doubted their efficacy. However, under civilian pressures, the War Department was forced to develop special programs. Dissatisfied with the response of the War Department, the leading figure pressing for political indoctrination of the military was Colonel Edward Munson, a member of the Medical Corps described as having "the backing of the Surgeon General and of a large number of civilian psychologists."[10] He was able to have a Morale Branch established under his command with a specialist assigned to each regiment and training base to teach "patriotism and love of country."[11] There is no evidence that these efforts had a positive effect, but it is unlikely that they caused any serious tensions. By 1921 the army had replaced the Morale Branch with a more conventional Welfare Branch.

In World War II, certain political leaders and mass media specialists again demanded that the armed forces undertake programs of information and civic education. Before the Japanese attack on Pearl Harbor there was a deep split in U.S. public opinion about involvement in World War II. A strong isolationist segment in the civilian population was mirrored in recruits mobilized both in the call-up reserve units and among conscripts. Legislation authorizing conscription had to face determined political resistance. Although the attack on Pearl Harbor fundamentally changed U.S. attitudes, the military services, despite considerable internal resistance, recognized that they had responsibilities to assist in informing the troops of the background and developments of World War II. General George C. Marshall gave crucial leadership in developing a program which

9. For one approach to the history of troop indoctrination in the United States army, see Stephen D. Wesbrook, *Political Training in the United States Army: Reconsideration*, Mershon Center Position Papers in the Policy Sciences, no. 3 (Columbus, Ohio: Mershon Center of the Ohio State University, March, 1979), 64 pp. See also Morris Janowitz and Stephen D. Wesbrook, eds., *The Political Education of Soldiers*, forthcoming.

10. Stephen D. Wesbrook, "Political Training in the United States Army," pp. 23, 14.

11. Ibid., p. 14.

fitted the needs of the U.S. citizen soldier. Marshall's staff sought to avoid a heavy-handed indoctrination program. There were civilians in U.S. information and propaganda operations during World War II who believed that U.S. forces required ideological indoctrination. They argued that the German military was strengthened by Nazi indoctrination. Such a viewpoint grossly overstated the role of ideology in the fighting effectiveness of mass conscript armies, including German forces.

During World War II, ideological indoctrination did not prevail in the U.S. military. If it had been attempted, it would have received little attention from soldiers, sailors, and airmen in the field. Instead, a low-key program was organized on a worldwide basis which stressed factual information, concrete strategic developments, and the pronouncements of U.S. political leaders who were unified in support of American war aims. The program rested in making available to military personnel the contents of the mass media produced by the commercial sector. As various studies have demonstrated, both civilian and military morale improved as the final goals, with the accumulation of victories in the field, became more real and closer to attainment.[12] In World War II, the armed forces were able to handle the day-to-day task of informing troops in the field without becoming deeply involved in political education. Policies of the military authorities were compatible with the citizen soldier concept. The news the troops received was very similar to that available in the mass media on the home front. There were outcries of censorship, slanted news, and mismanagement, but the system was viewed as relatively acceptable. The military were able to supply essential information and rely on the appeals of a unified political leadership without becoming involved in ideological controversy.

During World War II, however, the real citizen education came not from "troop information and education," relevant though such efforts were. To a limited extent in World War I and extensively in World War II, both ordinary recruits and citizen officers considerably broadened their self-conceptions and perspectives on U.S. society. The process was not complex, but the consequence was profound in that these military experiences prepared the groundwork for the acceptance, after 1945, of the expansion of mass consumption and, in turn, the emergence of the welfare state. The same phenomenon took place in the United States and in Western Europe—both in victorious Great Britain and in defeated Germany.[13]

The rank-and-file military, as well as wartime officers, thought of themselves as citizen soldiers, whether conscripts or volunteers, and not as

12. However, as discussed later, Korean and Vietnam limited warfare presented for the U.S. a problem of declining civilian and military morale.
13. See Richard M. Titmuss, "War and Social Policy," *Essays on the Welfare State* (London: Allen and Unwin, 1958).

mercenaries. They were undertaking a national obligation, the outlines of which they saw with some clarity, although they lacked knowledge of the details. At the same time, they had become members of an organization of considerable efficiency, certainly as compared with many institutional sectors of civilian life. This was especially the case if they were of lower-status background. They were living and working in a "mobilized" societal environment. In their view, progress had taken place. They received medical treatment superior to their civilian experience. Food was allocated on a "fairer" basis. Their families had superior social services. The system as a whole operated with greater "justice" than in peacetime. The individual soldier experienced a "taste of a better life." The hardship and trauma of war were a different matter, of course. If with the burden of armaments such progress could be made and welfare better organized, certainly a peacetime civilian society should be able to produce a better administered and more adequate life. Wartime experiences consequently helped generate political and social attitudes in support of the welfare state in the period after the war. Military service had therefore served well as a form of civic education for socially deprived elements of society.

Some of these welfare rights were justified as benefits for veterans—for those who had served the nation in World War II. This was particularly true of loans to enable veterans to purchase housing and to underwrite the cost of college and graduate education. The scope of educational assistance embodied in the GI bill was immense; indeed, government funding transformed access to higher education. Approximately 2½ million veterans of the Second World War attended 2,000 institutions of higher learning at a cost to the federal government of about 5½ billion dollars.[14] A major reason for passage of the World War II GI bill was fear of extensive unemployment among veterans, which did not take place. The result was to broaden the base of recruitment into colleges and universities. The basis was established for federal and state subsidy to individual students to attend institutions of higher learning—a policy that continued. Linking these welfare programs to the civic obligations soldiers, sailors, and airmen had fullfilled greatly facilitated passage of the necessary legislation. There was an obvious interplay of rights and obligations. This linkage was gradually weakened and finally broken as conscription declined.

THE DECLINE OF CONSCRIPTION

What caused the political demise of conscription in the United States? The ability of the armed services to demonstrate the advantages of conscription after 1945 declined sharply. The most widespread but hardly

14. Keith W. Olson, *The G.I., the Veterans and the Colleges* (Lexington: University Press of Kentucky, 1974).

adequate explanation was Vietnam. Vietnam was an unpopular war which provoked dramatic opposition in the United States and even in the field. It was a war without clearcut and readily discernible goals. Yet the idea that Vietnam ended conscription is no more than an observation of the "proximate" cause. Deeper attitudes come into play.

Five basic trends that influenced the decline or transformation of conscription are not adequately recognized. First, there is the growth in the destructive capacity of modern weapons systems during and after World War II. The outbreak of general war—which would include the use of nuclear weapons—is considered by major political parties in the United States as something that would not be in the national interest but, rather, a failure of NATO policy. Massive mobilization of conventional conscripts is no longer required. The actual manning of nuclear devices for purposes of deterrence has passed quickly into the hands of volunteer military formations. Conventional forces to deter the outbreak of limited war by other conventional forces are still defined as essential. However, among advanced industrial nations, experts believe that war, if it occurs, will be fought by highly powerful forces "in being" or very rapidly mobilized. Therefore, for nations such as the United States, mass conventional conscription is counterproductive to the military mission to be performed.

The second trend is a decline in the Western powers' use of draft forces after 1945 in maintaining hegemony over their colonial territories. The British withdrew from most colonial possessions without military confrontation. In a few cases they made use of volunteer forces in an effort to create more stable, effective, and responsible local governments. The French rapidly learned that draftees were of limited value in their efforts to continue control over their colonies. Paradoxically, the United States, with its historical commitment to national self-determination, sought to make use of draft personnel to take over the French commitment in Vietnam with results which failed both militarily and politically. With the decline in the use of a draft military for intervention in the third world, another rationale for conscription was weakened.

Third, in advanced industrialized nations of the West (and correspondingly in the Soviet Union and Soviet-dominated nations), military service is more and more seen as counter to the desired style of life. Before World War II, peacetime conscription for military service was seen by many soldiers as having a strong element of "adventure." It has come to be seen as "boring," inhibiting personal development, and limiting the pursuit of personal pleasures. In the United States, draftees as well as volunteers complained of the intrusion into privacy and of the meaningless forms of discipline and petty harassment. Military service, even for sons of the "working class," lost its appeal as a passage to manhood and a personal challenge. The attraction of a short period of service as a personal experience weakened and, with it, popular support for conscription.

Fourth, national defense remains a national goal supported by the electorate through immense fiscal allocations. However, the welfare state and protection of the environment have come to compete with national defense for funds. This competition has further weakened the idea of conscription. Public policy is debated in economic and cost terms. The population comes to think of conscription as an unfair and hidden tax. Many young people accept this economic logic and support the idea of market levels of compensation for military service.

The fifth trend was felt directly by important segments of the population—both by youth and by their parents. Once World War II was terminated, the conscription system was characterized by profound inequality. Total mobilization was no longer pursued, even during the hostilities of Korea and Vietnam. The numerous exemptions were viewed as unjust, prompted extensive grass roots criticism, and reduced the legitimacy of the conscription system.

These five trends help to explain the decline as well as the shift in the forms of conscription in Western political democracies. The decline in NATO nations has taken various forms such as complete elimination, reduction in the number of draftees, or shortening of the length of draft service.[15] The contribution of the Vietnam war to the end of conscription diverts attention from the basic transformation of the use of force in international relations, particularly among the superpowers. For the Western powers, these changes have undermined and/or restricted reliance on conscription. The use of force has historically operated with self-imposed limitations, and these limitations have increased since 1945, especially for Western political democracies.[16] This does not imply that the threat of

15. The decline of the "mass armed force" has also led to the development of new proposals to deal with the problems of military manpower. One approach offered is to limit conscription to a brief period—six months, for example—followed by a longer period in the ready reserve. Another set of recommendations deals with a two-tier system; the first tier composed of volunteers manning the active duty combat "force in being," and the second of conscripts for local defense and support units. The revival of a militia concept has also been formulated, designed for defense of specific local territories. All these recommendations are oriented to reduce the time required for military mobilization and to make available manpower which can support effectively a "force in being." It should be noted that during the post–Korean War period of the 1950s, more than 75 percent of all eligible American men served in the peacetime military (either on active duty or in the reserves). This figure was 16 percent in the all-volunteer force period. The perceived likelihood of military service among men must have accounted for some of its acceptance and legitimacy of the conscript system.

16. Ellen Stern, ed., *The Limits of Military Force* (Beverly Hills: Sage Publications, 1977).

force or the use of force is, for Western political democracies, moving to the point of no return. Decline in the use of force is hardly the same as loss of utility.

But the long-term historical changes in military organization and service are manifested and fashioned in day-to-day politics. The selective service system during the Vietnam war became a focal point of criticism and hostility, but one cannot argue that defects in administration of the draft brought about its demise, although these defects were powerful contributory factors. Lt. Gen. Lewis B. Hershey, as he aged and rigidified, became an easy target of those opposed to involvement in the Vietnam war. The local draft board system during World War II had a strong grass roots base. After 1970, when public criticism led to greater centralization, the selective service system became more and more a "federalized" administrative agency in the hands of government clerks.

The selective service system was attacked for being unfairly administered. It was argued that educational and health standards worked to exclude members of the lowest socioeconomic strata from the armed forces. It was argued on the other hand, by those who saw avoidance of military service as more desirable than the opportunity to serve, that college deferment was unfair because it favored the more privileged strata. College deferment was eliminated during the Vietnam war, but critics still claimed that members of the middle class had an advantage in finding other means to avoid the draft. Research on inductions indicates no relation between father's social position and son's military service; lower-class sons were able just as frequently as middle-class sons to avoid military service.[17] Moreover, for the period of conscription as a whole, the system worked relatively fairly—as fairly as one could expect of a human system. Research data did substantiate the claim, however, that the very bottom of the social structure was underrepresented because of high rejection for educational and health reasons.

The most pronounced distortion was in assignment of enlisted personnel after induction; lower-class persons with limited skill and education tended to be assigned to combat units and therefore had a higher incidence of casualties. On the basis of the available crude data, blacks suffered disproportionately in this regard. If this were the case, the imbalance would have taken place during the years 1965–67. But the official data report that blacks accounted for 12.1 percent of all combat deaths in the Vietnam war and 14.2 percent of all army enlisted deaths. The claim that blacks suffered disproportionately remains a debatable proposition. Subsequent statistical analysis highlighted that socioeconomic position was more im-

17. Neil D. Fligstein, "Who Served in the Military, 1940–1973?" *Armed Forces and Society* 6 (Winter 1980): 297–312.

portant than racial background.[18] Still, public debate proceeded without regard to these findings. Interestingly enough, among officers, the higher their social background, the more likely they were to become casualties. In any case, inequality in the risk of combat by social position clearly served as a powerful focal point of criticism during the Vietnam war.

Since partial mobilization weakens the legitimacy of conscript service, how does a democratic society solve the issue? Who shall serve when all are not required? Full mobilization or effective universal service in peacetime eliminates many difficult political and moral issues of conscription. In nations such as France and Sweden, conscription is made as universal as possible for the relevant age cohorts. The theme of universal service is given equality to—even priority over—purely military considerations, at least over the short term. In the Federal Republic of Germany, the problem of universality is dealt with by making alternative civilian service available to conscripts.

Military service for U.S. personnel after 1945 was in the setting of the worldwide cold war. Debate about the importance of troop indoctrination was intensified in the cold war. The Korean war was a limited war in which there were serious reversals before a frustrating stalemate emerged. There was considerable debate, or rather clamor, in the mass media about communist expansion and infiltration as well as efforts to explain the United States' lack of success in countering the communists. The agitational activities of Senator Joseph McCarthy during the Korean war only exacerbated these concerns. Many political leaders came to believe that the United States did not lack the potential manpower or military equipment. What the United States appeared to have failed in was the indoctrinating of its personnel so that they could "stand up against" the combined political and military offensive of the communists. In other words, United States citizen soldiers did not know "what they were fighting for."

Such a stance is indeed paradoxical since, with the appointment of General Matthew Ridgway, the U.S. army forged the most effective fighting force it had produced in the twentieth century. But the performance of the citizen soldier was judged on the basis of the alleged behavior of American prisoners of war captured and interned by communist armies. The behavior of American POWs was judged to be weak and ineffective and even, occasionally, immoral. Their behavior reflected not only the lack of political indoctrination but also elements of weakness and immorality in civilian society. Mainly through the research of Albert D. Bid-

18. Gilbert Badillo and G. David Curry, "The Social Incidence of Vietnam Casualties: Social Class or Race?" *Armed Forces and Society* 2 (Spring 1976): 397–406.

erman, gross factual distortions in these claims were revealed.[19] Biderman found the behavior of American soldiers in captivity to be the same as any group of soldiers in the same circumstances. In his judgment, only additional realistic military training and specific training on how to survive in captivity were required. Nevertheless, a program of ideological indoctrination was pressed by civilians in the Department of Defense and by various public groups. Even before the outbreak of the Korean war, the Department of Defense had intensified its "Information and Education" effort. The Chaplains' Corps was involved in this enterprise, which continued to become more explicit after the Korean war. The civilian-dominated level of the Department of Defense, guided by the thinking of John C. Broger and his formulation of "Militant Liberty," argued for and established a heavy ideological dosage approach. Others, including many professional officers, were doubtful about such indoctrination. They considered political education the task of civilian institutions. The role of the armed force was to facilitate the spread of factual information in a format consistent with the national interest, following the model used during World War II. The U.S. navy outrightly rejected the use of material prepared for the Militant Liberty program; the marines were equally negative. But in terms of imagery, the strong indoctrination advocates had the upper hand.

By the end of the Vietnam war, the extensive indoctrination goals of the 1950s and their support resources had been reduced or had atrophied. This was the natural history of a program with unrealistic goals and elements incompatible with U.S. political traditions. At first, the troops themselves largely ignored the indoctrination programs. Gradually, official regulations limited their scope. In 1962, the U.S. Advisory Committee to the Secretary of Defense on Non-Military Instruction issued a report which further reduced indoctrination strategy.[20] In turn, the very nature of the Vietnam war and deep divisions within both civilian society and the troops virtually killed military leaders' interest in ideological indoctrination, and, by 1977, the military had removed itself from this responsibility. Policy had traveled the full circular course. Nevertheless, the all-volunteer force was to present new and difficult problems of morale and political perspective.

With the end of the Vietnam war, public attention and research efforts shifted to the questions of veterans' adjustment into civilian society. How deep were the personal and psychological wounds of those who partici-

19. Albert D. Biderman, *March to Calumny: The Story of American POWs in the Korean War* (New York: Macmillan, 1963).

20. U.S. Advisory Committee on Non-Military Instruction (Karl R. Benetsen, Chairman), *Report* (Washington, D.C.: Secretary of Defense, July 20, 1962).

pated, especially in combat, in that "nasty" military confrontation? Second, how adequate were government programs of transition and assistance? In addition, there was the persistent question of the impact of Vietnam on the political outlook of those who served.

By the end of the Vietnam war, the United States had accumulated a large veteran population and already had a prolonged and mixed record of dealing with veteran "problems." In 1973, a year when public concern about Vietnam veterans was at or near its height, there were 29 million living U.S. veterans of all wars. The *U.S. Statistical Abstract* for 1974 notes that 8,811,000 persons served in the armed forces during the Vietnam war.[21]

The citizenry at large was relatively unaware of the large numbers involved, but did believe that Vietnam veterans would be especially difficult to reintegrate into civilian life and would require special treatment. Jack Ladinsky's careful review of available documentation and research has demonstrated that the difficulty was considerably less than anticipated by the mass media.[22] The basic problem was the failure of Congress to legislate an adequate program and the parallel slowness of the Veterans Administration to meet the needs of the new type of veteran who emerged from the Vietnam war. Though deeply concerned with the trauma and suffering of military personnel who served in Vietnam, Ladinsky rejected the exaggerated projections that Vietnam would produce immense cadres of drug-addicted, violence-oriented, and alienated veterans. The conditions of combat and even garrison life have to be assessed against the adequacy of veteran rehabilitation and assistance efforts.

Ladinsky points out that the bureaucratic structure of the Veterans Administration, geared to the needs of older men rather than those of younger veterans, deepened the transitional problem. (In 1973, World War II veterans averaged 54.4 years of age; Vietnam veterans 27.7.) Benefits were neither adequate nor effectively related to other welfare programs. Educational assistance was especially circumscribed. Gradually the benefits were increased, and the need for specialized programs, including outreach programs, were recognized and implemented. Given the lack of a hero's reception, scars had their impact on the politics of distrust and resentment.

Examination of the socioeconomic position of the veterans raises the question of the impact of military service on civilian earnings of veterans in the twentieth century. Patricia M. Shields has reviewed the research

21. *Statistical Abstract of the United States* (Washington, D.C.: U.S. Government Printing Office, 1974), p. 319.
22. Jack Ladinsky, "Vietnam, the Veterans, and the Veterans Administration," *Armed Forces and Society* 2 (Spring 1976): 435–67.

findings.[23] The results are mixed; some studies show higher income for veterans than for comparable nonveterans; others show no difference. It seems to me that the evidence for higher income for veterans is somewhat, but not decisively, stronger. There appeared to be a decline in the advantage for veterans from World War II to Korea to Vietnam. In this view, with the growth of civilian educational opportunities, the educational benefits connected with military service could be gotten as readily in civilian life as in the armed forces. Moreover, the evidence indicates the benefits in earning power were present both for whites and for blacks.[24]

With the development of social research, we have highly relevant data about Vietnam veterans. One careful attitude survey has produced important findings on the Vietnam experience itself as a form of civic education. This survey, completed by M. Kent Jennings and Gregory B. Markus, pinpoints the concentration and location of embitterment among Vietnam veterans. The findings are based on a two-wave national panel, 1965 and 1973, of 674 males, which allowed comparisons to be made between the almost one-half who served with those who did not.[25] These social scientists built their study on existing research which had demonstrated that military service does not automatically increase authoritarian attitudes, especially under conditions of conscription.

Jennings and Markus demonstrated that soldiers who had long service in Vietnam (more than the usual twelve months) became embittered. This was less because of actual military experience than because of resentment in the treatment of veterans, including themselves. One interpretation was that they believed combat experience generated citizen rights that were not fulfilled. (The number of embittered soldiers was contained by rotation, which had the side effect of weakening combat effectiveness of field units.) What was the overall attitude pattern of veterans, recognizing that only a minority saw actual combat? It is striking that, despite the frustration and trauma of the Vietnam war, this panel study found that even during the war, almost twice as many veterans were satisfied with their service experience as were dissatisfied (63 percent versus 37 percent).

In addition, when the veterans surveyed were compared with civilians, they were found to be somewhat less cynical and to have broader "political

23. Patricia M. Shields, "A Comment on Veteran Status Earnings and Race: Some Long Term Results," *Armed Forces and Society* 7 (Fall 1980): 171–73.

24. See, especially, Wayne J. Villemez and John D. Kasarda, "Veteran Status and Socio-economic Attainment," *Armed Forces and Society* 2 (Spring 1976): 407–20; also Sally C. Lopreato and Dudley L. Poston, Jr., "Difference in Earnings and Earning Ability between Black Veterans and Non-Veterans in the United States," *Social Science Quarterly* 57 (March 1977): 750–66.

25. M. Kent Jennings and Gregory B. Markus, "The Effect of Military Service on Political Attitudes: A Panel Study," *American Political Science Review* 71 (March 1977): 131–47.

horizons." Military service had some specific positive consequences on a broad measure of civic tolerance. (This was not the case for long-term career enlisted personnel.) The authors indicate that they also found support for the "hypothesis that the diversity to which the enlisted man is exposed does indeed have a liberalizing effect" (p. 143). It is my estimate, even in the absence of comparable survey data, that military experience was much more broadening in the Vietnam conflict than in World War II and at least as much so as in Korea. The military experience of Vietnam did contain important elements of civic education.

THE MEANING OF THE ALL-VOLUNTEER FORCE

We now turn to the civic educational aspects of the new, all-volunteer military. Available data from the first ten years indicate important differences from the traditional citizen soldier perspective. Negative potentials are manifest.

The political movement to end conscription did not await the end of U.S. involvement in Vietnam. In the presidential election campaign of 1968, both candidates committed themselves to the end of conscription as soon as feasible. A draft conference at the University of Chicago in December 1966 presented a mass of background data and analysis, with position papers on alternative solutions. Publication of the proceedings in 1967 came at a moment of intense national debate about the draft.[26] Although the conference was hardly designed to be a representative body, it soon emerged that the all-volunteer force had dominant support. It was striking that the leading spokesmen for this position came from both the right and the left, namely Milton Friedman, and Richard Flacks of Students for a Democratic Society. The minority position, national service with military and civilian options, was presented by me and rapidly pushed aside on the grounds of infringement of personal freedom or impracticality.

Despite the fact that both presidential candidates in 1968 supported an expanded all-volunteer force, it was not until 30 June 1973 that President Nixon could officially terminate the selective service system. Enormous effort was required to bring such a transformation into being, especially since many military officers did not believe that it could or should succeed.

Even before formal implementation, the U.S. armed forces had been shifting to ever greater reliance on "volunteers." Such an observation is difficult to document since the definition of a volunteer is arbitrary. Many persons volunteer out of "draft motivation," to use military terminology. Despite defects in the data, the long-term trend downward in percentage

26. Sol Tax, ed., *The Draft: A Handbook of Facts and Alternatives* (Chicago: University of Chicago Press, 1967).

of U.S. military who were draftees during hostilities is striking. In World War I, the figure stood at 67.2 percent; World War II, 61.3 percent; by Korea it had fallen to 27.1 percent, and for the Vietnam conflict, the draft figure was only 19.9 percent. In effect, the ability of the selective service to draft those who were strongly opposed declined continuously throughout the Vietnam war.[27]

Introduction of the all-volunteer force after the Vietnam war was planned and executed by economists in the employ of the government. "Competitive pay" was emphasized—that is, military wages were to be made comparable to those of equivalent civilian occupations. The projections were far from the realities later encountered. The force was much more costly and the standing military much smaller than had been anticipated. The concentration of minority group members, especially blacks, had been underestimated. The official projection by the presidential panel (made without reliable methodology) was that, under the all-volunteer concept, the proportion of enlisted blacks would reach 15 percent in the total active duty force and 19 percent in the army.[28] In fact, by March 1981, eight years after the end of the draft, black enlisted strength in the armed forces as a whole reached 22.1 percent.[29] The navy had the lowest proportion, 12.0 percent; the air force 16.5 percent; the marines 22.0 percent; and the army, the highest, 33.2 percent. The concentration is highlighted even if one includes officers as well as enlisted men. In 1981, blacks accounted for 10.8 percent of the navy, 14.4 percent of the air force, 20.2 percent of the marines, and 29.8 percent of the army.

The expanded all-volunteer force conformed to the expectations of those students of the military who thought of it as a bureaucracy with features common to any large-scale organization as well as special features because of its combat goals.[30] Recruitment and retention of qualified personnel was difficult despite the marked increase in pay designed to make the military competitive. Enlisted personnel, both in the ground combat arms and among highly skilled specialists, were constantly attracted to civilian industry. During the first five years of transition, the desired numerical quotas could be achieved in part by the gradual decrease in total authorized strength, persistent high rates of civilian unemployment, lowering of educational standards, and the ability to recruit females. Military officers

27. G. David Curry, *Sunshine Patriots: Punishment and the Vietnam Offender* (South Bend: University of Notre Dame Press, forthcoming).

28. *The Report of the President's Commission on an All-Volunteer Force* (New York: Macmillan 1970), p. 147.

29. See Martin Binkin et al., *Blacks and the Military* (Washington, D.C.: Brookings Institution, 1982), p. 42.

30. Morris Janowitz and Charles Moskos, "Five Years of the All-Volunteer Force: 1973–1978," *Armed Forces and Society* 5 (February 1979): 171–218.

complained about the recruitment of personnel with limited educational background and low aptitude for technical training. Pay was inadequate. The recession of the early 1980s boosted recruitment and especially retention, but no administration can rely on a major economic slowdown in order to gain qualified personnel. Recruitment and retention also involve effective leadership, interesting work, and the quality of life in the military. Recruits from underprivileged minorities and whites with limited educational backgrounds were placed increasingly in combat units. This trend raised profound political and moral issues, as well as the problems of military effectiveness. A limited but important countertrend was the armed forces' greater ability to recruit the sons of career military.[31]

The recruitment of females has rapidly reached its limits because of the relatively few interested female recruits and ambivalent citizen attitudes toward women in combat units. Political leaders and the mass media express concern about the shrinking male personnel pool eligible for military service. In 1978, approximately 2.14 million males reached eighteen years of age; by 1992 the figure will have dropped to 1.61 million.

The work routine in the military force of the post-Vietnam period is very different from the leisurely pattern of the volunteer force between World Wars I and II. The U.S. military, after Vietnam, was officially "at peace." But the strategy of deterrence created immense pressure on operational personnel and their families. Military personnel move from one station to another and from one assignment to another with considerable feelings of frustration. The tasks of operational readiness, training, and reconnaissance seem endless. The military is much larger and much more civilianized than it was between World Wars I and II, although military tasks remain the core of all four services. The typical military person and his family have extensive contacts with the larger society, through the mass media, schools, and voluntary associations.

By the early 1980s, there were slightly more than two million persons on active military duty. This level represented a stabilization of military strength. For many, concentrated in the technical and logistical support units, the military was just another job. For a minority, military service was "special" because their assignments were related directly or closely to combat. But even combat personnel lived in massive organizations which converged in format with civilian institutions. As a result, the combat personnel were constantly seeking methods to keep alive "the

31. They were personnel with higher educational background and strong commitment to a limited military tour of duty but not necessarily to regular military careers. It is important that military recruiters pointed to a sense of patriotism as one of the aids to recruitment. This subject has not been extensively researched. Patriotic attitudes are at work in a minority who enter military service, but it is difficult to determine the extent and consequences of such military service.

fighting spirit." These people resisted the trend toward civilianization of the military.

During the first decade of the all-volunteer force, the drop in personnel in the reserves and national guard was more pronounced than in the active duty forces, further weakening the citizen soldier concept. In 1981 there were only 1,300,000 in selected reserve units, as compared with 2,500,000 in 1960.

It was appropriate that leaders of civilian society should ask a variety of questions of the self-selected active duty officers and enlisted persons. Were the armed forces creating a series of social enclaves detached from the larger society or more accurately, enclaves with merely selected links to the larger society? Was the all-volunteer force undermining or weakening conceptions of the citizen soldier because of emphasis on "marketplace" compensation?[32] Was the emphasis on marketplace compensation resulting in a socially unrepresentative military? What were the military and political implications of such social unrepresentativeness? Was the expanded all-volunteer force departing from traditional notions of a nonpartisan armed force? Was the recruitment system into combat units producing personnel with adequate educational backgrounds and abilities to manage the complex technology of the modern military establishment? Was the process of self-selection resulting in career personnel more and more "hardline" on the subject of military and foreign policy, representing a form of neoconservatism?

Answers came from unexpected sources. The all-volunteer force produced an unprecedented and unanticipated level of personnel turnover, concentrated among recruits with marginal social and educational backgrounds. Although competitive pay was supposed to reduce turnover, after 1973 the rate of turnover in the enlisted ranks was higher than under conscription.

One standard measure of turnover is the percentage of active duty enlisted force with more than four years of service. In fiscal year 1967, 31.3 percent had more than four years of service; by 1977, the figure had only increased to 41.4 percent. This level was due in part to very high levels of attrition during the first term tour of duty among men and women without prior military service. In particular units, the rate of attrition resulting primarily from the initiative of individual commanders reached 35 percent. Retention and reenlistment are especially problematical in the ground combat services. For the army, only 13.5 percent of those who entered the service in fiscal year 1971 had remained on active duty as of

32. Charles C. Moskos, "Social Considerations of the All-Volunteer Force," in Brent Scowcroft, ed., *Military Service in the United States* (Englewood Cliffs, N.J.: Prentice-Hall, 1982), pp. 129–50.

30 June 1975. Of new recruits into the army in fiscal 1973, after the introduction of the all-volunteer force, 17.4 percent had remained as of 30 June 1977—only a small increase. High turnover was also the result of lower-than-anticipated rates of reenlistment; many "first termers" were either not interested in or not qualified for a second term, or lacked aptitudes for promotion. (High rates of unemployment, in the first years of the 1980s, temporarily increased the rates of reenlistment and retention.)

A high price has to be paid for extensive rates of attrition and turnover. Training is part of the cost. There is also the immense social price of failure for young men and women who enter the service with marginal educational backgrounds and attitudes. This is often their second failure, many having failed in high school before entering the military. Between 1973, when conscription was terminated, and the early 1980s, more than 800,000 young people were prematurely discharged from the military for reasons of indiscipline, personality disorders, and job inaptitude. The armed forces are less prepared than they used to be to perform tasks of social education. Recruits who cannot perform effectively are more often discharged than retrained.

Concerned that extensive rotation and attrition would result in combat units lacking the social cohesion and solidarity essential for effective combat, military leaders have launched experimental preventive programs. These programs hold out real promise by emphasizing unit rather than individual rotation and by seeking to reduce the overall amount of turnover.

The converse to excessive turnover, a high degree of personnel stability, especially among noncommissioned officers, also presents a troublesome issue. Units detached from the larger society are likely to develop specialized and undesirable subcultures.

Another disadvantage of the all-volunteer system is that the pattern of recruitment has in effect eliminated college-bound persons. Under conscription, for example during the early 1960s, about 20 percent of enlisted personnel had some college education. These persons supplied important human resources for informal and formal leadership. The ability of the military to serve as an agency of civic and social education has in the past, under conscription, rested on the heterogeneity of personnel recruited and serving in the enlisted ranks. Virtual elimination of the college-educated from today's armed forces weakens that ability.

The organization climate of the military establishment, especially its combat units, must be supportive of tensions its personnel are required to face. The atmosphere in which the rank and file operate should not diverge too markedly from that of most institutions of civilian society. There has been concern with the extent to which the organizational climate of various military services either under the draft and or under the all-volunteer system has been authoritarian and likely to engender authoritarian attitudes among enlisted personnel. An all-volunteer force with an authoritarian subculture would tend to separate the new all-volunteer force from the larger society; it would undermine the notion of the citizen soldier ethos. The military currently recruits many persons who are socially marginal. If such recruits are trained in an arbitrary and highly authoritarian setting, the citizen soldier concept has been pushed aside. Those trained under such conditions, especially enlisted personnel, are removed from the mainstream of society.

Particular observers have emphasized that the draft produced a mix of personnel, especially among its better educated and college-bound, which forced the officer corps to temper tendencies toward excessive authoritarian styles of leadership. Two important studies reassuringly concluded that short-term service in the military—up to three years—produced a decline in authoritarian attitudes among draftees.[33] However, further research indicated that there is a sharp increase in authoritarian attitudes among reenlisted personnel—those who had more than three years of military service. One cannot avoid the most careful concern with this tendency. The process of self-selection is at work and, over the long run, could more strongly influence the organizational climate of an all-volunteer force than that of an all-draftee force with a greater degree of heterogeneity of recruitment.[34] The implications for civilian military relations are clear: increased divergence between the military subculture of enlisted personnel and the attitudes of the larger society.

One would expect that the combat arms would be the locus of increased authoritarianism—and such a pattern would create an informal civic education at odds with the larger society. There is also good reason to believe that excessive rigidity would prevent effective military performance of combat soldiers. Despite the importance of effective discipline, rigid compliance with rules needs to be mixed with sensitivity to the requirements of the modern battlefield.

In 1981, in addition to the almost 1,800,000 enlisted personnel on active duty, there were about 280,000 officers in service. Although senior non-commissioned officers set the tone and outlook of the newly enlisted personnel, it is the regular officers on extended active duty who maintain the

33. Donald T. Campbell and Thelma H. McCormack, "Military Experience and Attitudes Toward Authority," *American Journal of Sociology* 62 (March 1957): 482–90; and Klaus Roghmann and Wolfgang Sodeur, "The Impact of Military Service on Authoritarian Attitudes," *American Journal of Sociology* 78 (September 1972): 418–33.
34. E. M. Schreiber, "Authoritarian Attitudes in the United States Army," *Armed Forces and Society* 6 (Fall 1979): 122–31.

ethos of the military establishment and demonstrate the results of self-selection. Their attitudes are particularly important, not only because of their increased authority, but because there is a greater level of career stability among officers than enlisted personnel. However, many new junior officers only have limited obligated tours of duty, from two to five years, as "repayment" for their education at government expense. Most of these short-term officers return to civilian employment. Officers on active duty for nine to twelve years, on the other hand, are likely to complete a twenty-year career, and give a strong element of stability to the officer corps.

There is a second level of officers who become generals and remain on active duty. Since the end of conscription, a change is discernible: fewer officers have previously served as enlisted personnel; but those enlisted personnel who do become officers are highly effective and contribute to social cohesion. Under conscription, draftees contributed an important component of heterogeneity and were well informed about the culture of enlisted personnel. With the new pattern of self-recruitment, the services recognized that they had to make efforts to increase the heterogeneity of the officer corps by actively recruiting minority group members. Such efforts were not noticeably successful. Available data are limited, but it is clear that retention and promotion go disproportionately to those who "fit in" and accept the value orientation of active duty military generals. Those who remain are likely to be conservative and to accept a hard-line politicomilitary perspective.[35]

The most extensive body of data on attitude changes in the all-volunteer forces is presented in the findings collected and analyzed by Jerald G. Bachman, John D. Blair, and David R. Segal in their study *The All-Volunteer Force*.[36] Their findings are particularly relevant since their research covered the period 1968–76, including both the draft and the all-volunteer system. Significantly large samples were subjected to detailed attitude research. Long-term changes developed gradually. During the period of the study, these investigators "failed to find a clear and uniform pro-military stance among the military men as a whole." In short, three years after the termination of conscription, the military continued to reflect

35. Such findings have been extensively observed in the United States and documented in the Swedish armed forces. See Bengt Abrahamsson, *Military Professionalization and Political Power* (Beverly Hills, Calif.: Sage Publications, 1972), passim; Robert Priest, Terrence Fullerton, and Claude Bridges, "Personality and Value Changes in West Point Cadets," *Armed Forces and Society* 8 (Summer 1982): 629–42.

36. Jerald G. Bachman, John D. Blair, and David R. Segal, *The All-Volunteer Force: A Study of Ideology in the Military* (Ann Arbor, Mich.: University of Michigan Press, 1977).

the pluralism of the larger society, in part because of the presence of short-term officers and enlisted personnel, the modern equivalents of the citizen soldiers. But with the passage of time, this study found, as expected, that those with career interests in the military were, on the average, enthusiastically pro-military along virtually every dimension. In other words, self-selection and informal indoctrination in a three-year period were creating a relatively homogeneous attitude set among both officers and noncommissioned personnel.

On the other hand, the spirit and outlook of the citizen soldier have been maintained to some degree by the national guard and the reserves, which, as of 1981, included 1,360,000 persons. There is wide variation in the effectiveness and motivation of these personnel.[37] But there is no denying that some units, especially in the air force, are well trained, have realistic operational tasks, are effectively integrated, and play an active role in civil-military relations. These reservists think of themselves as "citizen soldiers." They have full-time jobs; military internal policing duties are considered important ancillary tasks. Leaving aside their military utility, they contribute to the sense of localism, pluralism, and institutional diversity which strengthen a democratic polity. The ending of the draft gave them added recognition, even as their military utility is being refashioned.

The military has changed its format from a mobilization cadre for conventional warfare to a "force in being" for the strategic mission of deterrence. Reliance on an all-volunteer force means that the United States has moved significantly, over the short run, away from the citizen soldier concept. Such an observation does not mean that the concept has ceased to be operative or that it cannot be adapted to the military of today.

37. Jacobs, "The Role of the Military Forces."

Four

Mass Education I: The Search for National Citizenship

ACCULTURATION VERSUS ASSIMILATION

I find it useful to take 1890 as the turning point in school-based civic education. Until 1890 the highly decentralized or, more accurately, fragmented school system had a very simple formal agenda for civic education. Implicitly, it was concerned with acculturation of the continuing flow of immigrants, and relied on a mixture of national patriotism and religious symbolism. The virtues of the United States rested not only on its legally guaranteed freedom but on its military exploits and achievements. History instruction was the key element in organized civic education.

After 1890, civic education became more pressing as the nation had to deal with the mass of foreign-born immigrants and their offspring. In the urban areas especially, the school system—public, private, and parochial—augmented the teaching of history with an increased concern with civics—the organization and functioning of government.

Until the outbreak of World War II, this combination of history and civics dominated the educational institutions. Of course, whether the acculturation of new immigrants was actually in process was open to question. But long-term and profound changes came to fruition after 1945, with increased interest in fusing "social studies" into civic education. The social studies approach, developed in the 1920s, sought to make use of political science, sociology, and economics, as well as psychology, to prepare students to deal with the dilemmas of an advanced industrialized nation.

In this chapter I shall overview the institutional changes in school-based civic education from 1890 to 1940. In chapter 5, the focus shifts to the impact of social studies on the civil rights and anti–Vietnam war movements. That impact has endured into the 1980s.

As the years of required schooling increased in the United States, educational administrators acquired more and more "teaching" time to implement their strategies of civic education. "Success" was expected to be gradual, but that presented no special problem. To the contrary, long-term inculcation was thought to be the effective basis for building citizen commitments. Each level of the educational system—primary, secondary, and higher—supplies continuing opportunities to pursue the goals of civic education appropriate for a democratic polity.

Earlier in this study, I stated that I preferred a relatively broad *means* of civic education and relatively clearcut and delimited *goals*. As far as means are concerned, it is inadequate to focus on classroom instruction. More important is the institutional life of the school, and closely associated voluntary associations which have appropriated for themselves an active role in civic education. Nor can one avoid attention to the youth-oriented content of the mass media.

There is a body of research on the social history of the U.S. schools. Nevertheless, assessing the organizational climate and milieu is a difficult task, and to describe historical trends is fraught with the dangers of oversimplification. But there is no alternative if one is interested in the realities of civic education.

I reject the idea that the goals of civic education are to be equated with the totality of human interpersonal relations—the "human relations" approach to civic education. Such a perspective is, in my view, too vague and general to be useful. Clearly, the effectiveness of a democratic polity is enhanced by "civil" and "restrained" interpersonal behavior, but democratic citizenship is not the same as effective interpersonal manners. I proceed on the basis of a relatively distinct set of concerns for civic education in the school setting, namely, the attitudes and behavior of the populace toward the central organs of government. Given my definition of citizenship, the crux of the problem is the ability of civic education to increase the capacity of the populace—including its leaders—to participate in the delimited aims and broad means. Such participation can be limited to irregular participation in elections and infrequent contact with local officials. The fullest participation involves persistent, intense, and varied political behavior, but with the potential for mutual accommodation and compromise.

In probing the role of the school in civic education, I take for granted two assertions. First, political democracy is enhanced if a nation-state displays an important element of cultural homogeneity or cultural integration. One can almost say that a basic minimum of cultural solidarity is required for a democratic polity. The United States has hardly surpassed this minimum. In the past, such a cultural base has been limited despite the commanding position of those cultural leaders who immigrated from England or descended from British immigrants.

Until 1940, the school performed an important function in civic education to the extent that it contributed to the fashioning of a common culture. Despite a pronounced level of cultural heterogeneity, the school helped to account for the remarkable capacity of U.S. society to integrate wave after wave of immigrants from abroad and from rural areas. This achievement is all the more striking because American society was culturally diverse from the beginning. There was no explicit set of cultural modalities to which new generations could turn for a cultural format to be emulated, in the way that immigrants to Great Britain or France might have done. This is not to overlook or downgrade contributions of New England society and New England norms which played a significant role in setting cultural standards.

In the United States, a sense of nationality and national culture developed fairly rapidly. No doubt the public school in the early nineteenth century with its relatively unified, or common, academic curriculum contributed to civic education. One cannot help speculate that the very looseness of the system and the absence of pressure on new immigrants to abandon their cultural traditions, except in the few years after World War I, assisted in the process of "nationality building." The toleration of prior allegiances had the unanticipated consequence of speeding up the process of integration into the increasingly urban society of new immigrants from abroad and migrants from the hinterland.

I am mainly concerned with the period from 1890 to 1940. I see that period as one in which the mass education system diligently, if only partially, succeeded in coping with the problem of acculturation. After 1945, the school's contribution to national cultural integration displayed pervasive discontinuity with the past. This reversal emerged in the 1960 decade, but the groundwork was prepared during the years of assumed quiescence immediately after 1945. The period of 1890 to 1940 represents "progress" in school efforts at ethnic integration and the development of hyphenated Americans. We need to explain not only the lack of "progress" after 1945 but also the fragmentation grounded in a variety of separatist ethnic nationalisms which, over the short run, produced widespread political turmoil and disruption, with the school as the focal point.

The achievement of the schools in teaching civics—that is, the workings of government and how the individual relates to these political arrangements—was less impressive between 1890 and 1940. The mass education system offered limited formal classroom education on these topics. At least a minority of alert and interested students exposed to effective teachers learned some American history and, by inference, learned

75

about civic virtue and obligation. Moreover, civic education during this period had a style which presented not only citizen rights but emphasized, in the name of patriotism, citizen obligations. Material published after 1945, by contrast, concentrates almost wholly on particular individual rights and how they can be achieved.

My analysis of the school's contribution to civic education centers on a rather precise distinction between acculturation and assimilation. This distinction is not sufficiently emphasized in the research literature. In the pioneer classic sociological study of ethnicity, *The Polish Peasant in Europe and America*, the senior author, W. I. Thomas, makes clear the continuing relevance of the distinction.[1] For Thomas, assimilation implies abandoning or rejecting one's cultural traditions and communal resources to accept completely a new set of values and norms. The assimilated Jew, for example, is no longer a Jew. Acculturation is much more gradual and less drastic. It implies continuity with one's background but involves learning and internalizing key elements of the new society into which the migrant has moved. Acculturation can be extensive without assimilation.

Thomas emphasizes that the Polish immigrant in the United States is no longer a Pole but a member of a Polish-American community, a group structure in transition. Members of such communities must adapt to new political, social, and economic settings. Assimilation is not the typical response of the newcomer; the immigrant family seeks to acculturate.[2] Immigrants make use of their ethnic background and contacts in the struggle for immediate survival. At the same time, they internalize cultural and normative patterns, as well as essential skills, in order to operate in the new environment. New perspectives and skills are incorporated while certain traditional ethnic patterns are kept and refashioned.

The new immigrant has an advantage if there are available effective communal organizations and leaders. The Polish-American community emerged as a new entity—not merely a collection of Poles in America nor a duplication of a segment of European Polish society. Members of the Polish-American community initially demonstrate strong loyalty to the "old country." In fact, their nationalistic and ethnic sentiment can at times become stronger than it was before they left Poland because they are in a setting which permits freer political expression and more pointed mobilization of ethnic nationalism. These immigrants developed Polish-type

1. William I. Thomas and Florian Znaniecki, *The Polish Peasant in Europe and America*, vol. 5: *Organization and Disorganization in America* (Boston: Richard G. Badger, The Gorham Press, 1920), Introduction and passim.

2. Eric Rosenthal, "Acculturation without Assimilation?" *American Journal of Sociology* 66 (November 1969): 275–88. For an alternative approach see Milton M. Gordon, *Assimilation in American Life: The Role of Race, Religion, and National Origins* (New York: Oxford University Press, 1964).

institutions less to keep old world affiliations alive than to assist transition to an acculturated status—to create hyphenated Americans. The immigrant must learn essential cultural patterns required of all persons in the host land. As these new forms are acquired, old world traits are weakened, selectively displaced, but hardly eliminated. In time, acculturation comes close to assimilation, though ethnic loyalties and nationalism for some groups continue to display powerful elements of persistence.

The U.S. mass school system never was assigned, nor did it assume, the task of contributing directly to assimilation. There was no "clearcut" model of the culture of the "American citizen," although dominant themes and values gradually emerged. Each nationality group was encouraged to incorporate elements found in the immediate locale and region in which it came to reside. Mastering the English language was a central route, but there were a hundred pathways to be explored in acculturation and, in time, full citizenship.

"Acculturation" as practiced and fostered by the school system in the United States has proceeded in a format very different from that encountered in most Western European nations, especially France. The school in Western European nations has traditionally, and explicitly, sought to develop a citizenry with strong national attachments and a pervasive sense of patriotism. Children have been taught the superiority of their national values in order to strengthen national allegiance. Until the outbreak of World War I, the centralization of Western European schools was a device for increasing uniformity of educational content and purpose. On the continent of Western Europe, the school system was organized to produce students prepared to enter the mass armed forces being built up in the last quarter of the nineteenth century by means of popular conscription. European advocates of a democratic polity believed that they had to be "on guard" against antidemocratic elements in the officer corps. Nevertheless, universal military service had widespread popular support, including support from the political left, for whom a "nation in arms" served to safeguard democratic political aspirations. It is ironic that the long-term consequence of these Western European school systems that emphasized nationalistic civic education was to produce a working stratum with strong populist, oppositional, and even radical attitudes.

In assessing the consequences of civic education, whether in Western Europe or in the United States, we should avoid a perspective that has gained much acceptance in social research. It is the view that the school system essentially reflects the social structure of which it is a part, and that any effects of education on that social structure are, at best, marginal. In particular, contributions to the fashioning of values, including those associated with citizenship training, are minimal. Much of this reasoning is grounded in research which focuses on the limited ability of the school system to solve social and economic problems of the "underclass." It reflects intellectual frustrations resulting from large expenditures in recent years for experimental programs to improve academic skills of children from lower-strata families. Because the school system in the United States has profound defects, it can hardly be concluded that it has only marginal influence on the social structure. To the contrary, the long-term difficulties the school has faced, in my judgment, highlight the conclusion that it has been assigned more functions than its organizational structure is able to execute. Nor can the school system compensate comprehensively for defects of other basic institutions—for example, weaknesses in economic and taxation policies.

To reject the view that education barely influences social structure does not mean exaggerating the school's ability to change social structure or to fashion value patterns. The observations of self-critical social research practitioners converge with, rather than diverge from, informed and commonsense lay judgments.

It is striking that the United States, with such cultural heterogeneity, became a nation-state with relatively stable democratic parliamentary institutions. Despite weaknesses in the U.S. educational system, schools until 1940 made a decisive contribution to the acculturation (and thereby to the incorporation) of diverse immigrants by pressing for common literacy and some common cultural content. I shall focus on two elements: (a) the goals and motives of educational leaders, expressed in the nineteenth century in terms of religion and in the twentieth century in terms of the moral as well as material benefits of education; (b) the highly localistic structure of the school system. I shall argue that both elements, paradoxically, helped the school to acculturate the expanding immigrant population, even though the black and native American Indian populations, until after 1945, remained at the periphery of the U.S. educational system.

RELIGION AND THE RISE OF MASS EDUCATION

The history of the U.S. school system as an agency of civic education starts with the earliest colonial period.[3] Already then, the religious motivations of educators and the local character of educational institutions were having an effect.[4] The United States Constitution sought for a separation of church and state with profound long-term implications for the school system. Although this constitutional provision is often interpreted

3. Lawrence A. Cremin, *American Education: The Colonial Experience, 1607–1783* (New York: Harper and Row, 1970).
4. Lawrence A. Cremin, *American Education: The National Experience, 1783–1876* (New York: Harper and Row, 1970).

as an essentially secular achievement, it was designed to ensure and to strengthen religious freedom. In any case, constitutional provisions concerning religion hardly served, during the nineteenth century, to eliminate religion or religiously motivated teachers from the school system.

The early immigrant population contained a high concentration of farmers and peasants, who tended to be devout. In fact, there was a noticeable Protestant revival, both in urban and rural areas, in the decades following 1830, with a strong interest in stimulating the growth of the public school system.[5] I cannot point to a satisfactory explanation for this religious revival, elements of which persisted beyond the Civil War up to the mass immigration of the 1880s. However, it is clear that the school system, or rather the conglomeration of schools, were mobilized into proselytizing. The school provided a natural vehicle for religious teaching. A wide gap persisted between the idea of the separation of state and church and the actual practices of the American common school. Particularly in New England, but throughout the expanding nation during the nineteenth century, the teaching of religion and the use of prayer and Bible reading were employed by dominant Protestant elements to teach and to underscore morality. This was due partly to tradition, partly to religious revival, and partly to political design. Clergymen and their political spokesmen believed that religion gave divine sanction to teaching and to learning, in addition to supplying moral content to the curriculum. Although evangelical Protestants, the overwhelming majority, had their feuds with the ever increasing number of Catholics, the school system generally served the aspirations of the Protestant resurgence.

David B. Tyack describes this Protestant religious thrust in the common school as a "robust force in American life."[6] Leading educational reformers, including figures such as Horace Mann, saw no discomfort in combining education with religious instruction. Mann and others did, however, have to face the question of the appropriate content of educational instruction, which should not be excessively sectarian. There was a real effort in the years before the Civil War to create, informally, a Protestant community and, in turn, a Protestant society.

Despite internal cleavages, Protestant clergy were able to maintain elements of nonsectarian religion in the common school until the turn of the century. Moreover, the nineteenth century, particularly the years 1830–80, saw rapid expansion of primary common schools and limited, but

5. David B. Tyack, "Onward Christian Soldiers: Religion in the American Common School," in *History and Education: The Educational Uses of the Past*, ed., Paul Nash (New York: Random House, 1970), pp. 212–44.
6. David B. Tyack, "Onward Christian Soldiers," p. 217.

important, growth of high schools. An important aspect of this trend was free education.

Careful statistical analysis by John W. Meyer and his associates suggests that school growth was part of a conscious social movement rather than a strictly economic phenomenon.[7] The data are particularly appropriate since they cover the period 1870–1930, the years of increased industrial development.

Meyer and his colleagues start with the observation that educational enrollments were high very early. Statistically, they found that urbanization demonstrated a consistently negative association with educational enrollment. Even when per capita manufacturing product is used instead of urbanization, the same consistently negative effect appears. However, for earlier decades of the study, as anticipated, their index of evangelical Protestantism showed consistent positive effects on enrollment. By 1910, however, this particular effect disappeared. For the analysis of the period after the turn of the century, they argue that "social movement" factors influential in educational expansion in the nineteenth century were replaced by factors related to increasing nationwide bureaucratization. By this, I believe they meant that the educational system was becoming more of a national bureaucracy with a self-generated interest in expansion.

Republican party dominance revealed consistent, but not statistically significant, effects on enrollment in the nineteenth century. After the turn of the century, this factor became negative. The Republican party, for forty years the party of nation building and social reform, underwent drastic change in 1896 in the outlook and strategy of its leaders.

As expected, the percentage of Catholic population showed a negative effect on school enrollment, which became large after the turn of the century. This finding reflects the fact that parochial school enrollments were not included in the analysis. These investigators also report that immigration per se was not directly related to expanded enrollment, a finding that undermines a simplistic explanation of the growth of the public school system.[8]

Meyer and his colleagues conclude that, for the nineteenth century, expansion of the public school system, especially in the rural North and West, can best be understood as a social movement connected with a

7. John W. Meyer, David Tyack, Joane Nagel, and Audri Gordon, "Public Education as Nation-Building in America: Enrollments and Bureaucratization in the American States, 1870–1930," *American Journal of Sociology* 85 (November 1979): 591–613.
8. See also John H. Ralph and Richard Rubinson, "Immigration and the Expansion of Schooling in the United States, 1890–1970," *American Sociological Review* 45 (December 1980): 943–54.

religious outlook and that it served the purpose of "nation-building."[9] In their view, the leaders of this social movement were not a narrow, economically motivated elite but, rather, "hundreds of thousands of people who shared a common ideology of nation-building."[10]

Public funds were used to support religious instruction throughout the nineteenth century. Opposition to teaching religion and religious practices in the public school was expressed by small groups of free thinkers. The fact that Catholics withdrew and developed a separate school system without public funds worked to further secularize the public system. After World War I, secularization increased, especially in the western part of the nation. The growth of freethinkers and a sharper emphasis on the separation of church and state helped to circumscribe Protestant religions in the public school system. Subsequent decisions of the Supreme Court about separation of church and state served the same purpose. In the period after World War II, however, it is striking to what extent religious activities such as Bible reading and extensive use of religious symbolism in connection with holidays still persisted in public schools. In 1980, with the emergence of a "moralistic political" revival, demands by parents for religious instruction in public schools received extensive coverage in the mass media. Despite gradual secularization, the public school system has retained more than a token connection with religious symbolism and organized religion.

We are dealing not only with religious instruction. Between 1830 and the 1890s, active Protestant sectarianism was linked to the growth of nationalism and to a sense of national citizenship. Protestant sectarianism was an active ingredient of the implicit civic education of the period, disrupted, of course, by the Civil War and its aftermath. Protestantism carried the heritage of the colonial period and the American Revolution. Leading citizens and prosperous folk of the community were generally outspoken Protestants until well after the turn of the century.

In contrast to the Catholic missionary apparatus, American Protestants had few foreign attachments or allegiances. The variety of Protestant groups, through their influence on the schools, well served the process of acculturation of early waves of Protestant immigrants from Great Britian and North West Europe. The ethnic diversity of the English, Scots, German, Norwegian, Danish, and Swedish Protestants could, relatively speaking, be subsumed under the unity afforded by the presence of a dedicated Protestant core. Tensions between Protestant groups about education and national identification were muted or resolved at the local

9. Meyer et al., "Public Education as Nation-Building," p. 597.
10. Ibid., p. 601.

level. The great divide was between Protestants and Catholics—again, often manifested at the local level.

The public school was not a foreign body intruding into the local community. There was no national or even state institution pressing the immigrant to become an American. It was not until about 1890, with the rapid expansion of urban centers and the marked increase in Catholic population, that more explicit approaches to the role of the public school in acculturation were sought and formulated.

Clearly, the school system created during the period 1840–90, regardless of the moralistic motives of public leaders, served real economic needs. Human-capital economists point to the increased productivity of educated labor and the increased benefits of education both to the individual and to society. Neo-Marxists are quick to add that the economic function can only be understood in terms of the class struggle and the benefits gained by the "bourgeois." But the gains that resulted from education in nineteenth-century America diffused to a marked degree through the social structure, although many immigrants had a grim struggle to establish themselves as "economically" viable farmers. Likewise, if the working conditions of many immigrants were miserable, even limited levels of education assisted immigrants' children to find a future in the urbanizing sector.

While schooling—and that means compulsory schooling by the nineteenth century—demonstrably served economic needs, economic motives hardly explain the drive to build and expand the system, either public or parochial. Nor was there extensive popular agitation by the rank-and-file citizenry, including the lower or working strata, to demand more education for their children.

Instead, cultural and moral factors were at work. Local leaders of the common school movement could afford to send their children to private school, but supported and used the public schools which they helped to build. They proclaimed the moral benefits of increased education for the individual and, in turn, for society. Most immigrants in the period 1840–90 eagerly accepted the importance of education. Their acceptance is particularly striking because the immediate economic advantages for them and their children in a predominantly agrarian setting were not easily apparent. The moral and cultural thrust in the expansion of public education can hardly be separated from vague aspirations to incorporate diverse populations politically into the nation. There was a growing spirit of nationalism, especially in the aftermath of the Mexican War, that paralleled the nationalism encountered in Western Europe. Schoolteachers and their supervisors, as well as many regional and national spokesmen for expansion of public education, displayed a strong attachment to that spirit.

Nevertheless, some schoolteachers who were strongly religious were indifferent and even hostile to militant nationalism and "old fashioned patriotism." These persons were either vaguely utopian or straightforward idealists. They were interested in the "brotherhood" of man or equivalent appeals. Thus, we have already the origins of a "conservative-liberal" split in school personnel which becomes institutionalized after World War II and persists in one form or another to the present day. Merle Curti speaks of the difference between military patriotism and civic patriotism in the civic attitudes that were propagated.[11] Although this terminology is hardly neutral, it is useful in identifying the early cleavage among schoolteachers.

In the absence of explicit policies of civic education, elements in the teaching profession served as a mild pressure group stressing nationalism in civic education, an emphasis which was to intensify after 1890. The message these activist teachers carried was that the United States should incorporate culturally as well as economically its diverse population. The sheer problems of building a publicly supported common school system consumed the energies of local leaders and of national spokesmen committed to the free school concept.

The teaching of American history and the development of appropriate textbooks were the main organized program. Surveys of the textbooks used in the public schools during the nineteenth century[12] reveal a simple or formal civic education during that period. They are also valuable sources about attitudes and values if their limitations are kept in mind.[13]

11. Merle Curti, *The Roots of American Loyalty* (New York: Columbia University Press, 1946), pp. 216–17.

12. Three surveys of pre–Civil War history textbooks have been summarized in George H. Callcott, "History Enters the Schools," *American Quarterly* 11 (Winter 1959): 470–83. See Henry Barnard, "American Text-Books," *American Journal of Education* 13 (June 1863): 202–22; ibid. (September 1863): 626–40; ibid. 14 (December 1864): 751–57; ibid. (September 1865): 639–75; William F. Russell, "Historical Text-Books Published Before 1861," *History Teacher's Magazine* 6 (April 1915): 122–25; Agnew O. Roorbach, *The Development of the Social Studies in the American Secondary Education before 1860* (Philadelphia: University of Pennsylvania Press, 1937), pp. 246–78.

13. Scholars have repeatedly sought to make use of textbooks as sources of information on public attitudes and the Zeitgeist of a particular period. These sources are particularly appealing since the contents reveal changes dramatically over time. But the problems of interpretation are complex. First, it is not always documented how extensively the text was used. Second, it is not clear how much reliance a teacher placed on the textbook. Third, and most important, it is difficult to assess the extent to which the textbook reflected the existing value patterns of the locality and period as compared with the extent the text was an active agent in influencing the student body by presenting new or different perspectives. Some studies are sounder than others, especially where an effort is made to study a large

By 1860, the teaching of history had penetrated deeply into the public school system. Making use of available surveys as well as his own data, George H. Calcott points out that the textbooks of the time strongly stressed military history, including that of the United States. These textbooks devoted one-third of their contents to military events, three times as much as appear in modern texts (that is, for the period of the 1950s).[14] In short, civic education through military themes was of importance and, interestingly enough, not thought to be incompatible or even in tension with the religious themes offered by the public school system.

A conspicuous theme of these textbooks was the superiority of America—"the glory of the United States, the greatness of democracy and the blessings of American liberty." Calcott describes this content as reflecting "romantic nationalism." I would label it old-fashioned patriotism. The teaching of history was designed to inspire nationalism and patriotism, and to give meaning to citizenship.

In the light of the strong religious context of public schools and the close link between religion and nationalism, I do not find it strange that these history textbooks spoke frequently of the duties of citizenship. Such a perspective persisted until the turn of the century, when the religious thrust in the school system underwent some constriction and transformation. Protestant religious sentiment of the nineteenth century strongly emphasized elements of duty in personal and family matters. Moreover, the individual had latitude in expressing his sense of duty since initiative was a central aspect of Protestantism of the period. No doubt such reasoning and thought spilled over to the individual's relationship to the government; the civic arena was another area of expressing a sense of duty and obligation.

But the discussion of the duties of citizenship was indeed general during this period. History was for inspirational purposes. The duties of the citizen were not spelled out. Practical information on citizenship developed only after World War I. Given the background of the typical student, the symbols—the flag and the flag salute—were as important as textual materials. Civic education was mainly oriented to fashioning generalized sentiments of patriotism and affiliation with the larger society. The Civil War, however, institutionalized sectionalism at the political level. Yet the

sample in depth, as in the case of Bessie Louise Pierce, *Civic Attitudes in American School Textbooks* (Chicago: University of Chicago Press, 1930). One of the most colorful and interpretative accounts of trends in history textbooks, with a strong emphasis on underlining social and political meanings which the textbooks reflected, has been prepared by Frances Fitzgerald, *America Revised* (New York: Vintage Books, 1980). The student of civic education would have welcomed some evidence, especially statistical evidence, of the generality of the conclusion.

14. Calcott, "History Enters the Schools," p. 476.

war did not permanently disrupt the idea that there was one nation. The idea of a nation was reaffirmed by the end of the century and incorporated into the teaching system with striking speed.

ETHNICITY AND THE PROFESSIONALIZATION OF THE SCHOOL

In the years after 1890, two trends transformed civic education in the school system. The first was the vast increase in new immigrants, especially between 1890 and the entrance of the United States into World War I. Since many of these immigrants were from Eastern Europe and more alien to existing cultural patterns, they were harder to acculturate. Nativist sentiment was rapidly strengthened, leading in the 1920s to a sharp reduction of legal immigration. Even pro-immigrant leaders stressed the need for increased intervention—both public and private—to assist the process of acculturation and thereby reduce the human misery of the new population. The limited and often informal efforts of earlier decades of the nineteenth century were obviously inadequate; new approaches in education as well as in social welfare were required.

During this period, the difficulties of the new immigrants, especially of their children, consumed a major share of organized efforts. Civic education became more formalized, but it encompassed more than special efforts to assist new immigrants. Pressure to strengthen national sentiments in the population at large was intensified in the aftermath of the Spanish-American War.

A second trend was the professionalization and bureaucratic development of the school system. Children of the immigrant population were attending school in increased numbers and for longer periods of time. The increased size of the school population and the expanded concentration of students in urban centers demanded a more explicit curriculum. School personnel, assisted by university-based colleagues interested in mass education, strove independently for greater professionalization and a more refined division of labor. By 1890, the urban school system, because of sheer growth and the problems to be faced, was becoming an ever more formal organization. The extension of social welfare tasks connected with the school contributed to this trend, since it was widely recognized that an important fraction of the student population was failing to learn basic skills. Complaints about the defects in "big city" schools were already commonplace by the 1890s.

Teachers and their supervisors were pressing for increased professionalization, partly to achieve higher salaries and better conditions of work, and partly because a minority of these teachers were genuinely interested in performing at a higher level of competence. School administrators sought to be more specific and more "operational" about the content of civic education. Their intentions were good, and although the tasks were well beyond the resources available, their performance can be commended.

Educational administrators were able to implement a middle-of-the-road strategy that avoided a monolithic "Americanization" program, which would have failed and would have produced sharp "nationalistic" reactions. On the other hand, they avoided indifference, which would have contributed to social fragmentation. In sum, the school system did contribute to the acculturation of the immigrant flow. Given the size and diversity of the population, this was an achievement of historic note. Protestant churches lost their dominant position in the linkage between school and society, but remained active. A bewildering host of voluntary associations, including religious groups of the social gospel persuasion, as well as a variety of academic associations, became a new interface between school and society. Exposure of the school system to external interest groups has remained a uniquely American format. In the urban community, ethnic leaders sought to mediate the interests of their constituents with organized political parties.

Response to the need for change was highly localized, though growing metropolitan, state, and national institutions were involved. The local organization helped to contain the scope of conflicts over educational policy and direction. The result, of course, at least by 1950, was an extensively fragmented system, which was dysfunctional. The school response reflected differing conceptions of the malleability of new populations from Central Europe, and the increasing flow of migrants from U.S. rural areas.

The range of opinions about immigrants was strongly conditioned by the social policies of the period. We must avoid imposing current thought patterns and terminology on these developments of the turn of the nineteenth century. The term *ethnic group* was employed neither by the citizenry at large nor by serious students or experts. It gained popularity only in the 1960s. In retrospect, the term is appropriate. By ethnic group I mean a particular type of descent group, based on a mixture of language, national or territorial background, and especially religion. In this sense, a racial group is a special ethnic category based on perceived and socially defined physical characteristics. The idea of a primordial trait is most useful in delimiting ethnic groups in their relation to the national polity. A primordial trait refers to group characteristics taken for granted and generally prized by group members. It is created not by rational reflection but by group experiences, especially those of interaction with other ethnic groups, and those experiences supply a cohesive basis of group belonging. If one thinks of racial groups as a special type of ethnic or primordial group, one must recognize the difficulties of permeating the boundaries of racial groupings.

Until 1890–1900, immigrant groups were referred to in a related but different popular language. There was a strong element of biological determinism in the terms used for these social and cultural entities. Often they were referred to as "nationality" groups and/or racial groups, or at least groups with a racial element. For some members of United States society, the biological metaphor meant that the acculturation of the new Eastern European immigrants would be more difficult than the previous flow of immigrants. But attitude patterns are not necessarily consistent. Most citizens, while accepting aspects of a biological metaphor, still believed that the immigrant population could be integrated into U.S. society. The past record showed the ability of the nation to accept "foreigners" of all types. At stake were the numbers that could be handled. Many citizens argued that the nation could not be expected to acculturate vast numbers of such immigrants.

At this time, stimulated by the logic of pragmatic philosophical thought, a critical approach to social biology was developing. University professors, educators, and social workers were increasingly rejecting popularized biological determinism. In Chicago, for example, sociologists at the University of Chicago such as W. I. Thomas and Robert E. Park, social workers Jane Addams and Grace Abbott, and educators including Charles H. Judd and John Dewey were stressing the social and economic aspects of acculturation. They rejected any notion of innate barriers to acculturation. Their influence was felt through their writings and their use of the mass media. It is striking that their social and cultural formulations did not make them unduly optimistic but led them to reject mechanical "Americanization" programs designed to produce a more homogeneous population in a short span of time.

Instead, these intellectuals and specialists pressed for a more pluralist "middle of the road" strategy, which, although remaining a minority point of view in education, materially influenced national trends. They were even more influential in social work. In careful observations, epitomized by Thomas Znaniecki in *The Polish Peasant in Europe and America* (1918), they showed understanding for the power of primordial attachments among new immigrants. They were also sensitive to the short-term strengthening of ethnicity among new arrivals as they moved into a strange environment. They understood the equally powerful social, economic, and political pressures on the immigrant family and its offspring to accept varying forms of acculturation.

Subsequent critics of these pioneer writers charged them with underestimating the enduring power of ethnicity. The term *beyond the melting pot* was used for such criticism. But I believe that the earliest writers on the persistence of identification were sound in their views. They saw the endurance of ethnic sentiments in the United States context, but they could not believe that the new immigration of the turn of the century could comprehensively resist acculturation and even assimilation. It was a matter of degree. They argued for a pluralist society which recognized the reality of continuing heterogeneity. The vitality of ethnic identification was not incompatible with widespread acculturation. Nevertheless, by 1980, despite post–World War II immigrants, I would estimate that 50 percent of the adult population had no ethnic identification of significant depth.[15] (This estimate places the blacks, the Orientals, etc., mainly in the group with ethnic identifications.) This was no sudden change, but the consequence of decades of eroding ethnic identification.

Thomas and the other early writers did not reify the notion of ethnic groupings. They understood that such identifications were not permanent attachments but, rather, subject to social and cultural change. Individuals could acquire, transform, lose, and regain their ethnic identification. Marriage, as well as political circumstance, produces change. Moreover, the persistence of ethnic affiliation is in part the result of the skill and organization of political elites with a vested interest in a particular constituency. The continued flow of immigrants after 1945 contributed to ethnic visibility.

The early intellectuals concerned with ethnicity realized that a homogeneous "Americanized" society was neither a short- nor a long-term possibility, nor even desirable. They did not want a society in which each person had to inscribe himself overtly as a member of a particular ethnic formation. They recognized that the outcome of the process of acculturation would be strongly influenced by the performance of the school system, voluntary associations, and the expanding mass media. They helped to fashion education and social work designed to assist acculturation based on recognition of ethnic differences. In particular, they took into account that the recent immigrant to the United States found himself most frequently at the bottom or near the bottom of the social structure.

The Protestant-dominated, rural-based school system of the nineteenth century operated with a relatively clear conception of social hierarchy, and with a sense of the moral worth of its authority. Those parts of the turn-of-the-century urban public school system which served the relatively acculturated segments of society—middle or working class—displayed both of these characteristics. However, some of the sons and daughters of new immigrants presented a challenge to the educational "authorities"

15. Edward O. Laumann, *Bonds of Pluralism: The Form and Substance of Urban Social Networks* (New York: John Wiley, 1973).

in the forms of resistance, apathy, and malresponse based on ignorance and suspicion. The schoolteacher who sought to act as if there were no difference between the reasonably acculturated and the new immigrant achieved little success. Efforts to meet the educational needs of these youngsters—including their pressing needs for civic education—took the form of a search for compromise. The minority of "progressive" teachers and administrators actively worked to close the cultural and social gap. They sought to accord a measure of moral worth to the heritage that youngsters brought to school; in exchange, they attempted to implant necessary basic skills for employment, as well as some formal instruction thought to be relevant for citizenship. They made an effort to reach out to these students.

The dedicated and innovative segments of the educational bureaucracy never abandoned their basic goals, as happened in inner-city schools in the post–World War II period. They insisted on the goal of basic literacy in English; teaching native foreign languages was secondary, usually in high school. Appropriate behavior within the school system was also required. The administration of the school was clearly in the hands of older-stock, native-born, white Anglo-Saxon school principals committed to cultural integration. They were opposed to nationality-based schools, which represented to them a form of segregation. The hold of this social type over the school system persisted until the 1930s, and they helped give the system its direction. Acculturation was the central goal. The teaching staffs were also from an English-speaking background, although already by the turn of the century they were more likely to come from urbanized families. In 1908, the Immigration Commission reported that 43 percent of urban teachers were second-generation, and mainly from the British Isles and Canada (non-French).[16] These teachers were optimistic about their ability to acculturate new cohorts of immigrants; indeed, they were often zealous to a fault.

In order to adapt to the student population, schools had to maintain and build the self-respect of youngsters and their immigrant parents. They had also to conduct business in a more personal manner than was the practice in large-scale bureaucratic organizations. The persistent strategy, which was overdone in the 1960s for minority groups of the period, was neatly summarized in 1913 by the United States Commissioner of Education: "For the enrichment of our national life as well as for the happiness and welfare of individuals we must respect their (immigrant parents') ideals and preserve and strengthen all of the best of their Old World life they bring with them."[17]

16. Quoted by David B. Tyack, *The One Best System: A History of American Urban Education* (Cambridge: Harvard University Press, 1974), p. 233.
17. Ibid., p. 238.

With the massive immigration of the turn of the century, active and positive programs were required. The leaders of the progressive education movement saw the building of self-respect, in immigrant children and their parents, not as an end in itself but as a transitional device in acculturation. Clearly, it did not require a social theory for teachers to be respectful to new immigrants; it required good judgment and the absence of prejudice. Such virtues were not necessarily in abundance.

Organized efforts were launched to deal with the problems of teacher-student relations. For example, Chicago became the center of a movement to "humanize" the school system, which involved training teachers to understand the "natural" process of learning among children.[18] The innovative Francis Parker, at Cook County Normal School, taught hundreds of teachers in the final years of the nineteenth century. John Dewey organized the Laboratory School at the University of Chicago to experiment with more appropriate methods of teaching. A most interesting leader was Ella Flagg Young, the educational equivalent of Jane Addams, who became superintendent of the Chicago Public Schools. Her agenda included considerable concern with immigrant students.

Such leaders, and there were perhaps a dozen, were men and women of genuine personal stature concerned with educational reform in general, not just with the difficulties of immigrant families. They varied in their interests and strategy. They were open and self-critical, yet united in their belief that traditional modes of education were inadequate for an industrial society. Moreover, it was central to their outlook that culture could be democratized without being vulgarized. They were deeply aware of political realities, but sought reform by means of building volunteer associations rather than entering partisan politics. Given the wide currency of the terms *progressive* or *reform* during this period, it was understandable that they, and especially their disciples, would be called progressive educators.[19]

By 1919, a Progressive Education Association had been organized, which endured until 1955. Teachers College (of Columbia University) became their central "higher" headquarters. In those years, the members were actively engaged on many fronts. In turn, the progressive educational movement came under bitter attack for undermining the fundamentals of sound educational practice. The lasting consequences of the progressive movement can easily be overstated, however, for certain changes would have come even without the progressive movement.

18. Ibid., p. 178.
19. Lawrence A. Cremin, *The Transformation of the School: Progressivism in American Education, 1876–1957* (New York: Alfred A. Knopf, 1961).

During the first decades of the twentieth century, the "posture" of progressive education was more a source of vigorous debate than of institutional change. Only very few schools implemented a comprehensive program of progressive education. This observation is hardly to deny the indirect influence the progressive education movement exerted as its ideas spread throughout the United States.

By 1900, the new pattern of urban education included the assumption of social work tasks by the public school—for example, health inspections, bath and shower facilities, and even outreach efforts to parents. The regular curriculum was intertwined with special forms of civic education. The school system was taking on new functions—a trend that led to an overloading of the tasks of the school. In fact, the belief that the school was too formalized and too narrow to contribute sufficiently to acculturation led Jane Addams to establish Hull House and give impetus to the settlement house movement. Here, parents as well as children could be exposed to programs of reasoned Americanization, which took into consideration the cultural background of the immigrants. Civic training and education, many educationists believed, could best be developed not in the school but by local community organizations. One of the most stimulating writers on the community as the locus for civic education was Mary Follett.[20] But the school never effectively articulated with the local community.[21]

Instead, the school remained the central educational agency for civic education, augmented by the growth of associated voluntary associations. Between the turn of the century and World War II, the history textbook continued to be the central tool. Two new developments in the textbooks of 1890–1920 may be noted. One is that the problem of the immigrant was introduced in books destined to be read by students at large. The subject was too conspicuous to be excluded. Many textbooks presented an element of social realism about the pressing issues of immigration. This is not to overlook the fact that the treatment of the immigrant generally concluded on a note of optimism. Second, in addition to historical materials, there was some coverage of the organization of political parties and governmental administration. There was also a more explicit discussion of the rights of the citizen than presented in earlier texts. Explicit linkage between rights and obligation was rare. It was not until after World War I that civics was dealt with in separate textbooks—the first step in

20. Mary Follett, *The New State* (New York: Longman Green, 1918).
21. For a review and assessment of this literature on the community as a center of civic education, see Philip Olson, "Urban Neighborhood Research: Its Development and Current Focus," *Urban Affairs Quarterly* 17 (June 1982): 491–515.

the movement to include other social sciences in the high school curriculum.

The entrance of the United States into World War I created an immense strain on ethnic relations and democratic patterns of citizenship. The Germans—the largest ethnic group in the United States and a vigorous and active civic group—were stigmatized by the war. The result was to divide the nation with the long-term effect of constricting the public presence and visibility of the German ethnic group. Among members of the group were old families with strong democratic traditions which could be traced back to the Civil War and to 1848, when the largest wave of political refugees came from German-speaking territories. On the positive side, during World War I, vast numbers of recent immigrants and their children demonstrated their civic loyalty to the nation-state. In part, this reflected the political circumstances of their former homeland, where old monarchies were breaking up under the impact of "self-determination" and Wilson's political stance. The struggles for political leadership in Europe served to involve immigrant groups in the United States and operated as a form of civic education. Likewise, the extensive economic and social integration of segments of diverse ethnic groups into U.S. society, as well as the consequences of schooling to which their children were exposed, contributed to a sense of patriotism.

After the end of hostilities, the immigrant flow started again, but encountered fierce resistance. Economic conditions were unsettled and employment opportunity declined, generating strong nativist demands for restrictions in immigration. Moreover, new immigrants were characterized as containing a marked concentration of "radicals." In reaction to the Russian Revolution and radical movements in Western Europe and in the United States, a "red scare"—a fear of communist agitation—swept the country, further increasing opposition to new immigration. There was a marked increase in political demands that schools more vigorously pursue Americanization programs and instruct students on the dangers of communism.

The term *Americanization* had its vogue until the advent of the Depression. It had a variety of meanings, however, and was used to justify a variety of strategies. For many educators it merely meant more intense efforts at acculturation. However, Americanization often was a code word for energetic opposition to radical movements in the public school system. In many smaller communities, such an emphasis was pursued. Tensions of the post–World War I period increased radical agitation, both of the right and of the left. But the Americanization movement of the 1920s chose to attack the radical left and was relatively indifferent to agitation of the radical right, especially of the Ku Klux Klan.

Advocates of ethnic pluralism criticized excessively rigid American-ization programs and the antidemocratic overtones of these efforts. These critics were outspoken in their judgment that "superpatriotic" pressure would not be effective in acculturating ethnic groups in the United States.

In the 1920s, school administrators had to deal with the substantive problems of expanding high school populations. Would the United States follow the pattern of Western Europe of a distinct college preparatory high school, or would there be a more open and less elitist format? Amer-ican educators, while concerned with school efficiency, were more inter-ested than their European counterparts in youngsters not headed for college.[22] Both administrators and teachers had to face the pressures and agitation of numerous voluntary associations to force a political and "moral" confrontation. The extent to which the schools became a "battleground" for sociopolitical movements should not be exaggerated, but neither should it be overlooked.

The many interest groups with explicit goals in youth education and "civic training" which came into being after World War I are documented in a detailed study prepared for the American Historical Society by Bessie Louise Pierce.[23] While Pierce makes no effort to assess their influence, her study assists one in developing a realistic overview of the matrix in which the public school operated during the period of the search for national citizenship. The pressures the school was exposed to were strongly status-quo oriented, but they foreshadowed the left and the ethnic nationalist upheavals of the 1960s. In the nineteenth century, public schools were penetrable by Protestant religious organizations. In the 1920s they were infiltrated by a variety of patriotic, military, peace, fraternal, religious, and racial groups, as well as movements of youth, business, and labor. Not to be overlooked, prohibition and antiprohibition groups, and even the Ku Klux Klan, had public school agendas. Pierce's description of these activ-ities underlines the conclusion that civic education in the United States after World War I was shared between the high school administration and voluntary associations which saw the school as a useful locus for agitation. Where barred direct access, these groups worked at the school's bound-aries.

The sheer "crossfire" of these groups in the years between the end of World War I and the arrival of the Great Depression probably limited their impact. But there was a hierarchy of access and prestige. Dominance rested with patriotic and veterans' groups augmented by various fraternal

22. See Raymond Callahan, *Education and the Cult of Efficiency* (Chicago: Uni-versity of Chicago Press, 1962).
23. Bessie Louise Pierce, *Citizens' Organizations and the Civic Training of Youth* (New York: Charles Scribner's Sons, 1933).

and religious youth groups. The daily flag ceremony was important. Armistice Day and Memorial Day, and the local equivalents in the South, supplied the stage for emphasizing national spirit and nonpartisan sentiments. The symbolism of these events outweighed in influence the formal course offerings in history and the increase in civics texts. (Even before Vietnam, such rituals had declined; I would place the decline in the years after the Korean conflict.)

Organized youth movements such as Boy Scouts, Girl Scouts, and Junior Red Cross represented the second level of penetration. These were vigorous organizations with strong status-quo perspectives. A major exception to that orientation was the peace movement groups, religiously rather than politically based. The structure of opinion of parents and children cannot be estimated from the patterns of organizational dominance. Radical movements organized youth activities outside the public school. Most reform movements were not oriented toward youth. However, there was considerable vigor in the municipal reform movement, which propagandized for various changes, especially public ownership of utilities. The result was that the school had a minor but steady flow of messages from both advocates for and against public ownership. Public relations efforts of business groups led more conservative labor unions to demand a "fair share" of representation and publicity. The American Federation of Labor emphasized the presence of labor movement history in textbooks and searched for evidence of distortion and omission. Comparison with Europe was revealing of the political patterns of American society. In Europe, the church and political parties, especially radical parties—left and right—organized large-scale youth movements. In the United States, the initiative and response came primarily from voluntary associations and specialized interest groups.

In an interesting analysis of "civic attitudes" found in high school texts, Bessie Pierce studied nearly four hundred texts published between 1915 and 1930, mainly history, but including an increasing number of civics books and some initial volumes which reflect the intrusion of materials from sociology, economics, and political science.[24] Some conclusions are hardly startling, but supply a basis for comparison with subsequent decades. The materials are strongly nationalistic. "The American is taught to respect and to venerate his forebears and the institutions which they designed and developed."[25] There was little criticism of American characteristics or activities. Instead, the textbooks were permeated with a "national or patriotic spirit." Most were pro-American, some were neutral;

24. Pierce, *Civic Attitudes in American School Textbooks.*
25. Ibid., p. 254.

a few included a critical outlook. None could be charged with disloyalty to American ideals.

It is well to keep in mind that Charles and Mary Beard had, in 1923, a text edition of *History of the United States* which emphasized economic conflicts operating in the development of the nation. In essence, by the 1920s, there were isolated books with a more critical orientation. But it was not until the Depression that there was an increase in "social realism," representing left-of-center perspective as against the dominant right. These books were by a limited number of educators, but received widespread attention—greater than the actual influence they exerted. But they did indirectly influence the textbooks of the 1930s and 1940s.

Concerning the balance between citizens' rights and obligations, Pierce's study shows that the theme of rights was clearly discernible. The student is reminded about the "freedom of opportunity, the right of liberty, life and property."[26] Obligation is presented as an aspect of allegiance, more taken for granted than elaborated. The long-term trend of increased attention to rights was thus already evident in the 1920s. There is no reason to believe that discussion of obligation has been constricted. It is rather that obligation, though acknowledged in texts dealing with civic education, never got much space.

Moreover, civic education, especially in the 1920s, involved more than an increase in formal course work and the reaction of the public school to external political pressure. In response to strong egalitarianism in the United States, together with the writings of progressive educators, there was heavy resistance to the European form of high school based on early selection and segregation of students who would be prepared for higher education. The 1920s was a period in which high school education was expanded, while college and university attendance also grew. The form of this expansion, which continued with increasing rapidity after World War II, had a direct impact on civic education.

The United States created a high school–college system more open in the social basis of recruitment than Western European preparatory high schools. Ultimately, the U.S. system came under heavy attack for serving too large a segment of the youth population, thereby reducing the level of academic performance. From the point of view of civic education and citizenship, the important aspect of the expanding high school system between World Wars I and II was the recruitment of low-income youngsters into college. This was accomplished in good measure by organizing comprehensive high schools. The essential strategy is well known: to include in a single high school complex both terminal high school programs

26. Ibid., p. 256.

and a high-level academic track. Such an arrangement facilitated the identification of bright youngsters from low-income families to raise their aspirations and to place them in the college preparatory track. If a high school did not have an academic track, recruitment of qualified low income youngsters into college preparatory programs was much less likely. To succeed, the high school required a competent teaching staff both to offer the courses necessary for the pattern of multitracks and to maintain an appropriate climate of civility and order.

The comprehensive high school became available in a variety of communities with considerable academic success. It required an ecological setting which enabled the school to draw a heterogeneous student population from the immediate surrounding area. However, by 1950, and especially by 1960, the growth of the metropolitan population reached such magnitude that the typical central-city or suburban high school was more and more drawing its students from relatively homogeneous populations. With such social change, certain high schools were recruiting middle-status students, while others served predominantly or even exclusively low-income students. Paradoxically, specialized high schools, including academic schools with citywide enrollment, became experimental models in the search to continue the goals of the comprehensive high school. These specialized schools, including those with concentration in mathematics, science, and literature, achieved some success but, with conspicuous exceptions, never duplicated the effectiveness and prestige of the comprehensive high schools. In any case, the issues facing the high school were redefined by court decisions to require racial integration by means of mandatory school busing.

Any assessment of the comprehensive school is at best limited because of the lack of research studies. But the comprehensive high school in its golden age—the 1930s and 1940s—despite the Depression and the dislocations of World War II, clearly made it easier for low-income students to enter colleges—including colleges of high academic standing.

Social mobility per se does not necessarily strengthen democratic values and practices. But the comprehensive high school helped to weaken rigid social-class lines and thereby reduced socioeconomic tensions. More concretely, it is also my estimate that the comprehensive high school—and other related educational programs—had a positive effect on the attitudes of even those students who were not destined for college. The fact that the students at large could directly observe the benefits that accrued to the "smart" student led to popular acceptance of the comprehensive high school. In short, the comprehensive high school operated in a period in which students reacted favorably to rewards based on merit and to the idea of the school being, to some degree, organized as a meritocracy.

FROM CIVICS TO SOCIAL PROBLEMS

The Great Depression resulted in profound societal strain. Rapidly the New Deal created a new web of linkages between the citizenry and organs of government. Unlike European countries, where the regulated economy and the welfare state developed over a long period of time, the United States became "overnight" a "modern" nation-state. It is striking that while the federal government intervened in almost every institutional sector of society, it barely touched the educational system.

President Franklin D. Roosevelt's Civilian Conservation Corps, although it had strong educational implications, especially civic education ones, was essentially an outdoor work program concerned with natural resources. A National Youth Administration was established to assist students to complete education by means of work-study arrangements, but the NYA was an agency separate from the school. When the NYA was terminated as the United States mobilized for war, it left no organizational consequence except to demonstrate the viability of government-subsidized work-study arrangements. Such programs were reestablished at a later date.

Roosevelt was suspicious of and hostile to professional educators. Moreover, he was pressing for social and economic reform which would produce rapid results, whereas educational agencies could best be approached on a long-term basis. New Deal programs in education would have involved federal aid to local schools and would raise the divisive question of aid to religious schools in the North and of assistance to black schools in the South. One cannot escape the conclusion that the "hands off" approach to public education by the New Deal compounded post–World War II social problems and contributed to ensuing tensions. When federal aid to education became a reality, there had been little prior learning experience to help fashion public policy. Nevertheless, the school system underwent extensive changes during the Great Depression, including important developments in the area of civic education.

Immense fiscal difficulties for schools—public, parochial, and private—meant extensive reduction in personnel and pay scales; there were even periods when salaries simply were not paid. In the major metropolitan centers, efforts to unionize teachers met with varying success. High and persistent rates of unemployment demoralized the adult population, with the optimistic face of FDR serving as the main counterelement. Teachers, while they did not fall into the near malnutrition category, were hard up like everyone else, but, unlike many others, they did have steady employment and high self-respect. Their students, however, could look forward to little gainful employment.

The quality of public education remained relatively effective, particularly for students in the academic track. Personnel recruited into teaching in the years after World War I were of good quality, since teaching was still a respected profession. The decline in high school instruction after World War II resulted largely from the drain of better personnel to junior colleges and colleges.

But the impact of the Great Depression was to strain and weaken, if only temporarily, institutional authority. The educational system was no exception. Gradually the nation struggled to return to increased levels of employment, either in the open market or by means of public works programs. The morale of the population, including the teaching profession, was again tested in the unexpectedly sharp recession of 1937. The advent of military mobilization brought the economy back to rising levels of employment and economic productivity.

The Great Depression and its aftermath produced two developments of long-term importance to civic education, which were to reach fruition in sociopolitical movements of protest in the late 1960s and early 1970s. First, civic education in public school, based on a format of undeviating patriotism augmented by praise for the "American way," was called into question. Changes were also underway, though on a lesser scale, at the college level. Yet traditionalists, despite the depth of the economic crisis, were able to maintain their dominance; sheer inertia was at work, together with a desire to avoid conflict.

A stream of materials involving social realism and specific social problems was introduced by a minority of the teaching profession, especially at the high school level. These new directions in civic education, seeds for which were planted in the 1920s, were compatible with and, in fact, supportive of the New Deal and its legislative program. The traditional goals of civic education, namely "Americanization" and acculturation as part of the search for national citizenship, lost their central place. National citizenship had not penetrated deeply into the most economically dispossessed minority groups. Civic education in public schools now began to emphasize loyalty to the political system and to offer elementary instruction in organization of government and partisan politics. Implicit was the goal of solving economic crisis by means of legitimate, noncoercive political and electoral behavior. Although the authors of these new materials believed they were setting forth an objective analysis of the United States, civic education in essence shifted from traditional patriotism to various forms of political dissent of the status quo.

Second, the Great Depression generated for the first time an activist, although fragmented, student movement in American universities, colleges, and high schools. The student movement was essentially left of center, with various cores of radical participants. Only a tiny fraction of the high school population and a small segment of college students were involved. Yet these movements were able to attract considerable mass media coverage. The articulate but divided leadership exercised influence well beyond the size of its following. The outbreak of World War II, and especially the Russian/German mutual assistance pact, halted the student movement, but only temporarily. The form and strength of the movement at any given time reflected the issues of the day. Particular factions of the movement were supported by a few teachers, either from ideological sympathy or because of previous membership. Civic education, in effect, was no longer the monopoly of teachers.

These two converging trends, the social realism of some official textbooks and the emergence of a student movement, meant the end of the "age of innocence." It meant the end of the cliché that the school reflects the values of larger society. The educational system after the Great Depression, while still dominanted by the conventional institutions of American education, contained vocal elements agitating in a fashion that can be called oppositionist.

The new social-realist materials can best be described, in retrospect, as social studies with liberal—sometimes left-wing—overtones and including elements of more radical ideology. "Radical" here refers to the extension of government ownership of selected key economic institutions. The content hardly implied an armed seizure of property, or even the style of strikes conducted by the industrial "sit ins" of the Depression period. It was an intellectual acceptance of "collectivist" or "socialist" thought because of the imputed failure of the economic system and the supposed superiority of a governmentalized solution.

Intellectual influences at work in the new social realism were diverse; it hardly represented a unified intellectual or ideological movement. Some of the new texts of the Great Depression period could be traced back to the Progressive movement. Native forms of dissent and intellectual radicalism from before World War I discreetly found their way into the writings of the new realism. But American left-of-center educators looked mainly to Europe for models. They were interested in socialist governments and experiments, especially in the so-called middle way of Sweden. Another group of educators and intellectuals, mockingly called fellow travelers, hailed the Russian experiment and asked for benign toleration to observe objectively those developments.

With the growth of advanced industrialism, teachers in Western democratic polities, because of training or because of frustrated personal ambition, often became critics of their national society. Their training and daily work predisposed them to criticism of society rather than to concern with maintaining a democratic polity. During the Depression it is not surprising that certain social science teachers looked with favor on differing forms of governing the economy. They used the Great Depression to confirm their belief that "capitalism was in trouble."

The new social realism and leftist orientations, of course, prompted sharp criticism from traditionalists. Many stressed that the progressive education movement was mainly responsible for the decline in the study of history and the growth of social studies. They asserted that this trend weakened the school's ability to perform its essential task in civic education—namely, transmitting enduring aspects of the political and cultural heritage. In particular, they believed that progressive education was enhancing personal authority at the expense of institutional authority. The result, in their view, was a gradual weakening of the authoritative institutions required to manage a modern nation-state. In my judgment, however, the progressive movement had little influence on social realism.

Some members of the Progressive Education Association accepted the new realism and helped to disseminate its implied left-of-center ideology. Others in the association separated personal political orientations from professional goals. They wanted to keep the school system free of direct partisan linkages and to prepare students for reasoned political decisions. For such persons, maintaining political freedom was just as important as ending economic depression. They tended to be skeptical of doctrinaire solutions to contemporary problems. John Dewey was in this category. For example, he was an international critic of the absence of personal and political freedom in the Soviet Union. As a pragmatist, he believed that the degree of collectivism in the economy was to be decided in the light of performance and an assessment of consequences. Ideological categories were not for him the core of civic education in a democratic polity.

More to the issue at hand, in my view, is the fact that the expansion of social studies into the high school and even into the elementary school was mainly the result of pressure by persons not directly connected with the Progressive Education Association. Most efforts were made by representatives of the various social sciences—political science, economics, history, and sociology—and by the national associations of these disciplines. After World War I, such associations already had organized commissions and committees concerned with bringing the social sciences into the high school. They were interested in objective investigation and increased employment opportunities for social studies teachers. Their interest in high school teaching outlived the Progressive Education Association. Social studies, though introduced into high schools in the 1930s, only became a major part of the curriculum after World War II, when the Progressive Education Association was defunct; on the other hand, national social science associations were expanding.

The idea that the social studies movement was a result of progressive education originated partly in the extensive textbook writing of Harold Rugg. Rugg was a remarkably energetic figure associated with Teacher's College of Columbia University. With a background in engineering and statistics, he was prone to overstate the accomplishments of social science. His writings were radical in their implicit acceptance of greater government ownership of economic enterprises.[27] Rugg started in the 1920s with a series of six pamphlets, which eventually grew into six volumes for junior high school, published between 1929 and the mid-thirties. Five were later revised and, by 1939, eight additional volumes had been produced for elementary grades.[28] These texts attracted much attention. They caused Rugg to be labeled socialist and radical and embroiled him in controversy with conservative business groups. Materials and books of the new social realism would have had wider usage but for the economic limitations of public schools, which sought to save funds by not replacing existing textbooks.

What overall assessment can be made of the school's role in civic education during the Great Depression? In my judgment—based on the limited available survey data, documentary material, informed specialists, and self-reports of articulate students—the result was a limited but discernible increase in attitudes of social dissent and criticism with long-term political consequences in support of left-of-center policies. That result foreshadowed similar consequences of social studies on attitude patterns fashioned in high schools and colleges during the post–World War II period and until the end of the Vietnam era. Such an assessment avoids overstatement since it points to school experiences, formal and informal, as a secondary factor in molding political beliefs as compared with the combined primary impact of historical events and imagery produced by the mass media. Moreover, the attitude patterns resulted in a diffuse social movement and not in hardened, self-disciplined youth organizations, as developed in Western Europe.

Civic education in the Great Depression took place in the context of movements of the radical right and the radical left. It is, therefore, useful to estimate the extent of popular adherence to such movements among adult and youth populations. Available survey data for the right (more detailed than for the left) indicate that at least 8–10 percent of the adult population had radical-right attitude patterns during the New Deal period

27. Peter F. Cabbone, Jr., *The Social and Educational Thought of Harold Rugg* (Durham, N.C.: Duke University Press, 1977), pp. 25–33 and pp. 72–92.
28. Ibid., p. 24.

of the 1930s. Ineffective leadership prevented extensive mobilization of this constituency.[29] From less adequate data for adult adherents to the radical left, I would estimate that they failed to reach 5 percent. The percentage would be considerably higher if the popular front and cooperating liberal elements were included.

Youthful adherents to the radical right were very few; there was no meaningful youth movement of the radical right. In contrast, the radical left developed a strong youth movement whose members outnumbered their adult counterparts. Youthful elements in the radical left demonstrated vigor and intensity, but were prone to fragment into splinter groups on issues of ideology. Leftist youth groups were able to make effective use of the Spanish civil war in mobilizing sympathizers. This military confrontation was the leading event in the political education of many young Americans, both in metropolitan high schools and in colleges throughout the country.

There were radical leaders in particular trade unions, but the trade union movement was hardly a radical instrument. It demonstrated outbursts of militancy and vigor which, despite a flurry of sit-in strikes, operated within the context of New Deal legislation. There were radical political organizations and student movements with effective linkages to the mass media. However, only one radical, or one who could be attacked as a radical, was elected to Congress.

These data can be read in a different perspective. Despite the discontent of the Great Depression, the overwhelming bulk of the citizenry, including high school and college students, persisted in positive and patriotic adherence to the political system. Not until the 1960s did the nation encounter widespread political negativism. In effect, the Great Depression years manifested continuation of old-fashioned patriotism, with signs of increasing strain. The traditional approach in the public school persisted, supported by numerous patriotic and nationalistic organizations.

Most parents expected their children to be educated to be law-abiding, loyal, and patriotic Americans. Yet teachers encountered increased frustration when teaching sociopolitical issues in the classroom. The nation was impatient with the prolonged depression, and time-honored emphasis on the virtues of the American way and patriotism met with growing indifference and even hostility. The declaration of war by Axis powers against the United States temporarily settled the issues of patriotism and of involvement versus isolation.

The introduction of new social studies was without influence. In part, the failure of these materials was the result of weakness in the traditional

29. Morris Janowitz, "Black Legions on the March," in Daniel Aaron, ed., *America in Crisis* (New York: Alfred Knopf, 1952), pp. 305–25.

historical approach. Given the depth of the crisis of the 1930s, the historically oriented curriculum failed to inspire or reassure the rank-and-file student. Clearly, civic education to strengthen a democratic polity under pressure required emphasis on the historical strength of the society in meeting previous economic crises, and emphasis on the political creativity of U.S. leadership. This was hardly the approach of typical high school and college history texts, which emphasized success in military engagements and westward expansion of the nation.

The implicit conclusion of such texts was that the United States periodically engaged in war and, although lacking a European military tradition or a large standing armed force, was generally successful. This conclusion had a certain relevance since another major military conflict was soon to take place. But the historical approach failed to supply students with a sense of relevant historical continuity. It failed to instill a positive regard for the capacity of society to adjust to sociopolitical change.

The social-problems perspective, on the other hand, neglected the historical background. Moreover, there was no great uniformity or even convergence in the social-problems perspective. The efforts at the high school level to make use of social studies can be judged a failure. Social sciences were not sufficiently developed to warrant infusion into the high school curriculum. Understanding the significance of social studies requires more maturity than many high school students have. There is also a question of the quality of teaching personnel.[30]

The premature introduction of social studies into the public high school (and even into the grade school) has stimulated popular dissent without understanding of the subject matter or appreciation of the complexity of the issues involved in collective problem solving. Outside of regular classrooms, the social-studies high school teacher in the 1930s often attracted a small group of students who became a center of diffuse hostility toward the status quo. Of course, value questions are not to be avoided, since the purpose of civic education is to help students clarify their own values. However, with the exception of teachers interested in economic analysis, social studies teachers tended to have liberal, left-of-center, and radical, or would-be radical, points of view. This state of affairs persisted until the late 1970s, when the "new conservatism" began to foster right-wing values among social-studies teachers.

The personal values of teachers is not the point. What is objectionable is the intrusion of personal values into the professional performance of social studies teaching. From the start, the level of professional teaching

30. This is not to assert that there is no role for social studies in the high school. I will return to the question of the amount and emphasis on social studies at the college level, as part of civic education, in chapter 6.

hardly achieved desired standards in the secondary school. It is also necessary to keep in mind that social studies were introduced not by the activities of parents but, rather, by the commitment of teaching and administrative personnel. Social studies in the context of a progressive education had some consequences that can be judged positive. A well-done piece of research, the so-called "Eight-Year Study"[31] of 1,475 college students, was designed to contrast those who attended progressive high schools with those educated at traditional high schools. Although the findings do not deal specifically with different types of civic education, it can be inferred that progressive high schools included stronger emphasis on social studies, but not necessarily of the new social-realism variety, than did conventional high schools. Progressive high schools tended to be of middle- and upper-middle-class social composition. Graduates of progressive high schools demonstrated more active concern with national and world affairs, indicating that curriculum makes a difference. Elements of self-selection could have been at work, although efforts were made to control for this in the research design by matching students on a range of variables.

The number of progressive high schools was limited, and the social-studies approach to civic education touched a majority of traditional high schools. I assert, on the basis of self-reporting of participants after the fact, as well as inference from the materials used, that the new perspective contributed during the 1930s to the politicizing, and even radicalizing, of a limited number of students. My emphasis is on the phrase *contributed to*, since family background and a social personality in revolt against existing authority were effective predisposing factors. Events of the 1930s stimulated left-of-center thinking, not only on the immediate issues of unemployment and social injustice but, in particular, on the communist-dominated, antifascist struggle in Spain against Franco and his German and Italian allies. Causes with an element of remoteness can be highly persuasive in fashioning civic and political attitudes of young students.

If the traditional curriculum failed to devote sufficient effort to deal with duties and obligations in a democratic polity, the new realism was heavily, almost exclusively, oriented toward rights of citizenship. A striking aspect of the new perspective was the incomplete and partial view of political institutions and compromise processes required for a democratic government. The new social-realism approach focused on the inequalities of contemporary society, not on the strengths and weaknesses of legitimate systems of political problem solving. Clearly, such issues are better handled at the college and university level, but teachers of civic education must address these questions for those who will not receive higher edu-

31. See Wilford M. Aikin, *The Story of the Eight-Year Study* (New York: McGraw-Hill Book Company, 1942).

cation. Moreover, a cognitive, rational approach is not enough to "move" participants in civic education. A democratic society requires symbolic content capable of stimulating students to a sense of pride and self-esteem. The Great Depression demonstrated that old-fashioned patriotism needed new elements if collective enthusiasm was to be generated by a student population with increasing levels of formal education.

In retrospect, it is clear that during the Great Depression a significant segment of potentially discontented youth—members of racial minorities and particular ethnic groups—were untouched by civic education based either on patriotism or on the new social realism. World War II did serve as a form of civic education for many from these groups, but mobilizing them did not result in a continuing search for national citizenship. Instead, it produced—in temporary forms of racial and ethnic nationalism—a modern form of communalism which led to deep political strain. The public school became the central arena for these agitations. After 1945, this communal nationalism focused initially on the demands of the black civil rights movement. It remained for the Spanish-speaking population with its ambiguous relationship to U.S. national citizenship to produce a deep and long-lasting cleavage, which presents profound challenges to present-day civic education.

Mass Education II:
The New Communalism

While the long-term trend of acculturation has persisted, the United States in the 1960s and 1970s experienced an outburst of ethnic, especially racial, nationalism. The most extreme manifestations were short-lived, but important residues persisted. If *nationalism* seems too comprehensive a term, *separatism* might be more appropriate, though it stresses negative aspects and not social solidarity, which was the goal. I use *the new communalism* to describe the strengthened ethnic/racial group consciousness that erupted during the 1960s and the 1970s. It was not a generalized trend. Its locus was mainly in black, Chicano, and American Indian communities.[1] Although *nationalism* was the self-designation which many activists employed, *communalism* is useful as a neutral term. Communalism broke with the long-term expansion of hyphenated "Americanization," or with acculturation. It is a central theme of this study that civic education weakened after 1945, particularly in the 1960s and early 1970s. The new communalism must be taken as dramatic evidence of this weakness of civic education, especially among the dominant groups in American society. These strong sentiments of racial and ethnic consciousness were to be found in middle-class and, more interestingly, in economically deprived groups who were touched only to a limited extent by the trends of acculturation. During the 1960s, black communalism was the most vigorous and elaborate of these movements, but over the long run I judge the

1. The "revival" of communal sentiments among American Indians during this period is dramatic. I have focused on black and Chicano nationalism, however. The numbers involved in communalism among the American Indians is limited, and the symbolism among this group is complicated to analyze because of the centrality of "blood" lineage.

Spanish-speaking variety to be most important from the point of view of the issues of citizenship and civic education.

The new communalism emphasized in varying degrees exclusiveness and opposition to the tradition of hyphenated Americans—the key formula of acculturation. Adherents uniformly believed that primordial elements of minority groups were enduring. They argued that blacks would remain black because of racial characteristics and cultural heritage, and Chicanos would remain Chicanos because of language and cultural heritage. They demanded that political parties recognize this basic "reality." The new communalism did produce an increase in political participation and in the number of elected officials from these minority groups. In this sense, one ideal of citizenship was implemented.

But the logic of ethnic/racial communalism raised fundamental dilemmas for a democratic polity. It presented the specter of a series of cleavages which would weaken national citizenship and democratic political institutions. The new communalism had a powerful impact on minority youth. The sociopolitical movements markedly altered civic education over the short run, especially "unofficial" civic education. Participation in and exposure to activist ethnic nationalism substituted for classroom American history and civics instruction. Paradoxically, efforts in compensatory education and desegregation of public education had the short-term effect of mobilizing sentiments in support of racial/ethnic communalism. Since minority-group leaders could now negotiate more effectively with public officials, communal cohesion temporarily increased.[2]

Fashioned by the stratification system and by political demands of communal activists, these movements had their own dynamics, but generally followed the natural history of protest movements.[3] Although there was variation from group to group, they first put forth moderate demands, followed by extreme ones, which in turn gave way to a measure of moderation, but which resulted in demands more extreme than the original aspirations.

These protest movements—black movements in particular—took place in the context of extensive anti-Vietnam protest. Organized opposition to the Vietnam conflict had its own leaders and participants. But there was a noteworthy overlap in the membership of these movements and some elements of coordination, if only because of immediate pressures. The Vietnam war protest movement offered a form of civic education to a

2. For an intensive case study of increased communal sentiments in an educational setting, see John U. Ogbu, *The Next Generation: An Ethnography of Education* (New York: Academic Press, 1974).
3. Lyford P. Edwards, *The National History of Revolution* (Chicago: University of Chicago Press, 1970).

large segment of American youth, not only middle-class youth at more prestigious colleges and universities, from which much of the leadership was recruited. Also involved were many "popular" elements, mainly seeking to avoid personal participation in the armed forces.

There is reason to believe that the United States would have experienced these communally based protest movements even if it had not intervened in Vietnam.[4] But there is also reason to speculate that the Vietnam war and the protests it generated served to strengthen and invigorate agitations of ethnic/racial groups. Student antiwar protesters played a role in confrontations dealing with racial and ethnic issues. It was hardly a matter of competition weakening protest but, rather, an atmosphere of crisis which served by contagion to produce a momentum of mass demonstrations and attendant violence. I have seen no careful estimates of the number of young people or adults involved, directly or indirectly, in these protest movements. But on the basis of available evidence, participants in mass demonstrations and associated forms of violence (leaving aside outright race riots) involved a higher percentage of youth than had ever before been involved. It is ironical that, at the same time, American high schools and colleges were expanding social studies precisely for purposes of civic education.

The social sciences gained prestige and institutional acceptance during World War II. The period 1945–80 saw continued growth in social studies at both high school and college levels. Only toward the end of the 1970s did the growth slow and signs of contraction appear. Early in this period, it was widely assumed that the social sciences, political science in particular, could and would make a significant contribution to civic education. By the end of the 1970s, this assumption was repeatedly challenged; formal civic education in the United States was in profound disarray.

In a reversal of the situation of the 1930s, the link between social studies and liberal, left-of-center, and radical thought weakened. A limited number of conservative social scientists and educators were receiving extensive mass media coverage and wide distribution of their educational publications.

During post–World War II years, student protest movements had an immediate as well as a long-term effect in fragmenting and radicalizing the civic education curriculum. The short-term disruption was so deep that, in particular schools, the faculty and administration lost control of social studies, both to their students and to adult off-campus political

4. Lewis Killian, "Black Power and White Reactions: The Revitalization of Race Thinking in the United States," *Annals of the American Academy of Social and Political Science* 454 (March 1981): 44. See also William J. Wilson, *Power, Racism, and Privilege* (New York: The Free Press, 1973), pp. 199–200.

associates. This was especially the case in black studies. As expected, reaction developed which, in effect, moved social studies back toward the mainstream of organized education, though residues of the student revolt have persisted.

It is reasonable to ask why the student outbursts of the 1960s and 1970s caught the United States so unawares. The same can be asked about the growth of ethnic nationalism. One reasonable answer to this question is that forecasting matters of this kind is beyond the power of the social sciences; I tend to accept this explanation. However, one can speculate that regular party political leaders, because of their own political outlook, grossly misjudged the potential scope and intensity of antiwar protests. These leaders were essentially motivated to support presidential policy— under both Democratic and Republican administrations—out of a strong sense of patriotism and a diffuse sense of national interest. But they were schooled in pragmatic political bargaining. Their pragmatism meant that there were limits to their support for presidential policy. The stalemated Vietnam war was, to them, a national crisis which could be solved by reasonable men and women publicly supporting the president as he worked for solutions compatible with their basic sense of national honor and international obligation.

Regular organization political leaders never really understood the dogmatism and strong ideological beliefs and language of antiwar protesters. They consistently underestimated the size of youth, and even adult, populations which would be openly antipatriotic. Although a minority, the antiwar group had considerable mass media support. Political leaders had little previous experience with such uncompromising opposition. Initially, the antipatriotism of war protesters led to some "backlash" support for the president. As the war dragged on, antiwar protesters became more and more effective and received increased support, both overt and covert.

Protest movements, though prompted by immediate events and shaped by the personality of their leaders, are strengthened (or, some cases, weakened) by ideological formulations. The intellectual content of the antiwar movement was more than a series of rationalizations or mere political propaganda. Indeed, the student "rebellion" of the 1960s and 1970s involved more than antiwar feelings and support for ethnic communalism. Elements in the student movement wished to reform the university and the economic organization of society. Much of the ideology concerning these issues was hardly profound, but it did serve as a basis for recruiting both students and faculty. It is important to recognize that, even after collapse of the student movement by 1974, many participants still adhered to ideological beliefs that continued to influence their political behavior.

As I previously sought to assess the American Revolution as a form of civic education, it is appropriate to view the extensive participation of students in the Vietnam protest in a similar fashion.

To assert that ideological elements influence contemporary protest movements does not imply that these elements are necessarily helpful in achieving political goals. To the contrary, in the case of the antiwar movement the ideological elements were counterproductive. Just as political leaders did not understand the antiwar movement, the protesters did not understand the popular mood of the country when it became clear that "victory" could not be achieved. "Typical" citizen opinion was that the United States had attempted a justifiable military venture, and, in effect, had failed. With the loss of the prospect of "victory," it was morally and politically justified for the United States to seek an honorable termination.

The core of the antiwar protest, however, developed a very different ideological stance, which served in part to strengthen the resolve of United States political leaders. The "radical wing" of the movement, including members of Students for a Democratic Society and representatives of radical religious groups, enunciated the belief that the United States had become an immoral and politically irresponsible society, one that was thoroughly corrupt. In their view, there was no legitimacy in the United States intervention, nor in its conduct of the war. It was necessary to withdraw unilaterally from Vietnam because our presence was venal. After withdrawal, the struggle to transform society should be pushed vigorously, especially by mobilizing war veterans whose experience served to inform them of the true nature of the intervention in Vietnam. While such ideological appeals were attractive to a limited but emboldened segment of the high school and college population, they offended a majority of the citizenry, including those no longer actively supporting military intervention.

This left-wing ideological stance reflected only part of the protest movement. But it was this ideological view of the "new left" that came to dominate the strategy and mass media imagery of the anti-Vietnam protest. Politically, such a strategy could only be counterproductive. The movement did not have to develop such an ideology; it could have been more pragmatic and realistic, or it could have been more religious. But left-wing students were interested in building an organizational cadre to continue "the struggle" after the end of the Vietnam war. Many rank-and-file members of the antiwar movement were merely students caught up in mass demonstrations because of their desire to avoid military service, or because they had relatives or friends who faced the draft. While not ideologically motivated, they strongly opposed the goals and strategy of the Vietnam intervention.

The antiwar movement was active in working with young people who wished to remain civilians. More and more people learned the procedures for avoiding the draft. Radicals were generally unsuccessful in recruiting such people for a political movement. Despite the variety of surveys conducted on public opinion about the Vietnam war, there is little basis for judging the size of the youth segment who were to some extent "radicalized" by direct and indirect experiences with the war. Many who were radicalized reverted to a more traditional stance.

The antiwar movement chose the school, not the workshop, as the locus for agitation and the object of its attacks. The movement disappeared with the end of United States intervention in Vietnam, having failed to produce a cadre of activists prepared to continue radical and confrontation politics. A few entered conventional political affairs. Perhaps the most important response of the leadership of the Vietnam "generation" was their weakened sense of citizen obligation. Since they viewed the war and the government as immoral, they felt free of collective responsibility. The Watergate affair only confirmed their outlook. The Vietnam war had instilled in them the belief that to criticize the political system was the most important goal they could pursue. It is interesting that many leaders and subleaders took jobs in the mass media and continued their agitations and political criticism.

For the majority of young people who did participate in military service, the impact of Vietnam was hardly profound since they filled rather routine jobs or did limited tours of duty.[5] But for those who suffered in service, either in combat or in the transition to civilian life, the aftermath was another grim "veterans' problem," which, like previous veterans' problems, was to endure. There was no special veterans' organization to commemorate this military engagement, although the number who joined existing veterans' organizations was impressive and clearly increased the longevity and political effectiveness of their lobby.

Unlike the antiwar protest, racial/ethnic nationalism movements demonstrated striking resilience and ability to adapt to changing political circumstances. There remain important differences between the black nationalist and the Chicano configuration. In the black movement, outbursts of extremism and militancy occurred in the 1960s. After 1968, the extremist stance was modified, which increased group identification. Black nationalism of the post–World War II period was a form of communalism, a phase in a long-standing tradition of black protest. Black protest was to continue after this phase. By contrast, communalism among the Spanish-

5. M. Kent Jennings and Gregory B. Markus, "The Effect of Military Service on Political Attitudes: A Panel Study," *American Political Science Review* 71 (March 1977): 131–48.

speaking population in the United States has grown gradually. Among this group there have been nationalist outbursts, but the general trend has been a gradual strengthening of a sense of identity and a resulting accumulation of political power. In fact, the Chicano population represents the epitome of communalism in an advanced industrial society. Acculturation, as I have defined it, has been of secondary importance. The contrast between black nationalism and Spanish-speaking communalism is of fundamental importance for the future of a viable national citizenship.

INTEGRATION VERSUS BLACK COMMUNALISM

Black separatism, including the "return to Africa" slogan, is hardly a recent theme.[6] Especially in the 1920s, under the leadership of Marcus Garvey, support of black separatism was particularly vocal, although it touched only a minority of the black population. As civic consciousness developed from the end of World War I until the 1960s, black political leaders were demanding full citizenship. Aside from those who served merely as paid agents for white political organizations, most black politicians supported acculturation in some fashion, which they believed would parallel the experience of other minority groups. Most black political and community leaders just were not separatists. Intuitively, they were searching to become hyphenated Americans. They wished to improve the position of rank-and-file blacks as quickly as possible, as they built their own political careers. More and more explicitly, they took an integrationist stance. The average black seldom pondered the complex problems involved in pressing for or implementing integration. Increased political activity of blacks as a result of World War I created a need to defend the black community against renewed white racist violence equivalent to vigilantism of the post–Civil War period. Nevertheless, black leaders continued demands for social and economic change, paralleling those stressed in the past, and contemporarily by other ethnic leaders. The blacks wanted a style of life in the mode of society at large. As late as the New Deal period, integration, even in sectors dominated by the federal government, had not been a major goal. But political demands expressed through electoral participation would clearly involve greater interaction with the white population.

Moreover, the bulk of the black community thought of themselves as Americans, though their popular civic consciousness was less intense than that of people with European origins. Despite formal and informal barriers and race prejudice, the desire of most members of the black community

6. Wilson Jeremiah Moses, *The Golden Age of Black Nationalism, 1850–1925* (Hamden, Conn.: The Shoe String Press, 1978); John H. Bracey, "Black Nationalism since Garvey," in *Key Issues in the Afro-American Experience*, ed. Nathan I. Huggins, Martin Kelson, and Daniel M. Fox (New York: Harcourt Brace Jovanovich, 1971).

to become full American citizens was indeed powerful by the end of World War II. This aspiration increased their political involvement.[7] From 1945 on, the demand to enter the mainstream of American society was stated directly and without reservation.[8] Of course, there were black men and women of accomplishment who had their reservations about integration, and there were those who doubted it would ever come. But an integrationist strategy—based on a format of acculturation of blacks—was the dominant goal in the search for effective citizenship. Improved education was seen as the major factor in assisting blacks to obtain and assert full citizenship. As we shall see, military service facilitated the achievement of important aspects of citizenship for blacks. But it was a form of citizenship which, for obvious reasons, emphasized rights and privileges more than civic obligations.

Given the integrationist perspective, how are we to explain the outbursts of black nationalism and communalism which emerged so rapidly in the 1960s?[9] Even more important, how do we examine the restrained and even accommodative response of the larger society to black nationalism and, in turn, the rapid decline—or, rather, the restriction and adaptation—of the movement in the later 1970s? It should be stressed that extremist black communalism came after the civil rights movement and that these partial successes served only to increase frustration in the black sector. Moreover, the political propaganda of black communalism rejected the existing conception of citizenship in a pluralistic society. It offered an image of the future which would be difficult to articulate with the economic realities of complex interdependency.

Black nationalism of the 1960s and 1970s was a sociopolitical movement based in the educational system, located mainly in colleges and universities. It was a young people's movement, with black high school and college students and young teachers as activists. Efforts made to reach the black "underclass" were mainly unsuccessful.[10] Many involved in the race riots of the 1960s made use of the rhetoric of black separatism; such verbalism was of little political import. The movement produced its most

7. Bayard Rustin, *Strategies for Freedom: The Changing Patterns of Black Protest* (New York: Columbia University Press, 1976).
8. David J. Garrow, *Protest at Selma: Martin Luther King, Jr., and the Voting Rights Act of 1965* (New Haven: Yale University Press, 1978).
9. Lewis M. Killian, *The Impossible Revolution? Black Power and the American Dream* (New York: Random House, 1968); John H. Bracey, Jr., August Meier, and Elliott Rudwick, *Black Nationalism in America* (Indianapolis and New York: The Bobbs-Merrill Company, 1970).
10. Some black nationalists sought to develop the Black Panther Party as a political device for organizing the black "underclass." The results achieved were hardly lasting since that particular movement did not supply a basis for political coalitions with the larger community.

sustained response from young "middle stratum" blacks. It became, in effect, a specialized education movement, not a labor- or community-based agitation, making use of the apparatus and real estate of institutions of higher learning.

The movement had its romantic sequences, especially in efforts to link itself symbolically to national liberation in the third world. Elements of the antiwar movement converged with black communalism; and, in turn, often unrealistic and overblown attention was accorded these groups by the mass media. Mass media staffs, especially from television, saw the black "revolt" as good copy and, neglecting professional standards, over-played the subject as a spectacle in violence. Indeed, one response of the mass media to the violent agitation of the period was to add young people to their staffs, especially young blacks, and to make use of them to cover the civil rights, antiwar, and black communalism movements. This series of steps hardly served to increase the objectivity of coverage. Mass media was encouraged, in fact pressured, by members of the federal executive to make appointments of this kind. Such recommendations were made by the Kerner presidential commission, for example. Participation in sep-aratist agitation, as in the antiwar movement, became a powerful if tem-porary form of civic education. Paradoxically, these agitations had a lasting, although indirect, effect in raising the self-esteem and group cohesion of older blacks who did not accept the separatist orientation but were con-cerned with a strong self-image and strong public image for the black population.

From the end of the Civil War to the present day, a major problem for the black community and political leadership was the elimination of vio-lence against blacks, including covert police brutality. But it is striking that, in the range of demands made by black leaders since the turn of the century and even earlier, the most persistent goal is improved education. No doubt, leaders emphasized education more than the rank and file, whose more immediate concern was access to employment or better jobs. Gradually the need for more effective education was felt by all levels of the black community. The obligations of citizenship and the need for civic education were not stressed.

In the American scene, concern with improved academic and vocational education is understandable. Education was believed to be the agency by which other ethnic groups experienced social improvement and attained better jobs and the status of citizen. Improved education, therefore, should enhance the moral and economic worth of blacks and, as a result, enable them to obtain the benefits of effective citizenship. Again, civic obligations were not stressed in such formulations.

Black communalism should be examined as a manifestation of the difficulties in improving black education. If good education enhances citizenship, as is generally believed, I contend that the reverse is even more relevant: that a sense of affiliation with the larger society, a sense of citizenship, facilitates commitment to educational achievement.

The stress on accumulation of human capital has a long tradition in the United States, from the very first colonization. It was the theme most acceptable to all factions in the black community. For example, opponents of Booker T. Washington had to accord him an element of support and legitimacy because of his performance in developing black vocational education. Most black families placed greater emphasis on educating their children than on being involved in the political process. Likewise, the larger society accepted, at least symbolically, improved educational opportunities, although implementation was extremely slow. Education was a goal which a person could strive to attain by his own efforts. Personal improvement by political participation lagged behind until the 1960s, especially until the passage of the Civil Rights Act of 1964.

Available research efforts make it possible to assess the use of education by different ethnic groups as a means of economic and social self-improvement.[11] There are marked differences, with Jews and segments of Chinese and Japanese populations being heavy consumers of education in the United States. Cultural traditions are offered by way of explanation. No doubt, slavery helped prevent the development of such traditions, but the low levels of education among blacks represent generations of restricted opportunity after the formal end of slavery. (Although blacks served in the military, they did not have access to educational facilities operated by the armed forces until World War II.)

My purpose is not to account for levels of education in the black community. It is rather to emphasize that black leaders have long struggled to improve the number and quality of educational institutions used by blacks. Moreover, the inferiority of black schools has been fully recognized by the black community, including the most deprived members. In the language of the ghetto, it was traditional to assert that a white school is a good school and a black school a bad one.

The fact that blacks during World War II received technical and vocational training in addition to literacy instruction served only to increase the pressure for change. But resources came slowly and improvement was retarded by the bureaucratization of public schools, especially in the big-city ghettos.

11. For a detailed historical analysis of the role of education and ethnic group progress see Stanley Lieberson, *A Piece of the Pie: Black and White Immigrant Groups Since 1880* (Berkeley: University of Calilfornia Press, 1980).

The pressure for change in public education was also stimulated by polemical books by a number of white authors, social critics, and even mainline educators. Their arguments rested as much on humanistic values as on the ability (or inability) of schools to teach basic skills. Paul Goodman emerged as a leading figure in the construction of utopian solutions.[12] He was followed by authors such as John Holt, Ivan Illich, Herbert Kohl, Jonathan Kozol, and George Leonard, whose main contribution was to supply an effective vocabulary of criticism of existing educational institutions.[13]

Two strategies to improve education were available to the black community. One was desegregation and the second was a restructuring of the teaching process. Restructuring included increased community control of local schools. Selective experimental programs in community control received extensive mass media coverage, as in the Ocean Hill–Brownsville case. But there were few lasting results. Despite criticisms of the entire public school system, a white school was generally defined by blacks as superior. In order to make attendance at white schools available to blacks, the desegregation strategy was pressed. The Supreme Court in the Brown case in 1954, less than a decade after the end of World War II, ruled that a separate school system was not an equal school system. Mandatory public school integration became the central agency to improve education. The decision has been debated continuously, but the vast literature on the educational, social, and political consequences unfortunately does not permit pointed conclusions. What *is* clear is that the changes achieved were limited.

The school integration strategy did not satisfy the aspirations of the black community—including activists, the middle and blue-collar strata, and the so-called "black underclass." My reading of available research leads to the conclusion that, for a small segment, mandatory busing was clearly beneficial; the students involved in busing were, of course, already among the effective performers. On the other hand, for some the experience was difficult and even counterproductive. For most students, the gains were at best marginal.[14] But busing became a political issue, which pro-

---

12. Paul Goodman, *Growing up Absurd* (New York: Random House, 1960).
13. John Caldwell Holt, *How Children Fail* (New York: Pitman, 1964); Ivan Illich, *Deschooling Society* (New York: Harper and Row, 1971); Herbert R. Kohl, *The Open Classroom: A Practical Guide to a New Way of Teaching* (New York: Random House, 1969); Jonathan Kozol, *Death at an Early Age: The Destruction of the Hearts and Minds of Negro Children in the Boston Public Schools* (Boston: Houghton Mifflin, 1967); George Leonard, with W. H. Van Hoose and Mildred Peters, *The Elementary School Counselor* (Detroit: Wayne State Press, 1967).
14. Derrick Bell, *Shades of Brown: New Perspectives on School Desegregation* (New

duced support and at times fierce support from its political leaders.

As Gerald Suttles concluded from his examination of the literature on school desegregation, not only the consequences of the education process are at stake but also those of redefining the status of black Americans.[15] Successful school integration, in effect, implied to black leaders the improved social position of blacks.

One should be alert, however, to unintended consequences of "social engineering." In my judgment, programs of school desegregation were expected not only to deal with educational defects but to contribute to the acculturation of blacks. They were considered potential tools of social integration. Over the long run, this will no doubt continue to be true. In the short run, however, the social-psychological impact of school integration increased communalism, mainly in the North, Midwest, and Far West. The school integration movement contributed to the rise of black communalism, complicating the task of citizen education. The reasons are complex and, of course, speculative. First, opposition to school busing was so persistent that it resulted in counterhostility and defensive group solidarity among young blacks and their parents. Although most programs to integrate schools were accomplished peacefully, there were sufficient cases of violence—incidents widely covered in the mass media—to have negative consequences for intergroup relations. Second, the distance between residence and school greatly increased travel time. The result was to limit the potential of extracurricular programs and to complicate the management of school-community relations. Third, school integration was designed to enhance student self-esteem. Enhanced self-esteem was assumed to be an asset in civic education and citizenship performance. Individuals with adequate or strong self-esteem are more likely to have personal resources to develop a balance of citizen rights and obligations.

In 1964, Bruno Bettelheim and I argued that the requirements of black education could not be met by the assumption that only by moving into a white school would black students obtain a good education.[16] To avoid a feeling of psychological inferiority, it was necessary to have, along with integrated schools, at least some black schools that offered effective education. In effect, we anticipated the Black Power movement, which,

York: Teachers College Press, Columbia University, 1980). See also Nancy St. John, "The Effect of School Desegregation on Children: A New Look at the Research Evidence," in *Race and Schooling in the City*, ed. Adam Yarmolinsky et al. (Cambridge: Harvard University Press, 1981).

15. Gerald Suttles, "School Desegregation: The Agenda for Ethnography," forthcoming.

16. Bruno Bettelheim and Morris Janowitz, *Social Change and Prejudice* (New York: The Free Press, 1964), pp. 93–95.

despite basic opposition to democratic civic education, recognized the near-racist posture of those who insisted on school integration as the central solution. Bettelheim and I pointed out that, for some youngsters, moving into a white school—although better in facilities, teachers, and educational content—would necessarily result in lower self-esteem. It would reinforce the notion that blacks are a deficient group for whom special arrangements must be made.[17]

While mandatory busing was implemented, the larger society and leading black educators were also pursuing the second strategy—to improve urban education facilities, mainly by increased resources and by reduction of classroom size. Again, it proved very difficult to produce discernible changes on a large scale. For example, the More Effective Schools Program of New York City involved twenty-one schools, for which costs per pupil were nearly doubled.[18] In the fall of 1967, an evaluation was issued. Ten of the schools had been in operation since 1964 and eleven others since 1965. The report concluded that the program had had no significant effect. Overall school climate, staff attitudes, and community relations had improved, but there was no marked improvement in academic achievement.

The War on Poverty became the main agency through which school improvement goals were pursued. There were impressive increases in operating funds from the federal government. In addition, innovative educational approaches were tested and special efforts made to link the school to the other local community agencies. Much was learned from experimental strategies. Effective procedures were identified—procedures which were not, of course, completely new but had been used selectively in the past. Heightened expectations were not satisfied. In particular, there was little emphasis on group identification and issues of citizenship. The federal organization supporting these experimental approaches was highly unstable. The rhetoric of the War on Poverty contained exaggerated slogans of self-determination, while many programs were poorly managed at the national level. In any case, it was impossible to achieve basic institutional change, especially to change rapidly, given the rigid but fragmented structure of the educational establishment, including the barriers raised by teacher trade unions.

17. For support of this perspective, see Nancy St. John, *School Desegregation: Outcomes for Children* (New York: Wiley Interscience, 1975). An alternative conclusion is presented by Edgar G. Epps, "The Impact of School Desegregation on Aspirations, Self-Concepts, and Other Aspects of Personality," *Law and Contemporary Problems* 39 (1975): 300–313.
18. David J. Fox, "Expansion of the More Effective Schools Program: Evaluation of New York City Title I Educational Projects, 1966–1967" (New York: The Center for Urban Education, 1967).

The limitations of school integration and of the War on Poverty temporarily strengthened the separatist reaction. It remains to be explained why separatism took so long to develop after World War II. For militants, "Black Power" became a central symbol. The new communalism was dramatized by a wave of rioting—an increasing trend from 1964 to 1967. After the summer of 1968 the number and intensity of riots dropped sharply. The mass media and selected black nationalist leaders, during this period, made frequent references to revolution, revolt, and insurrection. But the actual burning and looting did not demonstrate black power. Previous riots had been the result of white-initiated violence in the form of an invasion of the black community. However, the rioting of the 1960s took the form of explosions within black residential territories against symbols of "white government." One response of the larger society to the riots was to contain the violence and increase social welfare and economic programs mainly for blacks. Efforts were made to get federal funds for worthwhile projects and to increase the number of appointed and elected black officials. By 1968 the rioting was contained, having caused immense hardships for underclass blacks. Black Power advocates were able to benefit, over the short run, by gaining temporary access to limited amounts of resources. Such access was blocked in good part by the intervention of more moderate and realistic black leaders.

At the same time, as mentioned above, black communalism found a power base which affected educational settings, with important results for civic education. In high schools and colleges, black students organized themselves on an avowedly separatist basis, at times romantically separatist and, on occasion, armed. Third World symbolism was frequent. Frantz Fanon, with explicit emphasis on the "therapeutic" benefits of violence, was an intellectual fountainhead for the extremist.[19] However, the typical black student nationalist thought of the use of intimidation far more pragmatically.

No doubt, the movement had ample justification for dissatisfaction with the position of blacks in the educational establishment. In a democracy there is no need for a tyranny of the majority. Advocacy of a form of self-rule need not be feared, certainly not actively opposed by harassment. The striking aspect of the new communalism among young blacks was the threat and, at times, actual use of force to obtain resources for constructing black communal centers on college campuses and in high schools.

At the high school level, genuine converts were recruited; frequently black nationalists turned into another youth gang, with fancy political language and bits of uniforms. At the university, much effort was spent

19. Frantz Fanon, *The Wretched of the Earth* (New York: Grove Press, 1963).

by the administration in working out the details of segregated dormitories and the preparation of soul food.

It was at the colleges and universities that black communalism had its most extensive, disruptive impact, by means of black studies programs. As defined by sensitive black scholars, black studies would have been a legitimate and enriching aspect of higher education.[20] The purpose was to improve scholarship about Afro-American peoples in the academic tradition of regional and civilizational studies. Instead, black studies initially emerged as a student-led coercive campaign oriented toward black separatist politics. In essence, it became an experiment in black communalism on college campuses and in selected high schools in opposition to existing definitions of "citizenship."

The speed with which the movement spread and the extensive mass media coverage is striking. A minority of activist black students, prepared for militant roles by participation in demonstrations and sit-ins, now found themselves in a setting temporarily congenial to black separatism, or at least not strongly opposed by the bulk of the white faculty and students. The goal was to construct separatist black enclaves on campuses which, in effect, would serve as models for blacks in the larger society.

Polarization between blacks and whites emerged as the outlines of the new communalism developed. Blacks would teach blacks, as far as feasible, by means of a curriculum that blacks would create. Blacks would live on campus mainly with other blacks, for their citizenship commitments were to other blacks. During the height of the movement, collegiate black communalism even denied the legitimacy of "civil" citizenship. Some distinguished scholars, a handful at most, refused to participate. Most black faculty members cooperated to varying degrees. Some were in favor of the goals of the black studies movement; others thought of it as an appropriate bargaining device. Among students, leadership was dominated by militants, prepared to make short-term concessions as long as they thought that progress was being made toward their long-term goals. There was a complete absence of organized black student opposition. The majority of black students supported the program and agitations, most with vigor and enthusiasm, with a minority following more passively.

The social ecology of campus life helps explain the rapid spread of this student movement. The leaders were interested in creating an all encompassing community—a closed community. They were assisted by the fact that students went to class, conducted their political work, and slept and ate in the same delimited social space on campus or nearby. The residential

20. Jim Haskins, "Black Studies: Is a Valid Idea Being Invalidated?" in *Black Manifesto for Education*, ed., Jim Haskins (New York: William Morrow and Company, 1975), pp. 116–27.

college or university is ideal for a militant movement, at least over the short run, since students are separated from their parents throughout the full daily cycle. Reality testing in the "real" world is sharply reduced; students are a "captive" audience.

Militant black student leaders were not afraid to make use of intimidation and even coercion. Over the short run, black communalism on campuses disrupted orderly governance. For example, the demand that only blacks could teach black studies, and the preference for a black faculty for other subjects as well, horrified a segment of the white faculty. It created a cleavage in the ranks of the teaching profession which was slow to heal.

Wilson Record, a sociologist, has traced the destructive impact of the black studies movement on white professors who had been teaching sociological subjects related to race relations.[21] Almost all universities gave in to black studies demands in varying degree and in a fashion which very often violated established procedures. Whites interested in race relations were harassed and threatened; not infrequently they stopped teaching. In many instances black students exercised considerable influence in the selection of personnel and in shaping particular programs of black studies.

The rapid growth of the movement was matched by an equally rapid decline. Separatism did not articulate with enduring aspirations of most black students. Even limited reality testing in the "outer world" demonstrated that training in black studies and a separatism perspective hardly facilitated entrance to many careers that blacks were increasingly entering. Support of black studies declined; enrollment dropped. It became just another segment of the college curriculum. But militant student separatism was not without consequences.

Solidarity among black students was heightened and informal self-segregation endured. It is striking that there was no backlash in attitude or practice, either formally or informally. To the contrary, colleges and universities intensified recruitment of black students and other minorities and organized a variety of compensatory high school programs designed to assist blacks to enter higher education. The most powerful instrument of change was the federal government's program of affirmative action, resulting in increased black faculty—an underlying goal of the new black communalism. Black attendance in colleges and universities increased rapidly, converging, percentagewise, with that of whites.

The movement was, in effect, a different kind of civic education, not only for students, but for the larger community exposed to extensive media coverage. One can only speculate about the white population. Sympathetic

21. Wilson Record, "White Sociologists and Black Students in Predominantly White Universities," *Sociological Quarterly* 15 (Spring 1974): 164–282.

whites—those who shared belief in the importance of education for blacks—had reservations. Prejudiced whites had their biases confirmed. The long-term trends toward greater acceptance and acculturation of blacks was hardly broken. When a minor backlash did develop later in the 1970s, it was limited to opposition to mandatory busing, a feeling widely shared in the black community. Most black adults did not take the black studies movement very seriously. Those who did gained some temporary satisfaction that blacks were standing up for their rights. More typical was the belief that black students did not mean what they said but were bargaining, or that they "ought to hurry and get back to their school work if they wanted to make something out of going to college."

From the point of view of civic education, consequences were mixed. Clearly, the long history of slavery and the continued postslavery oppression, as well as the putative durability and high visibility of color, meant that blacks were unable to become acculturated as quickly as other minorities. Experiences which heightened group solidarity, without unduly emphasizing separatism, contributed, paradoxically, to effective acculturation. Groups with effective internal cohesion are readily able to achieve the transitional status of hyphenated Americans. The black community did not accept separatist goals. For the white community, this result was reassuring; built-in limitations against separatism among blacks meant that race tensions were manageable.

The new black communalism indirectly improved black college education by developing compensatory and remedial programs. Important segments of the black nationalist movement became transformed into regularized middle-class college attendance. William J. Wilson has underlined college achievement for individual socioeconomic progress.[22]

But, at the level of the underclass, the new communalism often became a rationalization for purposeless violence without a facade of educational aspiration. Efforts at education of the sons and daughters of the underclass by busing, increased expenditures for public education, and black communalism, have not produced decisive results. Moreover, the struggle over black separatism diverted attention from underlying issues of education for civic responsibility. The demands of blacks and the positive response of whites operated only to further emphasize rights at the expense of obligations. This is an issue of special relevance for black youth with college educations as they press for full citizenship, since, understandably, they often come from families with limited civic consciousness.

For the lower stratum, participation in military service may be a more important employment and civic education experience than public school-

22. William J. Wilson, *The Declining Significance of Race* (Chicago: University of Chicago Press, 1978).

ing. Although aliens are permitted to serve as enlisted personnel in the United States in the twentieth century, the arming of a minority group member is a powerful sign of acceptance and trust of that minority by the larger society. In turn, armed military service is viewed by the minority group member as an important aspect of citizenship. This is especially important for members of the black community, who look back on a history of enslavement.

During World Wars I and II, minority leaders pressed civilian and military authorities to establish units organized by members of ethnic groups. Among other reasons, they were searching for an opportunity to display loyalty and fitness for citizenship by visible military service. As mentioned previously, both military and civilian leaders generally viewed such proposals as contrary to the traditions and goals of an effectively integrated polity. It should be stressed that black leaders were supported by the rank-and-file black when they made parallel demands. During World War I, there were repeated requests that more blacks be organized into armed combat units. Given the structure of military forces, blacks served in segregated units, mainly under white officers. The prime goal was not integration but to demonstrate the loyalty of the black population.

During World War II, civil rights organizations protested the extensive practice of employing blacks mainly for menial labor. The military remained segregated, with considerable racial tension and strife. As the war progressed, the black community was even more vocal in demands for change and improvement of the position of black recruits. These civil rights organizations backed the agitation among some black soldiers for "the right to fight."[23] Black and white liberals spoke of the desirability of integration of military personnel; the result was some upgrading of blacks. Equality was defined as including equality of opportunity in the military. On 28 July 1948 President Truman issued an executive order abolishing racial segregation in the armed forces. It was during the Korean war that comprehensive integration was extensively, if imperfectly, implemented. By the middle of the 1950s, desegregation had been accomplished in the military.

Tracing the participation of blacks in the armed forces reveals the limits of separatism and black communalism in the United States. Before the American Revolution, blacks were barred from bearing arms. The French and Indian Wars, however, forced the colonial militia to permit enrollment of blacks, mainly in noncombat tasks. With the end of the French and Indian hostilities, most states, particularly South Carolina, with heavy concentrations of slaves, rescinded such regulations.

23. Charles Moskos, *The American Enlisted Man* (New York: Russell Sage Foundation, 1970), p. 110.

During the Revolution, the revolutionary forces at first prohibited black recruitment, no doubt from race prejudice and fear of insurrection. But even among the revolutionaries there were some who believed it "incongruous and morally wrong to expect slaves and free blacks, whose status was severely limited, to share in the defense of freedom."[24] Again, manpower shortages reversed the restriction, and more than five thousand blacks served. By the end of hostilities, most Continental regiments had an average of fifty blacks integrated with white troops.

But there was no consistency of policy or practice. In the War of 1812, blacks were excluded from the army by law, despite acute troop shortages. Some states permitted blacks to serve after 1814; 600 were in Jackson's forces at the Battle of New Orleans. Because of the ban in the army, many blacks joined the navy; it is estimated that between 10 and 20 percent of naval crews were black. Interestingly, one argument used in the Dred Scott decision by Chief Justice Taney was that blacks did not have citizenship because no state allowed them in their militia.[25]

The Civil War represented the first decisive change. Although there were some misgivings about black service in federal forces, rising casualties and abolitionists' arguments undercut this opposition. In the Union forces during the Civil War, 180,000 to 200,000 blacks served; this figure does not include civilians in support roles. By the end of the Civil War there were sixteen all-black regiments; blacks served as soldiers mainly in segregated units. The Confederates agreed to raise black slave units in the final years of the war, but very few slaves were mobilized.

The Civil War was a turning point because of the establishment of permanent black combat units. After the Civil War, periodic Indian wars and continued patrolling involved the use of black troops. Four black regiments were operated, with a total of 4,159 enlisted men; with few exceptions the officers were white

In the Spanish-American War, in addition to four black army regiments, some 8,000 to 10,000 blacks volunteered for military duty. One company of blacks saw combat, and two regular army regiments reached overseas destinations. Thus, by the turn of the century, blacks represented a small but visible niche in the military that included combat tasks and assignments in segregated units. But there were numerous cases of racial friction and pressure from whites to limit the use of black troops.

In World War I, black mobilization was greatly expanded. Although most were assigned to manual labor and support duty, noteworthy numbers were organized into large-scale combat units. Despite the inferior

24. Jack D. Foner, *Blacks and the Military in American History: A New Perspective* (New York: Praeger Publishers, 1974), pp. 7–8.
25. Ibid., pp. 25–26.

position of blacks, the sheer numbers involved constituted a second turning point in the full incorporation of blacks into the armed forces. Prior to World War I, of 750,000 regular army and national guard personnel, about 20,000 were black. A total of 380,000 blacks were mobilized, reflecting massive recruitment. It is important to note that there was little, if any, opposition in the black community to the draft and military service. And as noted above, there was pressure to assign more blacks to combat units in order to demonstrate their commitment to the nation. A total of 42,000 were assigned to combat units. Equally significant as a sign of the massive national effort, 200,000 blacks were sent to France in World War I.[26]

This expansion was in a segregated military. The marine corps accepted no blacks; the navy used them only as messmen, and blacks amounted to only 1 percent of naval personnel. What was striking was the sheer increase in numbers of blacks. Performance in combat was allegedly mixed. One regiment of the all-Negro 92d Infantry Division was criticized for leaving the field of battle at Meuse-Argonne. On the other hand, Moskos reports that black units operating under French command, in a more tolerant situation, performed well.[27]

Between World Wars I and II, black participation decreased, and the armed forces remained segregated. The army adopted a quota system to limit blacks to their percentage in the total population, but during this period the quota was never filled. When the United States entered World War II, blacks constituted 5.9 percent of the army; there were only five black officers.

Trends begun during World War I continued during World War II. By the end of the war, more than one million blacks had been inducted. The concentration of black soldiers did not exceed 10 percent, and they remained in segregated units. More precisely, three quarters were in the quartermaster, engineer, and transportation corps. But there were genuine efforts to respond to civilian pressure to upgrade their position. These included highly successful literacy training, assignment to technical training installations, and increased utilization in combat units—not only in ground forces but in other branches, especially the air force, where blacks were admitted to pilot training and air combat.

Combat records of black troops in World War II have been subject to much argument. There was much racial tension and public concern about minority groups. Dramatically, in the closing hours of World War II, military events forced an experiment in racial integration of combat units. Dangerous shortages of combat personnel developed in Western Europe as a result of the Ardennes offensive in the winter of 1944–45. Black

26. Ibid., p. 121.
27. Moskos, *The American Enlisted Man*, p. 109.

volunteers were recruited from the ranks. The procedure was to assign a platoon of blacks to serve in a white company. The result of that pattern of integration was highly successful and led to further steps toward integration. It is essential to keep in mind that, after World War II, the black experience in the military was more and more an integrated one.

Despite the hardships of battle, military participation in World War II meant that a million blacks had meaningful experiences outside of the ghetto—just as white soldiers were exposed to totally new experiences. Most soldiers—white and black—accepted the "patriotic" need to defend the nation and press on with destruction of the enemy. Participation by the rank-and-file whites increased popular demand for social equity and strengthened political participation leading to expansion of the welfare state. For blacks, the consequences of military service were similar, if to a lesser degree.[28] The rhetoric and reality of World War II politicized a tiny but important segment and broadened perspectives and aspirations of most. The preconditions for a more effective civil rights movement were created.

It is, therefore, striking that two military study boards after World War II, in 1945 and in 1950, recommended maintenance of segregation and the quota system. These reports emphasized the low mental test scores of many black recruits and the complexities of supervision and discipline. Drastic social change is generally initiated from the outside; this was the case with racial integration in the military. President Harry S. Truman's desegregation order of 1948 set the stage for integration of the armed forces, although it was manpower needs in the Korean war that produced strongest pressure for integration of blacks, including combat units.[29] Blacks who entered previously all-white units performed well in combat. Observers pointed out that the fighting abilities of blacks differed little from those of whites. Procedures and patterns developed for integration in Korea spread rapidly through the armed forces; three years after the Korean conflict, segregation in the continental United States and at overseas stations was eliminated.

In all, more than 5,700,000 persons served in the Korean war, of whom at least one half million were black. Although a limited war with unclear objectives, it was accepted by most citizens as a legitimate, if unpopular, enterprise. Service in the Korean campaign produced no special or widespread resentments beyond the expected miseries and human costs of

28. Richard Titmuss, "War and Social Policy," in *Essays on the Welfare State* (London: Allen and Unwin, 1958).
29. Leo Bogart, ed., *Social Research and the Desegregation of the U.S. Army*, with introduction by Leo Bogart (Chicago: Markham Publishing Company, 1969).

modern war. This meant that the human cost, not the economic cost, was borne by a small group of young men and their families.

Fighting was still thought of as a civic duty. For the black community, it represented a major "breakthrough" in the movement to full citizenship. Blacks fought as equals with whites. This was effective civic education. Although the reasons for military participation in general, and in this war in particular, are varied and often ill defined, or no more than a mechanical response to a draft board decision, the bulk of participants felt, and manifested, a sense of obligation. As noted, only 27.1 percent of those who served in Korea were draftees; most were volunteers. The meaning of "volunteer" is difficult to isolate since many enlistees were just one jump ahead of the draft board. In effect, the Korean war was viewed as legitimate enough so that participation was an affirmation of one's citizen obligation, not mercenary behavior. In short, blacks were conspicuous in the Korean conflict, gained military honors, and rose in rank; so the conflict assisted integration of those blacks involved.

It was the Vietnam experience that completed the erosion of the idea of military service as a form of civic obligation and civic education. But the negative consequences of Vietnam on the sense of citizenship among blacks should not be exaggerated. It was a war in which blacks figured conspicuously and were overrepresented in the crucial category of ground combat soldiers killed in action. Blacks were active in the leadership of anti–Vietnam war movements within military ranks, and there was much disgruntlement among black enlisted personnel. It should be remembered that only a minority of those who served in Vietnam were draftees (19.9 percent); the number who volunteered because they were draft-motivated is difficult to estimate. In any case, sacrifice breeds loyalty as well as resentment and hostility.

In the years 1964–73, the period of the Vietnam engagement, more than 8.8 million persons served (about one-half as many as in the masssive mobilization in World War II). The number of blacks sent to South Vietnam is not reported in detail. The question of inequalities in casualties, previously discussed, remains debatable, but the black community believes in general that blacks suffered disproportionate casualties.[30]

Full assessment of the consequences of Vietnam on political perspectives, especially for blacks, has not been helped by the bitter public debate. In chapter 3, research findings on the limited impact for the military as a whole were presented. The same pattern holds true for blacks.[31] In fact,

30. Gilbert Badillo and G. David Curry, "The Social Incidence of Vietnam Casualties: Social Class or Race?" *Armed Forces and Society* 2 (Spring 1976): 397–406; Moskos, *The American Enlisted Man*, p. 216.
31. M. Kent Jennings and Gregory B. Markus, "The Effect of Military Service," pp. 131–48.

the Vietnam experience was a relatively broadening experience for the bulk of those who served. For those who had longer-than-usual Vietnam tours, especially combat tours, negativism and disruption was discernible. I would agree with Charles Moskos, who concluded that, for the rank-and-file soldier, antiwar and anti-army protests mainly served to reinforce progovernment and patriotic attitudes. In other words, "The combat soldier is an anti-peace demonstrator rather than pro-war."[32]

Because the war divided the nation, the returning military were accorded little honor. Programs of transition and assistance were initially limited; increased benefits came later. The result was that blacks did not receive their "just" reward.

The weakness of education for underclass blacks has been only partially compensated by military experience. Realistically, serving in the all-volunteer force is no guarantee of a successful personal experience. To the contrary, in the early 1980s, one-third of all recruits failed to complete their first tour of duty; only two-thirds completed the three-year term of enlistment. Those who failed to complete the first term were heavily from minority groups. But without military experience young men and women with limited education would have fared even worse, and black nationalism would have become more strongly entrenched. (Veterans both black and white, as we saw in chapter 3, earn more as civilians than their nonveteran counterparts.) This is not to suggest that military service should be used as a social corrective.

SPANISH SPEAKERS: THE CHOSEN PEOPLE

One would expect Spanish-speaking immigrants to encounter fewer barriers than do blacks in becoming integrated into the social structure. A variety of factors are at work: length of residence, different "racial" characteristics, family structure, education level, and group norms and values. Moreover, the history of slavery and continued repression and prejudice linked to skin color would appear to be powerful determinants in the slower pattern of acculturation for blacks than for the Chicano population. However, close examination reveals strong resistance to acculturation among Spanish-speaking residents. The strength of communalism—drawing on a long historical tradition among Latinos in the United States—in fact exceeds that found in the black segment. Discrimination against the Spanish-speaking in the United States is a central factor in the sense of communalism one observes. But it is essential to examine internal factors as well.

32. Moskos, *The American Enlisted Man*, p. 164.

Obviously, Spanish speakers are not a single sociocultural group. In this analysis I will focus on immigrants from Mexico, who are the most numerous of the Spanish speakers. There are also various dimensions to acculturation, no simple continuum, so that comprehensive assessments are not easily made. But the Mexicans are unique as an immigrant group in the persistent strength of their communal bonds. This contemporary communalism is likely to endure for decades and to modify the pattern of ethnic relations in the United States. Strong communalism is not universal among Mexican-Americans; some have become acculturated, and acculturation of all continues to a degree. To speak of the special character of the Mexican immigrants is not to deny the profound changes that have taken place and are likely to continue. It is, rather, to seek clarification of the idea of the melting pot and its limitations, as it applies to Mexican-Americans.

Mexicans, together with other Spanish-speaking populations, are creating a bifurcation in the social-political structure of the United States that approximates nationality divisions. In the 1960s and 1970s, communalism led to outbursts of militant Mexican-American political action, such as the Brown Berets and the Raza Unida party. They were relatively short-lived. Of greater importance is the day-to-day resistance of Mexican-Americans to acculturation to United States society. Latinos are the most pronounced exception to the absorptive capacity of the American social structure; they are likely to modify American society as much as they adapt to it.

It remained for an "Anglo" professor of cultural anthropology to claim, in exaggerated language, the superiority of Mexicans with their rugged communalism. Professor Jack D. Forbes's formulation of his research conclusions should not detract from recognition of the validity of the underlying theme. He declares in a handbook for teachers:

> In summary, the Mexican heritage of the United States is very great indeed. For at least six thousand years Mexico has been a center for the dissemination of cultural influences in all directions, and this process continues today. Although the modern United States has outstripped Mexico in technological innovation, the Mexican people's marked ability in the visual arts, music, architecture, and political affairs makes them constant contributors to the heritage of all of North America. The Mexican American people of the United States serve as a bridge for the diffusion northward of valuable Mexican traits, serve as a reservoir for the preservation of the ancient Hispano-Mexican heritage

of the Southwest, and participate directly in the daily
life of the modern culture of the United States.[33]

Of particular relevance in the assessment of the "citizenship" of Mexican-Americans is Forbes's reference to the Mexican's ability in political
affairs. One is not detracting from Mexican political accomplishments to
point out that the political process in Mexico has not produced a viable
democratic system. Forbes is no doubt speaking of the tenacity of Mexican
political leaders in the face of monumental social and economic problems.

In focusing on Mexican immigration to the United States and the resulting communalism, at least four elements are involved: (a) size and
pattern of immigration; (b) emergence of massive illegal immigration, which
deprives one of citizenship or resident alien status; (c) perspective of the
immigrant as "colonizer" rather than settler, thereby building powerful
resistances to acculturation; and (d) goals and accomplishments of Latino
political leaders in the United States. To explore the level of political
participation of Mexican-Americans is not enough; the goals of Mexican-
American politics must be examined.

The overwhelming majority of immigrants to the United States, certainly until 1945, came as settlers, not colonizers. By settlers I do not
limit myself to those who settled on the land but include all who came
with the intention of starting a new life in a new environment. They were,
in effect, departing from their homelands for economic, political, or religious reasons. Expectations were of a permanent and lasting break. By
contrast, the colonizer is not departing from his homeland. He is, in fact,
transplanting a segment of his society to a new and expanded locale. In
some cases he is returning to an area which was dominated or under the
control of his homeland at some time in the past. This is particularly the
case for selected Chicanos who reside in Texas and the Southwest. Their
land was won by the United States in battle, and they look forward to
its return to Mexican-type rule. Such a Chicano does not see himself as
breaking with the homeland but looks forward to close linkage with it, or
even return.

Colonization is helped by contiguity or closeness of one's homeland.
The German and Russian eastward colonization represents such patterns.
Distance weakens colonial ties. The United States had its settlers who
failed and returned home, but they cannot be thought of as colonizers,
rather, as failed settlers. It also had its immigrants who came to a political
haven with the aspirations to return to a free homeland; they often became

33. From Jack D. Forbes, *Mexican Americans: A Handbook for Educators* (Berkeley:
Far West Laboratory, 1967), as reprinted in Henry Sioux Johnson and William J.
Hernandez-M., *Educating the Mexican American* (Valley Forge: Judson Press, 1970),
p. 53.

settlers. Most immigrants were successful—in varying degree—as settlers. Settlers tend to acculturate; colonizers resist acculturation.[34]

Mexican immigration into the United States is, of course, fashioned by the long physical border between the two countries and by fluctuation in the demand for unskilled, cheap labor. Since the period after the Civil War, when this immigration started, Mexicans have not generally entered the United States as settlers. To the contrary, patterns of immigration have worked against settlement, which might have led to effective acculturation. Economic demand for labor produced three waves of legal immigration, and a long-term increase in illegal immigration. The resulting configuration is closer to colonization than to settlement. Education, especially civic education relevant for acculturation, has been difficult for migratory workers, who rarely attend school.

The first large wave started at the turn of the century, when Mexicans were engaged in railroad construction as well as agriculture and mining. These types of labor isolated them from the mainstream of American life. This wave persisted for three decades until the Great Depression resulted in massive reverse movement of Mexicans, much of it involuntary, back to their homeland and a temporary withdrawal of their involvement in the U.S. labor market. A second wave was generated by the World War II expansion of the economy. As in the Great Depression, the end of wartime economy resulted in repeated expulsion of large numbers of Mexicans. The third wave, starting in the 1960s, has continued to the 1980s. It has the potential to continue at least until Mexicans outnumber blacks. The sheer size of this ethnic group contributes to its ability to resist acculturation. The third wave represents not only continuing poverty in Mexico and the absence of family planning, but a move toward short-term political accommodation between the United States and Mexico, in which immigration opportunities are exchanged for a first call on Mexican energy production. Thus, Mexican immigration has been characterized by two-way movement, which interrupted permanent settlement. Nevertheless, legal immigration and a very high birthrate have resulted, by 1980, in an estimated five million Mexican-Americans, constituting one of the largest ethnic groups in the United States. To this one must add the illegal population, whose number cannot be ascertained. Estimates range from four to twelve million. It has been estimated that the Spanish-speaking population, mainly Mexican, will reach 20 percent by the end

34. One can speak of a third type of immigrant to the United States—that is, persons who hope to earn money and to return home. They could be called sojourners. No doubt there are such immigrants among the Mexicans. But the sojourners are closer to the colonizers rather than to the settlers in outlook. At present, the central question is how many Mexicans who appear to be sojourners will put down roots and become settlers.

of the century. Given the likelihood of continued massive illegal migration, this ethnic group differs markedly from other immigrant groups. Leo Grebler, Joan W. Moore, and Ralph Guzman succinctly introduce their massive overview, *The Mexican-American People*, with the following statement:

> As a group, Mexican-Americans in the Southwest are highly differentiated from the dominant society on nearly every yardstick of social and economic position. A profile of their main demographic characteristics, such as age, family size, fertility, and the incidence of broken families reveals variations from Anglo norms. Their educational attainment shows an especially notable gap. Associated with this gap is an unfavorable occupational structure and a low average income. Their housing conditions reflect not only poor earnings, but the pressures resulting from extremely large families.[35]

In 1976, Joan Moore and Harry Pachon assessed the educational resources and attainment of the Mexican-Americans in stark terms, despite the discernible amount of progress which had been made. "Mexican educational accomplishment offers only little hope for those who suggest that southwestern schools will soon be able to end the Mexican-American labor market handicap."[36] But the statistical profile of immigrant groups is replete with unanticipated findings, especially if one focuses on economic income as a measure of the extent to which an ethnic group "has made it" and is being acculturated. The family income of Mexican-Americans, for example, is higher than that of blacks (18 percent higher in 1979, according to one source). Official statistics for 1980 indicate that the mean income for blacks was $15,806 (median, $12,674). For "Spanish origin families" (which include Puerto Ricans, who have a lower income than Mexican-Americans) the mean income was $17,615 (median, $14,716).[37] Moreover, despite higher income among Mexican-Americans, communalism, including political separatism, is more pronounced among Mexicans than among blacks.

35. Leo Grebler, Joan W. Moore, and Ralph C. Guzman, *The Mexican-American People: The Nation's Second Largest Minority* (New York: The Free Press, 1970), p. 13.
36. Joan W. Moore with Harry Pachon, *Mexican-Americans* (Englewood Cliffs, N.J.: Prentice-Hall, 1976), p. 66.
37. U.S. Bureau of the Census, "Money Income and Poverty Status of Families and Persons in the United States: 1980," *Current Population Reports*, series P-60, no. 127 (Washington, D.C.: U.S. Government Printing Office, August 1981), p. 13.

As a result, Mexican-Americans are more concerned with their rights than their obligations. No doubt, the patterns of immigration and return to Mexico in the past worked against acculturation. In addition, cultural patterns and specific political achievements have in fact produced something of a colonization outlook. Mexican immigration—both legal and illegal—is supported by the Mexican government and by the U.S. government in the enactment of national and local legislation for bilingual education and bilingualism.

Since the Mexican Revolution, the Mexican government has in effect stimulated, or at least tolerated as justified, the migration of Mexicans into the southwestern section of the United States. The Mexican migration is seen as a return to lands which traditionally belonged to the Mexican people. The colonizing definition of the immigration to these geographical areas has spilled over to Mexican enclaves throughout the United States. This sociopolitical perspective has been compatible with policies of repatriation, which, however, have declined in scope. In the meantime, more and more Mexicans leave their homeland.

The pull of Mexican values and traditions slows absorption into American life patterns. Mexican familism is a powerful factor in resisting acculturation. The Mexican family which comes to reside permanently in the United States seeks the American standard of living but not at the cost of Mexican life styles and values.

The value patterns of Mexicans and, in turn, of Mexican-Americans are complex.[38] Since Mexican-Americans display a strong sense of communalism, it would be in error to assert that we are dealing with a "cultural lag" that can be expected to attenuate. Increased education and income will not dissolve Mexican communalism, although it has already refashioned and weakened it in specific segments of the Mexican-American population. Communalism among Mexican-Americans is not likely soon to atrophy. It is linked to political initiative and trends, both in Mexico and in the United States, which very often reinforce elements of separatism. Ruth Horowitz, a student of Chicano culture in the United States, emphasizes that economic progress among Mexican-Americans generally strengthens Mexican-American communalism.[39]

Mexican-Americans as colonizers have strong self-esteem rooted in family patterns and supported by nationalistic and communal political institutions. These immigrants think of themselves as special. Their communalism is a vital adaptation of a large-scale ethnic grouping which demonstrates the combined persistence of traditional values and a struggle

38. See Ruth Horowitz, *Honor and the American Dream: Culture and Identity in a Chicano Community* (New Brunswick: Rutgers University Press, forthcoming).
39. Ibid., *passim.*

133

to adjust to contemporary economic realities. Mexican-American self-esteem is not related to one's socioeconomic status in the minority group but is spread throughout the social hierarchy. However, the strong sense of group identity has not prevented considerable criminality and deviance among the young. These forms of social pathology do not lead to a rejection of Mexican identity and do not inhibit parental support and toleration for their "wayward youth."

Mexican-American couples have traditionally produced large families. In the past, comparable birthrates were found among Polish-American and Italian-American families. But, by 1969, fertility rates for most ethnic groups were drastically reduced. Mexican-Americans emerged as easily the most fertile, with 4.4 children per woman between thirty-five and forty-five years of age. Most Mexicans marry within their group although there is a trend toward intermarriage in the large metropolitan centers, especially Los Angeles. In 1910, the rate of intragroup marriage was assessed at 90 percent; it now stands at 75 percent.

Much has been made of fragmentation in the Mexican-American community resulting from differences in length of residence in the United States, levels of education, and income. Such fragmentation has not, however, prevented the emergence or persistence of communalism; and I believe there is less fragmentation than there was. In any case, Mexican-American communalism rests on a strong sense of family and attendant self-esteem.

Unlike immigrant families of Orientals and East European Jews, Mexican-Americans have not been preoccupied with educational achievement, although progress in education has been made.[40] As of 1960, it was reported that only 13 percent of Hispanics in the Southwest completed high school, compared to 17 percent of blacks, 28 percent of whites, and 37 percent of Japanese-Americans. With the emergence of a new (or third) generation of Mexican-Americans, these figures have grown, although the educational level of young Mexican-Americans remains the lowest.

Education levels, of course, are intimately related to levels of income. About 24 percent of all Spanish-surname families counted by the 1970 census fell below the "poverty line" as defined by the federal government. In 1960, that figure had been about 35 percent.[41]

Some social scientists concerned with comparative analysis of ethnic relations in the United States have, in recent times, strongly opposed a cultural pespective. Cultural explanations smack of prejudice and bias. Instead, these scholars have emphasized ecological factors, population flow,

40. Thomas Sowell, *Ethnic America: A History* (New York: Basic Books, 1981), p. 266.
41. See Moore, *Mexican-Americans*, p. 63, for a discussion of family income.

education resources, and opportunity structures.[42] Such a perspective supplies a useful corrective to an overstated cultural determinism, but runs the risk of oversimplification. Cultural modalities cannot be overlooked. Trends in ethnic income and education are crucial for an examination of communalism, civic education, and civic obligation. Thus, it is my view that the lower educational level combined with higher income and a strong sense of communalism of Mexican-American families, compared with black families, requires some attention to cultural factors. The cultural factors in this comparison center on attitudes toward work and involvement in commercial entrepreneurism. These cultural factors, of course, change over time.[43]

The rate of Mexican naturalization has been low. In the past, political interest and participation, including voting, has been low, though political participation has increased since the 1960s.[44] The mobilization of Mexican-Americans to elect Hispanic representatives has been relatively less effective than the ability of blacks to elect political officials. But sheer trends in participation do not reveal basic patterns or interests. The one issue which has produced increased political interest and involvement relates to Mexican communalism. There is limited but impressive systematic survey data on the acculturation of various generations of Chicano children into the United States political system. Generational experience structures the political attitudes of these children.[45] According to James W. Lamare, this is the case even with controls for socioeconomic status, language, environment, and education. He found that there is a linear progression of political integration from the newcomers through the second generation. However, third-generation Chicanos recede in their political acculturation, according to his data.

Of central importance is the ability of Spanish-speaking groups to develop national and local legislation in support of bilingual education and bilingualism generally. The achievement is clearly unique. The standard pattern among other immigrants to the United States has been to stress

42. See, especially, Lieberson, *A Piece of the Pie.*
43. I am not impressed with the claim that cultural arguments are circular since they have no independent measure of cultural content.
44. One study, based on interviews conducted between late October 1967 and mid-March 1968, presented data which indicated little difference between Mexican-Americans and other segments of the electorate. But the author points out that these findings should be considered "suggestive," because of the problems of comparability of the data "on Mexican-Americans and other Americans." Marilyn H. Buehler, "Voter Turnout and Political Efficacy among Mexican-Americans in Michigan," *Sociological Quarterly* 18 (Autumn 1977): 504–17.
45. James W. Lamare, "The Political Integration of Mexican-American Children: A Generational Analysis," *International Migration Review* 16 (Spring 1982): 169–88.

the importance of learning English, especially at primary school level. Language was considered basic to acculturation. The format of hyphenated Americanization meant that English was the "first" language of the public school system. The mastery of English was central for economic advancement and for sociopolitical commonality in a democratic polity based on citizenship. As a result, foreign language instruction was an optional element of public instruction, designed to serve the desire for cultural continuity and a measure of group identity. Foreign languages were "second" languages. Instruction was often in the high school, on the assumption that students had achieved the rudiments of English. It was often offered after school hours by representatives from the ethnic group residing in the locality. Attendance was voluntary, and the declining relevance of such instruction meant a decline in engaged students.

Bilingualism reversed these priorities. Spanish, widely used in Mexican homes, became the basic language—the first language—or rather, that was the political goal. In turn, English was the second language. In effect, bilingualism, introduced in the 1960s and expanded during the 1970s, represented the epitome of communalism. It was a national program to be implemented for any ethnic and racial group and included "black" English. These national programs involving educational programs and foreign language contents in the specialized mass media had varying degrees of success. In the Hispanic case, the movement encountered considerable community support, especially among Mexicans. A few advocates of Spanish bilingualism saw the program as a short-exposure enterprise to assist new cohorts of immigrant youngsters to make the transition from Spanish to English. But, in general, the goal of bilingualism programs was to keep alive the use of Spanish. These efforts are at variance with the political goals of hyphenated acculturation. Their long-term effectiveness is not to be measured only in terms of foreign language, since a sense of separatism can also be transmitted via the English language. The crucial measure is the dissemination of the cultural content of communalism, with its sense of group pride and colonizing spirit. In fact, since Latinos do not speak Castilian Spanish but various dialects, administrative problems of launching instructional programs were conspicuous, but the effort was extensive. There was considerable dissatisfaction and tension when Anglos or Spaniards taught Spanish. Bilingualism, it is essential to keep in mind, is not only a language program, but a cultural one as well.

The thrust of bilingualism was not limited to public school education, but involved communications with agencies of government and the election system. An extensive group of civil servants and teachers were appointed to implement these programs, which have been supported by generous federal grants. Budgetary restraints resulting from the prolonged recession have begun to cause cutbacks, and future funding will be increasingly state and local. Bilingualism programs generate an educational milieu and a network of public employees and subsidized voluntary association leaders with a vested interest in the use of Spanish. It should be stressed that commercial television and radio broadcasting in Spanish, as well as Spanish-language newspapers, are powerful adjuncts to these efforts. The media are clearly agents of bilingualism and represent traditions more effective than the foreign language newspapers of previous generations. In short, not only does Mexican communalism work to retard acculturation, but extensive and widespread efforts of the bilingualism movement are an active ingredient in strengthening nationalistic separatism. Bilingualism emerges as an aspect of the demand for "rights," including the rights of resident aliens, and even illegal immigrants. Spanish-speaking persons have come to believe that their rights of access to welfare and social programs require that they be able to approach these agencies in Spanish. Unless they can use Spanish, they believe they are unable to obtain their rights and benefits. This includes dealing with public utilities, reading traffic signs, and taking a driver's test. One counterelement to the development of Mexican communalism is military service, especially during periods of actual hostility. In World War II, Mexican-Americans served in the armed forces of the United States in noteworthy numbers for the first time and with distinction. However, in contrast to black participation, there is only limited research on the consequences of military service on the Hispanic minority. Available research reports that military service increased the civilian earnings of those Mexicans who spent time in the armed forces.[46]

Thus, the presence of Mexico at the border of the United States, plus the strength of Mexican cultural patterns, means that the "natural history" of Mexican immigrants has been and will be at variance with that of other immigrant groups. For sections of the Southwest, it is not premature to speak of a cultural and social irredenta—sectors of the United States which have in effect become Mexicanized and therefore, under political dispute.

Mexican-Americans, of course, as well as those Mexicans who remain in the homeland, will be increasingly subject to urbanization and industrialization. Social and political change is far more certain than convergence with American political patterns. Social scientists have learned to speak about the third world without the notion of a uniform process of "mod-

46. Harley L. Browning, Sally C. Lopreato, and Dudley L. Poston, Jr., "Income and Veteran Status: Variations among Mexican-Americans, Blacks and Anglos," *American Sociological Review* 38 (February 1973): 74–85; Dudley L. Poston, "The Influence of Military Service on the Civilian Earning Patterns of Blacks, Mexican Americans and Anglos," *Journal of Political and Military Sociology* 7 (Spring 1979): 71–88.

ernization." Mexico is a third world nation which is hardly destined to develop in a European-American format of "modernization." Mexico is undergoing widespread political turmoil. Few experts are prepared to anticipate the outcome of the agitations and political demonstrations, but they will no doubt influence the pattern of immigration to the United States in the years ahead. The important conclusion of comparative analysis is that the institutions of urbanization and industrialism can be accompanied by powerful elements of traditionalism. Perhaps the term *neotradition* is more appropriate. The homeland of Mexico has five to six thousand years of history, which have produced traditions and neotraditions of long enduring consequence. Social scientists have generally underemphasized the strength of these traditions. It would be in error to call these traditions peasant, although there are peasant value patterns which figure in the cultural configuration which endured through a revolution of "national liberation." The pride that one encounters in the Mexican enclaves in the United States is in part a reflection of the sheer endurance and continuity of Mexican society. It is a mixture of peasant culture, Catholic residues, absorption of a variety of invaders, plus the aftereffects of national revolution. They supply the format for elements of continuity during a period of change generated by industrialization and urbanization.

Mexican-Americans are not likely to be profoundly influenced by an American type of civic education. The effective content of citizenship among these people will be influenced by the communalism of Mexico. If effective citizenship involves a set of internalized civic obligations, neotraditional values of Mexican-Americans stand as powerful barriers.

The Delicate Balance of Toleration

The issues of acculturation versus communalism obviously extend beyond blacks and Spanish-speaking minorities. They can be raised about all nationality immigrant groups, especially those which give little indication of a discernible reduction. In the light of persistent unemployment and serious social problems in segments of the "new" immigrant population, it is understandable that public interest in immigration has increased markedly since 1970. By new immigrants I mean all those who have arrived since 1945, many of whom came since the 1965 amendments greatly broadened the basis of immigration.

Three trends warrant discussion. First, increased public interest failed to generate significant consensus about appropriate national immigration policy or to highlight changes considered necessary. Second, in view of American history, one would expect much stronger popular opposition to continued high levels of immigration. That such opposition remained contained is not an assessment of potential trends in the future, although major changes in the 1980s appear unlikely. Third, and most striking, has been the almost complete lack of concern among political and community leaders about forms of civic education for new immigrants and their offspring. In fact, the realities of partisan politics have instead led to strong emphasis on bilingualism and related ethnic institution building. Policies and practices, especially under the Carter administration, were designed to strengthen communalism. The traditional formula of the hyphenated American was at least temporarily modified in the direction of emphasizing stronger primordial attachments.

The United States presents a pattern at variance with that of most Western democratic multiparty countries. These nations have political regimes, including socialist ones, which regulate immigration on the basis of economic goals and trends. Most, including those with effective traditions of social democracy, have imposed restrictions on immigration when confronted with rising levels of domestic unemployment. One approach is simply to impose limitations or stop immigration when unemployment reaches a given level. Such an approach has not been used by the United States. Instead, in the post–World War II period, the United States reinstituted an expanded version of its long-standing comparatively open policy. The enlarged opportunities for immigration into the United States because of the 1965 amendments increased internal fragmentation of the two major political parties; this has led to legislative inertia on these issues. While there is no one-to-one relationship with party politics, liberal elements in the Democratic party stress the open society perspective and seek to maintain existing levels of immigration. In this view, immigration is of limited importance over the long run in population growth, and a positive asset in economic development. A form of comprehensive amnesty for existing illegal aliens is envisaged, with United States policy driven by humane considerations of family reunification and by the political consequences of foreign policy. It is proposed that nonfamily immigration be dealt with by ad hoc standards of availability of employment. Control of illegal immigrants and repatriation efforts are given little support.

On the other hand, the conservative approach—both Republican and Democratic—is to limit immigration. However, since various and important economic enterprises press for cheap labor, conservative political leaders must deal flexibly with immigration policy. Immigration is seen in economic terms, including the socioeconomic costs of welfare and health service needed by low-income and low-skill workers and their families. The conservative approach, despite the cross pressures to which it must accommodate, includes strong concern with the control of illegal immigration through more effective enforcement of existing law and by making employers responsible for hiring only legal immigrants.

A wide variety of minority group leaders are pressing to increase immigration. In the American scene, individual families make effective lobbyists. Yet the national heritage has extensive nativist elements; this segment has increased political strength because of the decline in size in the older foreign-born population. Moreover, leaders of minority groups who suffer from open immigration, particularly blacks, have failed to confront the dilemmas of United States immigration policy at the national level.

One can note a parallelism between the postures of conservative and liberal political leaders. Conservative leaders who oppose immigration must confront employers who want cheap labor. Liberals who want open immigration and some form of amnesty must confront labor leaders who do not want the economic competition from the continued flow of immigrants. A stalemate results.

The United States, in absolute terms, accepts more immigrants than does any other nation. In relative terms, only Australia, Canada, and New Zealand have higher annual percentages of immigrants, and there are signs that immigration is declining in these Commonwealth nations as a result of explicit government policy. Since 1976, both Canada and Australia have enacted immigration statutes tied to their national goals of population growth and economic development. According to federal officials, "in contrast, the U.S. immigration policy is based on traditional humane considerations and the principle of family reunification rather than on any recognized economic or demographic need."[47] Such a characterization neglects the pressure for "cheap" labor and demands of minority leaders for admission of more of their kin in exchange for electoral support.

Immigration into the United States after the 1965 Immigration Amendments (1967–76) averaged, officially, 358,000 annually; that is, about 100,000 higher than the decade before. Geographical origins of immigrants changed drastically. Fewer were from Europe. Immigrants from Southern and Eastern Europe replaced those previously coming from Northern and Western Europe; many more come from Asia. The Interagency Task Force, in March 1979, described the sources of immigration as follows: "Asians, Latin-Americans and Southern and Eastern Europeans predominate in the present legal immigrant flow to the United States. Mexico, the Philippines, South Korea, Taiwan, Cuba, India, the Dominican Republic, Jamaica, Italy, Greece, and Portugal have been the major sources of legal immigrants since 1965. Northern and Western Europeans, who

47. Interagency Task Force on Immigration Policy, *Staff Report*, Departments of Justice, Labor, and State, March 1979, p. 27.

enjoyed a large plurality until 1965, have become only a small fraction of the flow since then."[48]

Official statistics indicate that immigrants contribute substantially to U.S. population growth. In 1965, the total U.S. population was 193,223,000; by 1979, the figure had risen to 219,699,000. For this period, the lowest annual increase was 1,494,000 (1973) and the highest was 2,315,000 (1965). Over 20 percent of that increase was due to immigration, with only slight fluctuation.[49] However, the figures of the federal government do not take into consideration illegal immigration. Estimates indicate that if illegal immigration were included, the percentage of annual population growth by immigration would rise to 30.

While there are a number of thoughtful studies, there is no adequate body of research either on the overall adjustment of new immigrants, or on the different experiences of immigrants from particular regions. This lack of data is striking, given the rich tradition of sociological investigation of immigration stimulated in the past by intellectual and policy concerns of Jane Addams and the "Chicago school of sociology." Under Public Law 95-412, a Select Commission on Immigration and Refugee Policy was established to study existing law and procedures dealing with immigrants and refugees, and to make administrative and legislative recommendations to the president and Congress. The report, *U.S. Immigration Policy and the National Interest: Final Report and Recommendations*, was issued in March 1981. It tended to continue the "open society" perspective.

This commission built its effort on the previous work of the Interagency Task Force on Immigration Policy (Departments of Justice, Labor, and State), which reported in March 1979. The research and documentation for both groups, especially the prestigious Select Commission on Immigration and Refugee Policy, leave much to be desired. It is a remarkable achievement that such massive numbers of immigrants were received into American society during the period after World War II. But the achievement should not prevent examination of profound problems, both now and in the future.

The staff reports and supporting appendices seem more concerned with justifying past performance and ongoing policy than in analyzing the impact of new immigrants on U.S. society and vice versa.[50] In my view, these reports mute central, controversial issues. For example, the interplay

48. Ibid., p. 1.
49. U.S. Bureau of the Census, *Statistical Abstract of the United States: 1970*, 91st edition (Washington, D.C., 1970), tables 2, 4; 96th edition (1975), table 9; 101st edition (1981), table 4.
50. *United States Immigration Policy and the National Interest*, Staff Report of the Select Commission on Immigration and Refugee Policy, April 30, 1981. Supplement to the Final Report; see also Appendices to the Staff Report.

between immigrant and domestic unemployment requires fuller treatment. Likewise, the reports avoid discussion of the wide difference in adjustment of new immigrants to the United States, the difference between rapid acculturation and painful adjustment which produces only marginal survival. In particular, they hardly deal with the remarkable success of particular groups of immigrants to perform with distinction in college. Some of this performance clearly surpassed the achievement of long-time minority groups. The staff approach appears to avoid any invidious comparison. The research effort took place in a highly politicized "Select Commission." At best, they were prepared to admit that older people had a more difficult time adjusting, while the position of the younger generation was described in optimistic terms. "In any case, acculturation is mainly a problem for the older members of an immigrant generation. For their children, who are subject to powerful acculturing influences including television and the schools, the process of Americanization seems inexorable regardless of ancestry."[51] But perhaps in this regard the most fundamental weakness of the research efforts (and in turn the recommendations for policy) is the limitation of the scope to "legal immigration." The difficulties of the illegal immigrant are profound and cannot be separated from the issues of total immigration flow.

Older immigrants find an absence of agencies and educational institutions concerned with skill instruction and civic education, which were available to former immigrants. Both older and younger groups faced tensions and dilemmas of an advanced industrial society, equipped with vast machinery of the welfare state, which was not functioning satisfactorily. The low-status immigrant with limited education had to take his or her place in the queue in a society with inadequate rates of growth in economic productivity. The amount of communalism varied greatly among immigrant groups. While the political formula of hyphenated American still operates, its implementation has become more difficult.

Even in the absence of research on acculturation, the basic statistics present an overview. As U.S. fertility rates have decreased, immigration has become an increasingly significant element of population growth. Moreover, projections into the future must take into consideration the higher birthrates of new immigrants. Finally, we must take into account a greater gap culturally between the new immigrant and the resident population than was true after the Civil War, until the temporary closing of the gates after World War I. Such observation is not nativist bias or an effort to inhibit the broadening of pluralism. It is, rather, an

51. Ibid., Appendix D, p. 5.

assessment of the resources required to maintain a balance between diversity and a core of central values essential for citizenship.

The somewhat surprising lack of popular opposition to open immigration in the United States is in part the result of the mass media, which have strongly supported a tolerant "definition of the situation." The argument offered by the mass media, in turn supported by academics, is that an open society of ethnic and racial pluralism is the tradition of the United States, which built the society and which keeps it strong. To close the gates is both morally wrong and not in the best self-interest. These "liberal" attitudes were in good part molded by the civil rights movement and the opposition to the Vietnam war. They are at variance with partially formulated and incompletely verbalized attitudes of rank-and-file citizens, who tend toward restrictive policies. A delicate balance of toleration is needed in order to reflect the tension that exists between the open society attitudes of the mass media and more defensive feelings operating in society at large.

There are strong pressure groups, formal and informal, on both sides of the immigration issue. The 1980 presidential election manifested a discernible but limited shift in national attitudes toward this question. Opposition to open immigration increased somewhat, though not to the extent of producing a new political basis for national policy.

It serves no real purpose to offer "predictions" of emerging levels of tension between the resident citizen and the new immigration who enjoys no more than a marginal subsistence standard of living, who is being threatened with repatriation, or who is deeply involved in a communal life style which blocks the development of a sense of citizenship. However, it makes sense to recognize that new immigrants find fewer resources than did turn-of-the-century immigrants to assist them in the crucial period of acculturation. Specialization programs of settlement houses and night schools for immigrants have weakened. Older efforts to create hyphenated Americans have given way to communalism. It is with Latinos that communalism—old and new—has the strongest impact and will have the most extensive effects on the political process. Elements of communalism can be found in most post-1965 immigrant groups, especially in the Asiatic populations.

It is striking to what extent academics and "intellectuals" accepted the bilingualism formula, which must of necessity weaken common democratic political institutions. Older programs of the night school and settlement house variety contributed to both skill and civic education, and, if effectively modernized, might be useful with new immigrants. But such education programs are being constricted under budgetary pressure. The illegal immigrant, who particularly requires such assistance, is deprived of it for plausible but nonconstructive reasons. The quality of personnel available for manning such programs has declined. In short, since 1945, civic education of new immigrants has not been an outstanding achievement. Yet no other outcome could be expected, given the state of inner-city education. The textbooks of the new social realism that came into use increasingly after the Depression failed to confront directly the issues of the balance between rights and obligations. But the decisive development after 1945 was increasing reliance on the social sciences, very often designated as the behavioral sciences, in a flood of research and academic experiments. This trend, which reached a high point in the years after the Vietnam war, almost completely avoided the issue of rights versus obligations.

Six

Academic Frontiers in Civic Education

The "Behavioral Science" Redefinition of Civics

Civic education in the United States after 1890 reflects the increased intrusion of university professors. But it was in the years after 1945 that academicians greatly expanded their influence on civic education. In fact, in the period 1945–75 they were able to transform the curriculum. If one uses the definition of civic education that I have offered, they were almost able to eliminate that part which deals with the positive and enduring heritage of the political system of the United States. In effect, civic education became mainly the study of a series of discrete "social" and "political" problems plus an overview of contemporary patterns of political participation and attitudes. Appeals to patriotism were no longer heard, and little attention was paid to their appropriate reformulation for an interdependent world community. The political message that generally emerged was that increased political participation was an essential goal. Political and election sample surveys were used in the study of specific social and political problems. In essence, after 1945, at both high school and university levels, the "civics" approach gave way increasingly to a "behavioral science" analysis of contemporary society.

Social and political realism cannot substitute for self-critical patriotism and enlightened nationalism—that is, exposure to the materials of civic education designed to enhance civic consciousness. In short, if civic education is designed to prepare the student for responsible social and political obligations, it must be more than a series of calls for increased political participation.

It is my judgment that the civic education of the post–World War II period has complicated the task of political "reconstruction." Let there be no misunderstanding: the profound problems of governance in the United

States were not caused by the school system, or by the weakness of civic education. But the tasks of institution building to solve societal strains and dilemmas were exacerbated by negativism and near nihilism, unintended consequences of civic education programs which prided themselves on "myth smashing" and their "critical" stance. Even more pointed, the social science base of civic education increasingly ignored the balance between rights and obligations.

The struggle between representatives of various disciplines to influence and control the "new" civic education was intense. Historians gave much ground, but showed considerable tenacity. Economics, sociology, and even geography sought with missionary zeal to improve social studies. But it was political science that contributed most to the transformation of the curriculum, especially after 1945. Within political science, involvement in issues of civic education is hardly judged a prestigious intellectual task. Nevertheless, the discipline produced extensive cadres prepared to involve themselves in one or another task of civic education. The explosive growth of undergraduate enrollment after 1945 meant that social and political scientists did not have to work through third parties to organize high school social studies. After 1945, they had larger and larger captive audiences of students on their own campuses.

Political science had a special claim to exercise leadership because its content was highly relevant. However, there was considerable debate within and outside the discipline as to which parts of the discipline were most useful for civic education in a democratic polity. In the end, I shall argue that the descriptive findings of survey research were of strategic importance in shaping civic education, although some critics sought greater emphasis on ethical and normative issues.

Starting in the 1920s, intellectual developments within the discipline of political science must be considered in examining the contemporary state and consequences of civic education in the United States. Before the 1920s, political science was a mixture of political philosophy, public law, and study of the formal structure of political institutions. In the 1920s the discipline was influenced strongly by the Chicago school, under the leadership of Charles Merriam, Harold Gosnell, and Harold D. Lasswell. The transformation was twofold. First, political science became increasingly empirical. The emp ricism was not antiquarianism but, rather, the search for reasoned and delimited generalization. This meant, in turn, that it became more and more a social science and developed closer linkages to psychology and sociology.

Second, the new political science of the Chicago school, although committed to "scientific methodology," was interested in a fusion of empirical and normative (value) analysis, which, it was heralded, would contribute to the reduction of human violence and social misery. These political scientists were not merely engaged in a refined form of muckraking. They believed that a realistic understanding of the political process would assist both political leaders and the rank-and-file citizenry in democratic institution building.

The systematic study of politics was a genuine scholarly undertaking, which could clarify the dilemmas of democratic society and increase the effectiveness of its political institutions. These political scientists were concerned with the classical and traditional problems of political philosophy, but sought to formulate an empirical basis to their assessments. They saw no incompatibility between the study of the great ideas of political philosophy and detailed empirical analysis of contemporary society. To the contrary, empirical research was designed to make possible the assessment of the vitality and defects of the political institutions of a democratic polity. Such assessment had to make use of criteria of performance derived from classic political and social philosophy.

Thus, it is understandable that a concern with citizenship and civic education was at the core of the Chicago school of political science. Under the driving leadership of Charles Merriam, a massive series of international studies on citizenship and civic education was completed in the early 1930s. The series remains of value precisely because of the fusion of classical issues of governance with rich, if unsystematic, descriptive materials.

Charles Merriam's introductory and summary statements represent an intellectual high point in the analysis of civic education and civic obligation. The trend toward increasing emphasis on the rights and benefits of citizenship was already developing. But Merriam, drawing on political theory, was outspoken about the centrality of obligations and duties. His statement was perhaps the last major formulation by a modern political scientist of an articulated (not mechanical) balance between rights versus obligations and service to the nation. Merriam and his colleagues recognized the power of economic incentive and reward but emphasized that a democratic society rested to an important degree on mutual obligations among political leaders and between political leaders and the rank-and-file citizenry. Merriam, in his citizen role, was a progressive, but both as a citizen and as a political scientist his statements on citizenship appear to be very old-fashioned. He was fully aware that, in most nations, citizen training was used to keep governments in power, especially to assist authoritarian regimes. But for him the underlying issue was that citizenship training for a democratic society was not self-generating but had to be effectively constructed.

147

It is worthwhile to be reminded of the common elements of citizenship training that he found in almost every country he and his group studied. His perspective was clearly that of a political realist in pursuit of "higher" moral goals. The list of key elements in citizenship training that Merriam offered demonstrates the changed political milieus in the United States over the last fifty years. He spoke of: "patriotism and loyalty," "obedience to the laws of society," "respect for officials and government," "recognition of the obligations of political life," "some minimum degree of self-control," "response to community needs in time of stress," "ordinary honesty in social relations."[1] Clearly, in the half-century that ensued, limits on the effectiveness of democratic political regimes have seriously weakened the citizenry's attachment to these standards of behavior. But one cannot dismiss the part played by educators and of social scientists in this weakening.

The work of the Chicago school of political science, while generating disciples, did not become the dominant intellectual force in political science in the period after 1945. The striking development was the massive growth of survey research methodology, with emphasis on description and statistical analysis. Critics of survey methodology make two points. First, studies of this variety do not deal sufficiently with the organizational and institutional aspects of politics and political behavior. Second, the approach is not intensive enough to reveal underlying values or latent ideologies.

But survey methodology was widely accepted and effectively developed. It was claimed that the information collected by the behavioral method contributed to an open and informed society, strengthened political debate, and supplied the background for exploring specific social and economic conflicts.

Thus, advocates of survey research believe there is an implicit political role for their efforts, although they emphasize the political neutrality of their work. Under advanced industrialism, they hold, surveys assist the democratic process. Political leaders have difficulty in judging the goals and preferences of a democracy. Sample surveys supply data on citizen preferences which assist the legislative process. Likewise, survey research generates a flow of information about the effectiveness of political leaders from the public's point of view, which also assists the democratic process. In effect, surveys, unless properly interpreted, serve to weaken democratic institutions. They shift the election contest from issues to personalities; thereby they serve to guide campaign rhetoric rather than to establish the extent of consensus and dissensus.[2]

1. Charles E. Merriam, *The Making of Citizens* (Chicago: University of Chicago Press, 1931), pp. 1–26.
2. Morris Janowitz, *The Last Half Century: Societal Change and Politics in America* (Chicago: University of Chicago Press, 1978).

The political implications of sample surveys run deeper. The political data they generate become central elements in contemporary civic education. Each social and economic problem rests on a configuration of political attitudes illuminated by sample surveys. Such research points the political scientist to the issues that need to be emphasized and clarified. The findings of sample surveys, while relevant for a political democracy if properly presented and evaluated, cannot substitute for the kind of civic education that highlights the enduring assets of the political system and focuses on the creative efforts to reduce the weakness of existing political institutions.

After 1945, social scientists no longer had to work indirectly through high school teachers and by means of the preparation of teaching materials. The immense increase in college enrollment gave them direct access to an ever increasing student body. They trained new cadres of teachers. They became active in commissions and study groups, and worked with publishers, foundations, and governmental agencies. An underlying assumption of the new civic education was that empirical survey findings contributed to the construction of a curriculum for a pluralistic society— especially for those deprived minority groups who had not gotten their fair share of the benefits of a democratic form of government.

In the name of the study of "political behavior," a massive program of empirical surveys was developed which extended for more than twenty years. Paul F. Lazarsfeld of Columbia University and his disciples were among the first academics to pursue the systematic application of the sample survey for the academic study of voting and political participation.[3] Then the University of Michigan became the center of this effort. The first monographs, authored by Angus Campbell and his colleagues at the University of Michigan, dealt with the 1945 and 1952 elections and set the perspective for a series of studies which commanded widespread attention.[4] Although the Michigan group, as well as other research teams in ensuing years, did not set out to transform civic education, they did influence it considerably. The Michigan group's work was not limited to their series of volumes and extensive flow of papers. They organized a national study group of interested social scientists who were given access to research data collected over a period of years. The purpose was to encourage reanalysis and more specific studies.

3. Paul F. Lazarsfeld, Bernard Berelson, and Helen Gaudet, *The People's Choice* (New York: Duell, Sloan and Pearce, 1944).
4. Angus Campbell and Robert L. Kahn, *The People Elect a President* (Survey Research Center, Institute for Social Research, University of Michigan, 1952); Angus Campbell, Gerald Gurin, and Warren E. Miller, *The Voter Decides* (Chicago: Row-Peterson, 1954).

One should mention a third group. Although much smaller than the Michigan group, the collaboration of Sidney Verba and Norman H. Nie, loosely linked to the National Opinion Research Center, commanded considerable attention. One important part of their work, published as *The Changing American Voter*, was an effort to synthesize more than two decades of survey research on voting studies.[5]

These bodies of data, and the analytic studies they prompted, enriched the study of U.S. political behavior, although they have been criticized for deemphasizing the role of the mass media and not giving adequate weight to the changing structure of political parties and election machinery. In terms of ability to adapt civic education to the fragmentation of U.S. political institutions, three decades of intensive and large-scale research were, I would argue, counterproductive. I do not argue from the point of view of particular scholars who hold that empirical research is irrelevant to the moral and political dilemmas which civic education in a democratic society must deal with. My perspective is that, within the framework of the sample survey, central issues of citizenship were, with limited exception, ignored. Two particular research studies, one by M. Kent Jennings and Richard G. Niemi and the other by John Reynolds, do contain some data relevant to these issues.[6]

In the range of books and articles I have reviewed, however, there are no trend data on attitudes toward the obligations/rights balance. In fact, the terms *obligation* or *duty* do not even appear.[7] In essence, behavioralists saw the polity as a collection of interests and rights which were not fully or equally attained. Obligation was barely referred to. The behavioralist approach to political participation represents a form of economic rationality.

We are dealing not only with sample survey research but with broad trends in the social sciences generally. The seminal *Encyclopedia of the Social*

5. Norman H. Nie, Sidney Verba, and John R. Petrocik, *The Changing American Voter* (Cambridge: Harvard University Press, 1976).

6. M. Kent Jennings and Richard G. Niemi, *Generations and Politics* (Princeton: Princeton University Press, 1981); see data presented by John Reynolds from study organized by Roberta S. Sigel and Marilyn B. Hoskin, *The Political Involvement of Adolescents* (New Brunswick, N.J.: Rutgers University Press, 1981).

7. In *The Voter Decides*, an index is constructed called "sense of citizen duty." While this index has relevance for the Michigan motivational type of analysis, it does not figure centrally in the conclusions in *The Voter Decides*. It is not a comprehensive measure of civic obligation, which would be relevant for my interests in citizenship. It is, rather, an index which seeks to measure the respondent's attitudes about the importance of election participation. It is defined as "the feeling that oneself and others ought to participate in the political process, regardless of whether such political activity is seen as worthwhile or efficacious" (p. 194). The index was included in national surveys from 1952 to 1978 with results which showed a limited increase in "sense of citizen duty."

Sciences, in its first edition published in 1930, had a thoughtful article on citizenship.[8] In the second edition, 1968, it had no entry on the topic. The absence of an explicit concern with citizenship meant that the individual's relation to the state was incompletely treated. There was a total lack of concern with political obligations required to make the contemporary system operate effectively.[9]

Behavioral analysis of citizen participation was of limited value not only because of the failure to deal adequately with political goals, which in a democracy need to be pursued regardless of economic reward. Personal preferences of research professors led them, in turn, to avoid the issue of patriotism. Basic affiliations of citizens were conceptualized in terms of occupation, plus a wide range of cleavages such as age groupings, sex, and religious attachments. As one reviews the body of survey literature on political participation, national and patriotic identifications do not receive sufficient attention, despite the centrality of such attachments and their relevance to democratic politics. For the thirty years under discussion, we have no estimate of the changing strength of nationalistic sentiments or patriotic attachments. "Liberal" social scientists abhor excessive nationalist "spirit" and therefore avoid study of this problem.

Nationalist sentiment and patriotic zeal have weakened, but not as much as is often believed. Members of the working class are more nationalist than members of the upper-middle class, especially those with graduate and professional education. Whereas military service traditionally strengthened nationalism, the all-volunteer military has a more limited effect. It is difficult to judge the impact of nuclear weapons on feelings of nationalism. The United States has not had, until recently, a strong antinuclear weapons movement. In some segments of the population there has been an increase in defensive nationalism; but in others, especially among the young, nationalism is regarded with growing indifference.

8. Carl Brinkman, "Citizenship," in *Encyclopedia of the Social Sciences*, ed., Edwin R. A. Seligman (New York: Macmillan, 1930–35), vol. 3, pp. 471–74.

9. In part, this imbalance of interest is reflective of the political predispositions of many leading figures in the field who were deeply committed to the expansion of the welfare state. Strangely enough, survey research studies on political behavior were undertaken during a period in which many political scientists, such as David Easton, sought to implement a "systems" approach. Clearly, a systems approach would have included not only interests and rights but obligations as well. Without both elements one could not speak of a system. No doubt, we are dealing with well-recognized problems of "theory construction" in the social sciences.

Nearly all the survey research on elections in effect focuses on the social, psychological, and political factors designed to explain voter decision and choice. It is, of course, possible to make use of the survey research approach to analyze the election in more institutional terms. Such analysis would be highly relevant to the study of elections as an aspect of civic education.

Nationalism and patriotism among youth have been weakening since the end of World War II. The ·emergence of the United States as an advanced industrial society has meant an increase in personal hedonism at the expense of collective affiliations. The values and benefits of the welfare state become widely accepted, not just among the middle strata but throughout the social structure. The desire for material comfort implies not moral corruption but the cultural diffusion of consumerism. The process is circular: the pressures against traditional nationalism and patriotism weaken civic education, which, in turn, weakens collective civic consciousness.

From the start, it has been my assumption that there can be no effective civic consciousness and no sense of political obligation unless members of the popular citizenry have a realistic and meaningful sense of nationalism. The exercise of political obligation cannot rest on purely localistic or provincial attachments on the one hand or on a vague and diffuse sense of world citizenship on the other. I regret that there is no adequate body of data from survey research dealing with attitude trends on these issues. The leading figures in survey research just have not been interested in nationalism and its implications—positive and negative—for the democratic process.[10]

I speak not of blind, mechanical nationalism but of an attachment to the state compatible with the realities of the contemporary interdependent world community. Nationalism of this kind requires that the bulk of the population display feelings of patriotism—not aggressive patriotism but patriotism reconstructed into responsible civic consciousness. The next step is to examine the limited number of behavioral studies on citizenship, for they do contain materials of relevance to civic education.

THE SOCIAL CONSTRUCTION OF THE "GOOD CITIZEN"

Political behavior research in university-based centers has generally avoided direct discussion of the meaning of citizenship. By exception, we have the specialized results of the National Assessment of Educational Progress, together with two relevant but limited bodies of data dealing with youth's definition of citizenship. For the years 1969–76, a series of extensive surveys completed on more than 630,000 thirteen- and seventeen-year-olds strove to measure knowledge and attitudes about citizenship. Unfortunately, the questions and research were not very profound. Educators, political scientists, and administrators, assisted financially by the De-

10. In any case, we require research which pursues a more intensive probing of attitudes, values, and latent ideologies than is the case in standardized survey research.

partment of Health, Education, and Welfare, launched a series of national youth surveys with limited numbers of items on rather large samples, in order to assess the cognitive and normative level of high school students and to infer their civic competence. This was an academic undertaking with significant implications for educational policy. Major findings are incorporated in *Changes in Political Knowledge and Attitudes, 1969–1976: Selected Results from the Second National Assessment of Citizenship and Social Studies*,[11] and in another report—a slim document given the more than $21 million spent—issued as a "Bicentennial Survey."

The investigators appeared more interested in large numbers than in young people's definitions of citizenship and civic responsibility. The period was one of considerable turmoil in U.S. society, especially in the school system. It is not surprising, though disappointing, that only one question in the battery of tests and interviews dealt directly with citizen obligation. While the question did not deal with a central issue in civic responsibility, it did address a matter related to youth culture, namely vandalism. The question was, "Suppose you see a stranger slashing the tires of a car, would you report and describe that person to the police?" The answer given in 1971 by seventeen-year-olds was: yes, 74 percent; no, 14 percent; undecided, 12 percent. By 1976, the acceptance of this civic obligation had slipped down to 67 percent, a statistically significant drop.[12] But the striking finding was that while those who replied "no" dropped to 10 percent, those who were undecided increased to 22 percent. The essential shift was an increase in vagueness about standards of effective citizen obligation.

The effort to probe students' understanding of "democracy" was oversimplified. Students were asked to describe very briefly, "What is a democracy?"[13] They were not required to give explanations of the concept. Phrases such as "run by the people," "where the majority rules," were acceptable. Using such measures, the findings showed that, for the sample of seventeen-year-olds during the seven-year period, the proportion with acceptable answers declined 12 percentage points (from 86 percent to 74 percent). It is not easy to explain this drop. No doubt the increase in the concentration of students in high school from culturally impoverished families is part of the explanation. Another part is the declining effectiveness of public school teaching, especially in areas with minority group students.

11. Citizenship/Social Studies Report No. 07-CSN-2. National Assessment of Educational Progress, Education Commission of the States, Suite 700, 1860 Lincoln Street, Denver, Colorado 80295, March 1978, 72 pp.
12. "Changes in Political Knowledge and Attitudes," ibid., p. 20.
13. Ibid., p. 24.

The range of questions on knowledge about law, civil rights, and the structure of government produced no startling results. One wonders to what extent the factual knowledge displayed could be used as a meaningful indicator of civic education. Perhaps more interesting is the limited number of questions on which youngsters increased their knowledge during the seven-year period, in contrast to the large number of questions on which there was slippage. Students knew about the rights of a person accused of a crime (p. 9), and the level of this knowledge increased some over the seven-year period. A simplified question on the rights of the president of the United States (p. 30) followed the same pattern. On the other hand, there were other questions on constitutional rights and the structure and function of government on which the national level of correct answers for seventeen-year-olds decreased (pp. 7–13, 23–30).

Where there was an increase in factual knowledge, the topic had had extensive coverage by the mass media, especially television. For example, the question on presidential rights was linked to the Watergate incident and the extensive TV exposure. Further evidence of the influence of the mass media on civic attitudes derives from the social attitudes of the young people sampled. Tolerant attitudes toward minority groups is most noteworthy. On the question of getting a job, tolerant attitudes toward skin color and religion were almost universal and no doubt far more so than for the adult population. Ninety-seven percent of both age levels said that skin color should not be a factor. Of course, one needs to keep in mind the gap between attitudes and actual behavior, but it is difficult to account for these data without crediting the mass media. The mass media have stressed racial integration, and the interracial aspect of TV entertainment is especially relevant for the youth population.

In addition, the findings of these surveys indicate that students in classrooms exposed to moderate-to-frequent amounts of classroom discussion about politics did better than those without such discussion. Students who had "studied how to acquire and analyze information about political issues" also performed better in answering factual questions.[14] Previous studies of the effects of civics courses or even of a series of civics courses showed such courses to have marginal or limited impact.[15] These data point to the plausible conclusion that the mass media and/or extensive classroom discussion do supply increased factual knowledge.

14. National Assessment of Educational Progress, *Education for Citizenship: A Bicentennial Survey*, Citizenship Social Studies Report no. 07-CS-o1 (November 1976), p. 2.
15. See for example, M. Kent Jennings, "An Aggregate Analysis of Home and School Effects of Political Socialization," *Social Science Quarterly* 55 (1974): 394–410; M. Kent Jennings and Richard G. Niemi, *The Political Character of Adolescence: The Influence of Families and Schools* (Princeton: Princeton University Press, 1974).

A revealing segment of the National Assessment study involved questions dealing with willingness to participate in the political process. Factual data were collected on this topic by asking seventeen-year-olds whether they had engaged in any of three types of political activity: signing a petition, writing a letter to a government official, or helping in a public election campaign. Following the format of the study, subjective motivation for such behavior was not probed. Of the seventeen-year-olds questioned in 1976, 57 percent claimed to have signed a petition, 15 percent to have written a letter to a government official, and 8 percent to have participated in a public election campaign.

As measured by these indicators, between 1969 and 1976 there was an overall decline in political participation. Reported participation in all three activities declined between 7 and 9 percent. The largest decline was in participation in public election campaigns, which dropped from 18 percent in 1969 to 9 percent in 1976. During this period, the United States withdrew from Vietnam, and the resulting decline of political agitation in turn contributed over the short term to reduced political participation.

We do not know the scope and intensity of the 9 percent participation in election campaigns; still, the data make it difficult to speak of fundamental apathy. Two questions about the importance of voting did reveal, as expected, that younger Americans shared some of the disillusionment of the adult population about participating in elections. In general, the National Assessment study was limited by its focus on overt behavior and its neglect of subjective meanings.

Authors of the various reports avoided political controversy as to whether it was appropriate for government-sponsored research to ask politically "loaded" questions and to make judgments about the results. But with respect to elections the authors could not contain themselves. They offered the assessment that the figures on the conceptions of the importance of elections to seventeen-year-olds "could be considered disconcerting when one realizes that within a year, they will be of voting age."[16] Such questions and the resulting data have relevance mainly to the extent that patterns can be traced over long periods of time. However, the instability of government-sponsored research of this type undermined this goal. In due course, the National Assessment program was abandoned.

A more holistic analysis with emphasis on the subjective meaning of citizenship was pursued in two independent studies, in both of which citizenship was defined as involving important elements of civic obligation. The first study, *Generations and Politics*, by M. Kent Jennings and Richard G. Niemi, was based on a 1965 panel study of a national probability

16. National Assessment of Educational Progress, *Education for Citizenship*, p. 17.

sample of high school seniors and their parents, followed up eight years later in 1973.[17] The findings on the social definitions of citizenship and the changes encountered should be viewed in the context of the authors' overall findings on attitude stability and change. They concluded that "despite eight exciting, tempestuous years, and despite a good deal of individual and aggregate change, a remarkable degree of intergenerational continuity, or of only short lived discontinuity, was present."[18]

The approach of these authors to citizenship converges with mine. For me, citizenship is an expression of the political relations between the individual and the state. For a democratic polity to succeed, the citizen must fill his civic obligations; the basic question is the nature and content of these obligations. Jennings and Niemi see citizenship as a more generic category, wider than the political categorization of the citizen. Their task is to chart the full range of meanings the public, and especially youth, allocate to the term *good citizen*. In their perspective, the good citizen may be many "things"—a moral, ethical person; a good, kind, considerate person, etc.[19] They come close to my approach when they assert that "the good citizen may also be described in terms of the individual's role in a democratic polity."[20] I was struck by the fact that Jennings and Niemi, members of the University of Michigan behavioral school, are prepared to use the classic notion on which my own analysis is built, namely, "civic obligation" (p. 35). Civic obligation is an expression of the political citizen.

These authors join political philosophy to empirical research when they speak of two subgroups of political virtue (how refreshing it is to have the members of the University of Michigan school use such old-fashioned terminology as *political virtue*). On the one hand, they speak of one subgroup whose members stressed political allegiance—obeying laws, being loyal, honoring the country, paying taxes, etc. The second group stressed the more active participant component of the political "repertory"—being interested in and paying attention to politics, voting, taking part in campaigns and in the variety of forms of political participation.[21] Even though I have my reservations about their twofold categorizing, Jennings and Niemi are clearly pointed in the right direction if one is concerned with the virtue of citizenship in an advanced industrial society.

They seek to identify the concentrations of different types of citizenship. The fact that political roles are mentioned as frequently as they are testifies, according to these authors, to the fundamental role of civic obligation in

17. Jennings and Niemi, *Generations and Politics*.
18. Ibid., p. 229.
19. Ibid., p. 26.
20. Ibid.
21. Ibid., p. 36.

the vast repertory of citizen roles. "Commitment to a sense of duty is by no means ephemeral, even when tapped in [such] an indirect manner."[22] In particular, they were interested in comparing the members of the high school class of 1965 with those of the class of 1973 on the basis of attributes the students used to describe a "good citizen."[23] The students sampled selected three out of a list of six attributes. Unfortunately, the list was incomplete; it did not include activity in community affairs, or some form of national or community service. Thus, the basic question of the "citizen soldier" was not investigated. Nevertheless, it is useful to examine the results, which are set forth in table 1.

Despite discernible changes from the first to second period, a surprising measure of continuity persisted in view of the turmoil of the period and the imputed volatility of youth attitudes. Combining these data with others from the study, Jennings and Niemi categorize the 1973 students as "distinctly less imbued with the traditional virtues associated with civic training. Politics was less central in their lives and the participant culture was less valued."[24] The drop in "vote in elections," from 70 percent to 56 percent is essential to their argument. One can speculate, however, that this decline would be stabilized and even reversed as Vietnam receded and as the agitations of minority groups gave way to electoral politics. The essential observation is that the amount of change did not represent

TABLE 1. Attributes of the Good Citizen
(M. K. Jennings and R. G. Niemi)

	Class of 1965	Class of 1973
Obey the laws	72%	74%
Proud of their country	73	67
Vote in elections	70	56
Tolerant of other races, nationalities, religions	64	72
Go to church	12	9
Mind their own business	5	16

Respondents were asked to select three of the list of six. Totals do not add to 300% due to rounding and to the failure of some respondents to make three selections.

Source: M. Kent Jennings and Richard G. Niemi, *Generations and Politics* (Princeton: Princeton University Press, 1981).

22. Ibid.
23. Ibid., p. 225.
24. Ibid.

a "profound transformation" or "political revolution" for the Vietnam generation.

In any case, there is a contrast between the Jennings and Niemi findings and those reported by John Reynolds. The Reynolds study, on the basis of data collected in 1974, reports greater student emphasis on voting as an attribute of the "good citizen."[25] No doubt, the differences between these two studies are partly the result of differences in sampling procedures, as well as the format and text of the questions. Taking these differences into consideration, I would assert that Reynolds is closer to the mark in estimating the continued importance given by young people to voting as an attribute of the "good citizen." As is painfully well known, the level of voting in the United States is much lower than in Western Europe, and the level fluctuates more extensively. Thus the data on voting as part of the social construction of the "good citizen" need to be interpreted in the context of long-term patterns of United States electoral behavior. Without denying the decline reported by Jennings and Niemi, I would stress, as Jennings and Niemi do, continuity rather than change in their findings.

One should also note that Jennings and Niemi report on emphasis placed on an expression of patriotism—"proud of their country"—as an attribute of the "good citizen." The class of 1965 showed that 73 percent believed this attribute to be an element of the "good citizen." The figure dropped to 67 percent for the class of 1973. Despite agitations of the Vietnam period, this attribute displayed less decline than the voting measure.

Jennings and Niemi use their attribute data to construct a typology of citizen roles. I find it difficult to accept their simple dual typology of loyal patriots on the one hand and active participants on the other. Such a distinction undoubtedly characterized an important portion of the sampled population, but I have directly encountered numerous persons who represent that segment of the citizenry who combine loyalty and elements of active participation. I cannot disregard the existence of mixed types. With the development of an advanced industrial nation-state, and greater complexity of the social structure, the range of mixed types increases. In fact, the Reynolds study, based on a reanalysis of a body of survey data collected by Roberta S. Sigel and Marilyn B. Hoskin for their study *The Political Involvement of Adolescents*,[26] presents a broader range of popular definitions of citizen types.

25. John Reynolds, "The Normative Regulation of Citizenship Participation," unpublished paper delivered at the Northeast Political Science Association, 20–22 November 1980.
26. Sigel and Hoskin, *The Political Involvement of Adolescents*.

The data used by Reynolds were gathered by a stratified random sample survey of 1,000 high school seniors in twenty-five public schools in Pennsylvania. The interviews were conducted in 1974 and were followed by a questionnaire three weeks later. The students' characterizations of the "good citizen" are set forth in table 2. The convergence with the Jennings and Niemi survey is striking. In both studies "obeying the law" ranks very high as do the measures of patriotism. However, the wider range of attributes reported by John Reynolds is more revealing of the popular definitions of the "good citizen" held by young people.

It was not surprising that the item "keeping informed about public affairs" fell markedly below "obey the law," "vote in most elections," and the two items indicating patriotic sentiment. There was an even greater falling off for the item on participation in the political process ("trying to influence government decisions and policies"). The low emphasis on participation in the political process was due to the high concentration of students with no opinion. It was not that political participation was rejected outright as an attribute of the "good citizen" but, rather, that it was regarded with widespread indifference. The fact that one-third fell into this group highlights the limitations of contemporary civic education. However, the item of "volunteering for service to the local community" produced revealing results and reflects the potentials for filling citizen obligation. The overall results revealed low emphasis on this item as an attribute of the "good citizen." One-half the sample of young men and women surveyed in this study believed that such service was important; the overall low support resulted from the limited number (12.9 percent) who thought it was very important for being a "good citizen." Likewise, belief that such service was "not at all important" was very limited. I shall return to the issues on national and community service when I deal with the reconstruction of patriotism. It is clear to me, from these data and subsequent survey materials, that the attribute of service to the larger collectivity cannot be dismissed if one is interested in the potentials for developing civic obligation.

The data on the "good citizen" can be thought of not merely as attitude patterns but as emergent norms which must be dealt with by civic education. They are not a random collection of thought but, when subjected to factor analysis, present a threefold set of citizen roles (more complicated than the dual typology of Jennings and Niemi). Reynolds offered three elements: *The active-involvement norms* (voting in most elections, keeping informed about public affairs, trying to influence government policies and decisions); *the allegiant-compliant norms* (obeying the law, honoring one's country, not dishonoring one's country); *the personal character norms* (being

TABLE 2. Civic Obligations: Social Definitions Offered by Pennsylvania Youth 1974 (John Reynolds Analysis)

Below is a list of qualities which some people consider important for a good citizen. For each quality, check the answer which most accurately describes how important you think it is for being a good citizen.

		Extremely Important	Important	No Opinion	Not Very Important	Not at all Important	No.
a) Voting in most Elections	%	47.3	42.1	6.7	3.5	0.4	846
b) Obeying the law	%	60.4	33.1	4.6	1.8	0.1	846
c) Honoring one's Country	%	42.1	42.6	9.5	5.1	0.8	846
d) Working Hard	%	23.6	59.3	11.2	5.0	0.8	846
e) Being a good Human Being	%	45.6	42.2	8.8	2.7	0.7	845
f) Being Friendly and Helpful to our Fellow Men	%	46.9	46.3	5.3	1.5	0.0	847
g) Volunteering for Service to the Local Community	%	12.9	54.2	19.5	12.3	1.2	848
h) Not Bringing Dishonor to the Country	%	35.5	37.4	19.5	5.3	2.2	847
i) Trying to Influence Government Decisions and Policies	%	18.3	41.7	29.8	8.5	1.8	847
j) Keeping Informed about Public Affairs	%	23.5	55.7	12.3	7.7	0.9	848

friendly and helpful to our fellow men, being a good human being, working hard, volunteering for service to the local community).

Obviously we are seeking not a purely neutral formulation but one which is compatible with the definitions of democratic citizenship on which this study is based. In particular, the second category in which obeying the law is described as compliant seems to me to be an unfortunate selection of a label. It is a distortion to assert that obeying the law is in effect no more than a compliant act. It involves positive commitment and purposive action. Nevertheless, with this point in mind, the findings are revealing of the complexity of citizen attitudes and norms among youth.

In essence, we are interested in the overlap between normative types of the "good citizen." The strongest association (the highest overlap) is between personal character and allegiant-compliant norms (gamma is .40); the next highest is between personal character and active participation (gamma is .34); the third highest is active participation and allegiant-compliant (gamma is .29).[27] The first association calls into question liberal dogmas, while the third overlap questions conservative dogmas. Although these data can be thought of as a form of market research for teachers of civic education, they do not indicate the complexity of the student body's normative predispositions. In fact, Reynolds probes deeper by examining the symbolic dimensions of these citizen roles. He focuses on the "collective representations"—the symbolism—of citizenship and not merely with a set of individualistic self-interests. First is the simple but pervasive question of the level of political trust associated with different typologies of the good citizen.[28]

Naturally, important sociological differences were expected between the different citizen types. But some results, from my perspective, were most unexpected and demonstrate that, without empirical observation at crucial points, the analysis of "big ideas" can easily go astray. It can be reported that the students who emphasized active participation and those who emphasized allegiant-compliant—two very different conceptions of the attributes of citizenship—both revealed similar levels of political trust (active participation, gamma .26; and allegiant-compliant, gamma .28).[29] For these two groups, the amount of political trust was in effect average as compared to other items—neither very high nor very low. Reynolds uncovered two very different "ideological" groupings, but they displayed

27. Each relation is statistically significant at the .05 level.
28. I would have preferred a more intensive and comprehensive operationalization of this variable. The limited responses are not necessarily effective indicators of persistent and underlying attitudes and beliefs.
29. Both statistically significant at the .05 level.

converging levels of political trust. However, for the third grouping, those for whom the idea of citizenship is rooted in personal characteristics, the association with political trust was much less (gamma .10). The overlap between political trust and the personal character definition of the good citizen is very small indeed. In fact, one is safe to assert that the students' personal definition of a democratic citizen reflects their lack of trust.

Second, Reynolds characterizes the attachment to various key political symbols with a "thermometer index" (see table 3). The thermometer records how "warmly" the person felt about a short list of key political symbols. Of course, each person described political reality as he perceived it.

I would venture to assert that between the time these data were collected (1974) and the present, there has been some limited increase among high school students in attachment to the symbols of government and even a strengthening of patriotic sentiments. Interesting is their separation of the "current government" (the political party in power) and the underlying political system (the Constitution and the United States). As expected, the "thermometer reading" on "current government" was very low, reflecting the aftermath of Vietnam and the events of Watergate, for those students who defined citizenship in terms of active participation and personal characteristics. Only in the allegiant-compliant category was there a statistically significant and positive feeling for the "current government." By contrast, the Constitution and the United States got a warm but by no means overwhelming measure of support. The highest reading came in the positive sentiment expressed for "the flag" by the allegiant-compliant group (gamma .53). For me, these data indicate the long road to be traveled in civic education, but, because they supply a benchmark for the

TABLE 3. Symbolic Correlates of Perspectives of the "Good Citizen"

	Active Participation	Allegiant-Compliant	Personal Character
Correlate			
Political Trust	.26*	.28*	.10
Thermometers (feeling, tone)			
Current Government	.06	.27*	.07
Constitution	.26*	.28*	.14*
The United States	.17*	.48*	.16*
The Flag	.11	.53*	.20*

* Relationship statistically significant at .05 level.

immediate post-Vietnam period, they highlight the strength of human assets and indicate potentials for developing political maturity.

Exposing the "Hidden Curriculum"

Various explanations are offered by education experts to account for the limited effectiveness of academic programs. Each contains an element of plausibility. Family influences, particularly those that are in opposition to the goals of the school, have been stressed. Such explanations serve to relieve the classroom teacher of his or her responsibility for ineffective performance. But direct observation of the day-to-day social life of the "modal" classroom indicates that effective teachers can make a crucial contribution to the educational achievement of students regardless of the family background.

As a result, explanations have broadened from the personal and family characteristics of students to an overview of the organization of the class-room and local school. In this view, effective teaching rests on the efforts of teachers and support staff. The organization of the school emerges as crucial. Of particular importance in recent years has been the idea of the "hidden curriculum." The hidden curriculum is the actual organization and operation of the school system—and its classrooms. The explanation of the weakness of performance, especially in civic education, is the result of day-to-day power relations which prevent the school from transmitting democratic values essential for a meaningful civic education. Again, this is an explanation which relieves the classroom teacher for his or her per-formance. How can the culture of the American school—especially of the high school—contribute to democratic education when the school enforces constraint, hierarchy, and inequality?[30]

The writings of John Dewey are still used to support the hidden cur-riculum argument. In summary, the argument is that students cannot learn democracy in school because the school is not a democratic insti-tution. However, John Dewey would suffer if he had to listen to this version of his teaching philosophy. This is not to deny that the school—the high school in particular—except for a limited number with dedicated faculty, rests on a stultifying curriculum.[31] In any case, arguments offered in opposition to the hidden curriculum argument are numerous; the es-sential point is that the classroom is not the real world but a life space to prepare the student for the real world. It is certainly not a political arena

30. For analysis of the logic of this point of view, see Richard M. Merelman, "Democratic Politics and Culture of American Education," *American Political Science Review* 74 (October 1980): 319–31.
31. Philip Jackson, *Life in Classrooms* (New York: Holt, Rinehart and Winston, 1968).

or a locus for partisan politics. To the contrary, an important aspect of the teaching of skills and values required for a democratic citizen to be effective must take place in a specialized and protected environment of mutual respect between teacher and pupil, with humane rules for interpersonal relations. The classroom and school for the instruction of civic education is not an equalitarian "social system." Instead, it requires its own hierarchical structure—one appropriate for its goals. There are important carryovers from the civics classroom to the real world of politics. But the school most certainly is not a partisan political organ. The extensive writings of John Dewey and his disciples should have clarified the distinction in a democratic polity between education for civic and political participation and the actuality of citizen participation in the political process.[32]

Of course, the high school and college create specialized opportunities for interested students to have direct experiences in the political process of the local community and larger society. Below, I shall assess the very limited research on such institutional mechanisms. But at this point, I am concerned with the capacity of the present-day school—high school or college—to increase student understanding of the meaning of past political achievements of U.S. society. Clearly, this is a difficult task which requires considerable teaching skill. It also involves the risk and likely reality of open controversy between students and between the school and segments of parents. Past achievements and difficulties cannot be probed without reference to current dilemmas.

In general, it is not the hidden curriculum in my judgment which stands in the way of effective civic instruction, although there may be specific cases in which it does. To blame the hidden curriculum is a retreat from professional responsibility. To the contrary, the widespread demoralization of teachers, especially at the high school level, and their limited instructional skill largely explain the ineffectiveness of programs of contemporary civic education. No doubt, materials developed under the influence of the behavioral format, as I have described them, contribute to the limited level of performance. But only if teachers display energy and commitment can instruction be effective. There are profound barriers to such performance.

First, working conditions of high school and college teachers vary widely throughout the United States. A significant portion are employed in settings highly desirable and satisfactory, mainly in middle-class and "solid" working-class communities. In inner-city schools, however, pursuit of a curriculum in the social studies and civic education is exceedingly difficult—in some areas almost impossible. But whether in the suburbs or the

32. John Dewey, *Democracy and Education* (New York: Macmillan, 1916), p. 115.

inner city, teachers have been dissatisfied with their compensation and working conditions since the onset of stagflation. Student bodies receive an important form of civic education as they observe the overwhelming concern about pay among teachers, and as they experience the agitations and strikes to increase their pay. Such agitations, regardless of their goals, limit the effectiveness of high school teachers to pursue an attractive program of citizen education.

Second, there has been a long-term decline in the mental caliber, prestige, and authority of the high school teacher. In the 1920s and 1930s, public school teachers were highly esteemed and at the peak of their effectiveness. Continued expansion of the high school system, in my judgment, led to the decline. Many who would have been employed in the secondary schools became faculty members in post–World War II expanded community colleges and universities. Even the caliber of most of those recruited for colleges was generally ordinary, sometimes poor. By the 1960s and 1970s, the quality of the teaching profession in the United States could be characterized as mediocre, except at elite and near-elite high schools and colleges. Richard M. Merelman, in reviewing the available documentation, has stated this conclusion bluntly.[33] Equally unfortunate, it appears that social studies teachers—mainly responsible for civic education—are intellectually less qualified than teachers of other subjects.

Third, as a result of statutory provision, administrative regulation, and trade union agreements, it is almost impossible to remove incompetent teachers. Federal law resulted in the shift from sixty-five years of age to seventy as the age for retirement. This change served further to weaken teaching effectiveness. Declining student population and a surplus of teachers on the "payroll" in the first years of the 1980s served further to limit the recruitment of younger and more competent personnel. Prospects for raising the level of competence of the teaching profession, especially of social studies teachers, remain limited.

Fourth, I would place strong emphasis on the role of the mass media, especially television, in weakening effective civic education. Television viewing is extensive among high school and even college students. Classroom teachers must compete with television heroes, knowing they must lose out. As a medium of instruction, television can bring students into direct contact with events of historic importance, past and present. Sustained efforts to use television for civic education have achieved limited results, often negated by the massive dosage of popular culture supplied by television. Television has emerged as the media to be trusted by the younger generation. Of great importance is the role of media commentators

33. Merelman, "Democratic Politics and the Culture of American Education," pp. 328–29.

in defining in a subtle fashion who are the public persons worthy of condemnation.

If there is a hidden curriculum in the school system, it is the outlook of teachers of social studies and civics. The morale and perspective of these teachers is more important than the formal curriculum. At the high school level, the intrusion of professors of social sciences into the management of civic education has hardly, in the post–Vietnam period, served to improve the performance of regular teachers. To the contrary, their involvement has increased the sense of frustration and resentment of secondary school teachers, who come to believe they are as qualified as college professors but have been deprived of a more rewarding career only by their social background and circumstances, not by intellectual limitations. At the college level, many teachers of social sciences have parallel feelings. They believe they should be employed at more prestigious institutions. Joseph Schumpeter and others who have studied the history of social sciences stress the opposition of most social science teachers to the existing political system.

I have argued that narrow patriotism and ethnic acculturation formed the basis of civic education until the Great Depression. One decade after the end of the Vietnam intervention, I find that the dominant theme of civic education is the development in students of a "critical" outlook. It is not an inculcation of a set of values but, rather, an effort to make each student realistic about the facts of "political life."

A keen observer of inner-city educational institutions has offered the following summary statement about contemporary civic education:

> It seems to me that today there is an enormous emphasis on getting students to develop a critical view of this country: its values, activities, and leaders. Students are encouraged to question "myths." The ideal pedagogue is the one who "provides students with problem solving tools," that is, with the ability to look critically at a situation or assertion and imagine alternatives. This approach is supposed to prepare people for citizenship, by which we seem to mean understanding and actively participating in local and national affairs . . . In my view, the problems with the approach to citizenship education include: teachers themselves often fail to model a commitment beyond their financial well-being. Patriotism is unfashionable and receives little expression. Students' civic education suffers partially because of having few real responsibilities outside of school. There is no ethic of self-denial or encouragement to make a commitment to larger groups—community or country. There is an emphasis on the value of ethnic

pluralism, but no balancing emphasis on patriotism or
nationalism. Outside the schools, the media do little
that reenforces a commitment to the state. Boys Clubs,
4H and such groups retain an older form of citizenship
training, but they do not reach those young people
who are most disaffected.[34]

There is widespread commentary in the mass media that, after an era
of student unrest, the younger generation has moved toward conservatism.
I find no basis for such commentary. Benefits of the welfare state are
widely accepted, although there is debate about the magnitude, content,
and distribution of these benefits. At best we can speak of a middle-of-
the-road orientation among students. Rather than conservative, these students are better described as fiercely career-oriented and self-concerned.

Despite widespread frustration, some teachers have continued to perform with distinction. Some, in the Vietnam period, felt themselves in
opposition to dominant themes being stressed. Both older teachers, trained
in a more humanistic academic environment, and a few younger teachers,
not involved in the bitterness of the Vietnam period, raised the level of
performance.

Effective teachers of social studies at the high school level believed that
they had responsibility to stimulate extracurricular activities. Such activities in the years of student agitation and the new communalism ran the
risk of becoming disruptive focal points but, if properly managed, were
devices of civic education. There is no need to exaggerate the number of
the students who could be induced to participate; nor is there reason to
believe that unrealistic grants of "student power" were required to make
extracurricular activities beneficial for the student body. The demise of
the "student rights" movement of the 1960 decade and early 1970s was
not quickly forgotten. The task of the civic education teacher was to create
realistic opportunities for participation in the adjoining community and
in the wider arena of public and political affairs. Alert teachers, especially
at the college level, recognized that they were not seeking to displace
nascent social movements or partisan politics; rather, they were working
to extend the setting in which young men and women were learning about
the "real world" in a relatively orderly and reflective fashion.

We have one well-designed and tough-minded study of the consequences
of extracurricular activities. Michael Hanks and Bruce K. Eckland studied
a national sample of high school adolescents in 1955 and again in 1970,
at about age thirty.[35] Their data show that, independent of social origin,

34. Personal correspondence from Peter Kleinbard, 30 September 1981.
35. Michael Hanks and Bruce K. Eckland, "Adult Voluntary Associations and
Adolescent Socialization," *Sociological Quarterly* 4 (Summer 1978): 480–90.

ability, and academic performance, participation in extracurricular school activities had a strong effect on participation in adult voluntary associations. In turn, membership in adult voluntary associations increased voting behavior and decreased political alienation. In short, the potential of school socialization in generating a sense of citizen obligation is demonstrated. These data indicate that the school, in the mid-1950s, helped to fashion political orientations and civic participation. One can argue that the ability of the high school to stimulate meaningful extracurricular activity has declined since the 1950s. The unanswered question is the extent to which such activities by the high school can be expanded.

In exploring the research literature on the consequences of civic education, I was struck by a widely held, almost universal assumption, permeating formal programs of instruction which were explicit about their objectives. The assumption was that students must first learn basic academic skills—especially reading and writing. Once they learn these skills, they are prepared to take part in formal and informal efforts at civic education. The better they are prepared academically, the more successful the program is likely to be.

But the more I read, the more I questioned whether this academic priority was the best or the only appropriate sequence for the student and for society. Superficially, it seemed plausible, but did not appear adequately flexible. The reverse approach made better sense to me, under particular circumstances: to develop civic attitudes and a sense of group affiliation, which would stimulate the mastery of conventional academic skills.[36] I believe this proposition has real explanatory relevance and important practical implications. Inadequate academic achievement is linked to a lack of group identity and group spirit.

Although systematic data are wanting on these issues, I was impressed with the range of materials that supported my view that community and national sentiments and attachments are independent variables in the educational progress of individual students. Strong group affiliations, though not a prerequisite for academic progress, certainly stimulate it. This assertion is true of the whole social structure.

The relation of group cohesion to educational progress, including civic education, can be documented in a wide range of settings. Self-esteem, which is a function of group cohesion, is a powerful motivational element. Self-esteem is enhanced when students are first given tasks they can ex-

36. There is an interesting body of literature on the emergence of political attitudes among primary grade students. See for example, Fred I. Greenstein, *Children and Politics* (New Haven: Yale University Press, 1965); David Easton and Jack Dennis, *Children in the Political System: Origins of Political Legitimacy* (New York: McGraw-Hill, 1979); and Robert D. Hess and Judith V. Torney, *The Development of Political Attitudes in Children* (Chicago: Aldine, 1967).

ecute without elaborate classroom instruction and requiring few or no academic skills. In other words, "Everyone can play a tuba in the high school band." I have also encountered various upward bound and remedial programs which attempted to create self-esteem on the basis of territoriality as a precondition for effective academic instruction. Such an approach is relevant both for culturally deprived inner-city youngsters and for the sons and daughters of well-established suburban families.

Youngsters need group experiences that rapidly contribute to self-esteem. The illiterate or near-illiterate who enters the Israeli army is not first sent to school. To the contrary, he is sent to a military unit, which represents the larger society. The potential soldier is given a task he can perform. Such tasks build group spirit. After he has handled such tasks successfully, he is sent to school.

I have been struck by the diversity of educational programs using group affiliation strategies. One must recognize that communal movements of blacks and other minority groups have sought to implement such strategies in their educational programs. Work, including real-work programs, can contribute to the self-esteem of those involved. I shall examine a range of efforts to enlarge young people's civic education by immersing them in a social setting that emphasizes work and service in the context of symbols of national (or community) identification.

Seven

National and Community Work as Civic Education

WORK/STUDY VERSUS NATIONAL SERVICE

What does it mean to assert that work, properly organized and appropriately defined, can serve as a powerful agency of civic education, especially for young people? In one sense this idea is very simple. Effective education, formal and informal, for each succeeding cohort of young people involves mastering the skills and techniques required for occupational and professional employment. Education also involves understanding the social and moral content of work. Socialization into adult life implies the internalization of values that stress satisfactions deriving from an orderly career. Although people work for economic reasons, their work can also produce individual and group satisfaction. In an advanced industrial society, many occupational tasks, because of drudgery or sheer dullness, yield little satisfaction. Available evidence supports the conclusion that, in general, the better educated a person is, the more likely he or she is to derive positive stimulation from work.

Many types of work, however, even if not intrinsically exciting, may increase an individual's education. Work pursued on behalf of the community or nation is a form of civic education. Economic pursuit per se and the marginal advantages of more efficient and productive work increase the individual's income. But for the bulk of the population, economic satisfaction is insufficient as a basis for a satisfactory life style.

A broad formulation of education by means of community and national service was first offered before World War I by William James in his influential polemic *The Moral Equivalent of War*.[1] The power of his classic statement does not mean that he was never naive, utopian, and without

1. William James, *The Moral Equivalent of War*, International Conciliation, No. 27 (New York: Carnegie Endowment for International Peace, 1910).

sufficient concern with organizational details. But he did prepare a statement which has stimulated continuing efforts at reformulation along more practical lines.

William James proposed a form of universal service in order to create "civic discipline." The type of work to be performed would sample the tasks a modern society had to perform. Out of this broad perspective James gradually offered more concrete goals. These emphasized tasks we would label "human services." In seeking to spell out realistically the tasks to be performed, present-day thinking is still deeply influenced by the ideas of William James.

James believed that young men, especially the better-situated sons of the rich, should engage in real labor as part of their education. Such labor, he believed, would develop a sense of cohesion in a modern society. National service was to be a counterbalance to excessive "self-seeking." No doubt, James thought he was promoting altruism. Labor, with its resulting sense of solidarity, was to substitute for war and the solidarity that warlike tasks created. Details of his plan were of less concern than the underlying principle of using work as a technique for developing the moral consciousness of a society. James accorded immense importance to work in the development of civic responsibility.

With the growth of large-scale industrialism, however, the mass educational system at all levels has demonstrated limits in its capacity to develop and implant moral values. In part, this is the result of the separation of the classroom from work experience. Over the last century, the public education system has increased its emphasis on academic subjects and increased the years for required schooling. By the 1960s, with the separation between work and educational experience almost complete, work experience was no longer an integral aspect of moral and civic education. It became necessary for educational administrators to establish special programs to link the educational experience to an ongoing work experience. The absence of such linkage resulted in withdrawal and boredom or, even more dangerous, outright hostility toward education. Work/study and specialized work programs were developed as devices for improving skills, but also for stimulating motivation for successful entrance into the social world of work.

The quality and effectiveness of work/study programs are likely to increase. But such work experiences seek to attach an individual to a specific occupational setting in the existing social structure. National or community work, on the other hand, is designed to affiliate the individual into the larger social structure—to help make citizens out of students. The goal is less individual enhancement than the protection and well-being of the collectivity.

171

National work, as a form of citizen education, can be thought of as a social movement. As the individual participates successfully, his self-conceptions and values change; he feels himself more a member of the larger collectivity. An important element, not necessarily essential, is the temporary separation from family and local neighborhood to develop a sense of the larger society. The separation can be for a regular part of the work week or for a sustained period.

The consequences of national work, including community work, cannot be measured in terms of economic payoffs. There is little point in seeking to determine whether public or private property is enriched by such work. It is the collectivity that ultimately benefits. The property owner, the government official, or even the young men or women who participate may gain. But it is the various social groupings, including the nation-state, with which the participant is affiliated that ultimately benefit.

We live in a world in which effective literacy is a personal and national requirement. Therefore, the idea of work/study and national work as agencies of education are defined as particularly important for persons coming from deprived family backgrounds. But citizenship education by means of national or community work is especially applicable to students from the middle class, where civic responsibility seldom matches one's privileged position.

Explicit organization is required if there is to be extensive participation, whether the tasks be conservation, protection of the environment, assistance in the control of natural and manmade disasters, or involvement in educational and social work programs. Moreover, community and national work, since the time of Alexis de Tocqueville, has become more and more subject to the intrusion of "government." There are clear limits to this trend if the underlying goal of citizen education is to be achieved.

THE CIVILIAN CONSERVATION CORPS AS A SOCIAL-POLITICAL MOVEMENT

The Civilian Conservation Corps (CCC) makes an excellent point of departure for analyzing community and national work as forms of civic education. The CCC offers rich case material and systematic institutional analyses. In particular, there is Michael W. Sherraden's penetrating study "The Civilian Conservation Corps: Effectiveness of the Camps."[2] Sherraden has also undertaken a quantitative study of factors involved in accounting for varying organizational effectiveness of individual camps.

As a social demonstration, and a massive one, the CCC has a strong record of achievement; it is generally viewed as a success. Also impressive

2. Michael W. Sherraden, "The Civilian Conservation Corps: Effectiveness of the Camps," unpublished Ph.D. dissertation, University of Michigan, 1979.

was public respect for the program and satisfaction reported by the bulk of participants. As a result, both the reality and the symbolism of the CCC continue to stimulate efforts to adapt the original format to a more highly urbanized and industrialized nation. It is no exaggeration to say that the CCC continues to be a source of inspiration to political leaders and professionals concerned with defects of contemporary society, especially the inability of the welfare state to solve its "youth problem."

While there continue to be community and nationally based youth employment and job training programs of discernible success, the esprit de corps that the CCC created has yet to be replicated. Despite extensive literature on the CCC, the organizational climate it created is imperfectly understood.

The CCC was an instrument of the New Deal, organized as an outdoor program for young jobless men. Franklin Delano Roosevelt, as governor of New York, had created a similar conservation/work relief program. The U.S. Forest Service and the National Park Service were essential ingredients in the CCC and helped to transmit a "sense of purpose" to participants. Relief is designed to prevent starvation or extreme misery, so that broad "success" by relief projects is hardly conspicuous. However, to call the CCC an outdoor work relief project fails to describe its operations and effective achievements. While serving the needs of its clientele, the CCC evolved into an institution with its own collective "spirit." Its participants did not feel degraded but saw themselves as members of a group with worthwhile goals, which served themselves and the nation at the same time. Its conservation motif was crucial. President Roosevelt was personally interested in the CCC and his support was of great help.

The CCC evolved as a sociopolitical movement. Most participants were not obsessed with the idea that they were on outdoor work relief but felt engaged in an enterprise of practical and moral worth. They developed a collective consciousness—not to be exaggerated, but one that was realistic. What they were doing was not an egotistical act, although it supplied them with the basic necessities of life. They acquired simple work skills and, in a small minority of cases, more complex ones as well. They also learned habits appropriate for success in holding a job. They did not believe that they were building up equities for private profit or for particular public institutions. They were using their work efforts to conserve and improve resources for recipients yet to be designated.

Although the camps had their share of cynics and malcontents, the rank-and-file CCC participant felt that he was doing something worthwhile not only for himself but for "the country." If President Roosevelt originally saw the activity as a relief program, he was able to articulate and stimulate broader, and pragmatic, national goals. Work in these CCC camps was a

173

form of civic education because it joined together rights and obligations. The participants believed they were exercising their rights when they were given a job in a period of unemployment. In turn, they had an obligation to perform in the task of conservation of resources. The type of organization created was a loose, hierarchical agency. Although individual camp directors were military officers, it would be in error to describe the CCC as paramilitary. The top management was thoroughly civilian. The flexibility of the organization was strikingly successful. Part of its success may be the fact that it was terminated after a decade. Longevity might well have led to rigidity and a downgrading of the broad collective goals of the enterprise for a concentration on specific skills and techniques.

The Civilian Conservation Corps (initially called Emergency Conservation Work) operated from April 1933 to June 1942. It employed a total of more than three million young adults. Approximately 10 percent of the participants were black, assigned to segregated camps. Special programs were created for American Indians, and separate camps were established for U.S. military service veterans. The agency was based upon cooperation between government agencies under a complex organization, which under normal circumstances, might not have succeeded. The Department of Labor was responsible for the selection of participants, while the Veterans Administration selected the quota of veterans, not to exceed 10 percent of the total. The War Department administered the operation of the camps while the work programs were directed mainly by the Department of Agriculture (U.S. Forest Service) and the Department of Interior (U.S. Park Service).

Over the nine-year period, an average of 1,500 camps were located in all parts of the nation, more commonly in the Western states. Camps were typically limited to 200 men and remained small and relatively personal. Camps were usually under the command of a captain or a first lieutenant in the regular or reserve army. The officer was in charge of camp operations and had a major role in the participants' welfare.

One gets a flavor of life when it is recalled that in a CCC camp, personnel worked five days a week, eight hours a day, and received pay of $30 a month, of which $25 was usually sent home to the participant's family. Sherraden describes the average enrollee as being twenty years of age, Caucasian, equally likely to come from an urban or rural background, and never before having had a regular full-time job. Corps members were broadly "working-class," which meant some social mixture. The immediate motivation for joining was to help one's family financially. There was a mixture of intelligence and school achievement levels. The young man was likely to have an eighth grade education; at that time, only a minority of the population graduated from high school.[3] The average enrollee stayed in the corps for ten months. Interestingly enough, the average black participant stayed longer, fifteen months. Intelligence levels were nearly that of normal distribution.[4]

The range of conservation and construction programs was impressive. Given the low rate of pay, the accomplishments were worth many times the original cost. Such arguments were frequently used to support the CCC, but they missed the real meaning to participants and the public, who believed that conservation and development of resources were worthwhile goals per se. Even more important in terms of image building was recognition that the CCC contributed significantly to the participants' health, work habits, and self-esteem.

It should be stressed that the CCC did not make an impressive record in the two objectives of education and training. President Roosevelt and Robert Fechner, a prominent labor leader who served as director of the CCC, did not see classroom instruction as a central goal. No doubt, assembling an effective educational staff would have been difficult, if not impossible, and costly. It also would have made the CCC an organization with multiple goals and with resulting tensions and ambiguities. The CCC had a work task to perform, and in pursuing this task it was able to mobilize and strengthen commitments to work. Herein lies the essential lesson of the CCC: meaningful work on behalf of the needs of the larger collectivity was the basis of success and the means of reinforcing the social and moral meaning of work. As a result, the CCC enjoyed large-scale public support during its nine years of history, and was endorsed by both political parties in Congress. The annual cost per participant reported by Sherraden was approximately $1,000 per year, higher than the $800 per capita cost of the Works Project Administration and of the $400–700 per capita cost of National Youth Administration. In the early and middle years of its nine years of history, there were five applicants for every vacancy. At the height, one of every twenty male youths in the nation who turned seventeen years of age entered the CCC—a considerable national level of participation.

The program was not without its problems. One is struck by efforts to deal with these problems by giving the officer in charge of each site a considerable degree of discretion. The army did engage in some irregular inspections, but the primary inspection system was lodged in the CCC director's office and was nonmilitary. Primary authority for regulating the

3. One study revealed that 66.7 percent had completed primary school and 9.8 percent were high school graduates. W. F. Persons, "Selecting 1,800,000 Young Men for the C.C.C.," *Monthly Labor Review* 46 (April 1938): 846–51.
4. Kenneth Holland, "Conserving Human Resources," *Survey* 71 (March 1935): 81.

camps was clearly civilian. Contacts with the local communities often presented pressing problems. There were a few local advisory councils, the result of camp management or local community initiative. These local advisory councils were distinct from the Advisory Council in Washington, which had considerable influence.

Desertions and premature separations plagued the program; they were a concern to the administrators. Sherraden points out, however, that when one compares the early years of the Job Corps to the CCC in terms of desertions, the CCC rates were low.[5] On the basis of the mass of available documentation and records kept by the CCC, Sherraden was able to study participant satisfaction, camp productivity, and camp-community relations. In the case of participant satisfaction, many factors were involved, including camp leadership. But basically the participants responded well in terms of three factors: the adequacy of camp food, camp living conditions, and available outside employment opportunities.

Among its wide range of accomplishments, the CCC planted 2 billion trees, constructed 126,000 miles of minor roads, and put 40 million acres of farmland in condition to benefit from erosion control. The corps was organized with a strong emphasis on labor-intensive rather than capital-intensive activities. Yet Sherraden's study of CCC productivity demonstrates that camps made effective use of a limited supply of appropriate machinery (a capital-intensive measure). Camp machinery and equipment, in fact, was one of the two variables most closely related to camp productivity; the second was the camp distance from the work project. A second level of variables relating to productivity had to do with management of the camp, its age, and its location. New camps tended to be less productive, no doubt because of building costs and maintenance requirements in getting them organized. Location is an indicator of weather, a factor accounting for lost man-days. But the consequence of the "elements" is not to be overstated. It seems that lack of appropriate clothing was a more effective factor, but one which could be remedied.[6]

The effectiveness of camp-community relations could be and was improved by conscious efforts. The two variables Sherraden encountered as being most strongly associated with congenial camp-community relations were staff hired from the local area, and camp spending in the community. Often it took a few months for the economic dimensions to become visible, but, once they did, they obviously enhanced camp-community relations. Available research leads to no definite conclusions about the recruitment from the area versus from out of state on the question of camp-community relations. There is a good deal of impressionistic information, however,

5. Sherraden, "The Civilian Conservation Corps," p. 122.
6. Ibid., p. 221; also p. 295.

to imply that out-of-state recruitment had beneficial effects in giving the CCC worker a sense of the size and immense resources of the nation, thereby broadening his attachment to a more comprehensive or regional identification.

As opportunities for employment in civilian society increased, and as the United States began to prepare for World War II, the economic pressures supporting the CCC declined. The quality of the participants also declined, and dismissals increased.[7] But the program continued with reasonable effectiveness and continued public support until conclusion.

No doubt, the simplicity of goals, economic support for poor families through the labor of their sons, and effective contributions to conservation programs made possible much of the success of the CCC. But what is important is that it served, unanticipatedly, not merely as a relief program, but as a program which gave its participants meaningful citizen responsibilities and work obligations. It is striking that American society has not been able to adapt this experience effectively to contemporary needs.

The Failure to Update the CCC

During the rapid expansion of the "War against Poverty" in the early 1960s, strong emphasis was placed on youth work programs and skill training. A variety of professional and interest groups pressed for legislation which they believed would assist youth from extremely deprived backgrounds. If the original CCC legislation and its program were relatively simple, efforts generated by the War against Poverty were multifaceted and diffuse in the perception of the general public. Various pressure groups sought and got a stake in these youth programs. First, the administrators of the larger inner-city school systems were interested in work/study programs, which would offer financial assistance to hard-pressed families so that their children could complete their education. This was a relatively acceptable program to the mass of citizenry. Moreover, students under work/study programs would acquire work experience—"learn how to work" was the implicit slogan—and, where possible, pick up specific skills. The Neighborhood Youth Corps was authorized to conduct work/study programs. The work/study aspects of the Neighborhood Youth Corps were foreshadowed by the in-school component of National Youth Administration during the Great Depression. But these later programs did not have social and cultural elements. Second, vocational education specialists wanted to create job training centers outside the public school system which would teach basic reading and arithmetic skills and, in addition, specific skills which would make youth more employable. If

7. Alexander Lacy, *The Soil Soldiers* (Radnor, Penn.: Chilton, 1976), pp. 201–2.

possible, such programs would have a residential component. The approach was just the opposite of the CCC experience, where the emphasis was on participating in a work experience rather than on specific marketable skills. The "vocational education" approach led to the establishment of the Job Corps, which emerged as one agency which survived long after the apparatus of the War against Poverty was dismantled. In the Job Corps there was very little interest initially either in building self-esteem or in basic civic education.[8] Although the program became more aware of these issues, its goals remained "practical" compensatory education. It was an intensive remedial educational program with heavy emphasis on training in specific skills. Third, there was considerable support in Congress for an updated form of the conservation programs of the CCC. Some support came from conservation groups, but a great deal rested on the after-image of the success and popularity of the CCC experience. As a result, the original Job Corps legislation placed significant emphasis on "civilian conservation centers," but this segment of the program did not survive.

The original CCC format, essentially a resident work experience program, allowed participants to gain experience in "holding a job"; that is, in actually working. As far as possible, the skills the participant already had would be utilized. Training in specific skills and remedial education would be secondary. The assumption was that employers—industrial employers in particular—were more interested in work commitment than in specific skills which could be taught on the factory floor.

The residential centers in the 1960s, however, came to be thought of more and more as specific skill training centers. It is appropriate to compare the three types of programs—Neighborhood Youth Corps work/study, Job Corps skill training centers, and residential conservation centers—from the point of view of group values and as experiments in civic education.

Urban school boards, state governments, and federal agencies have in the United States a long tradition—especially lively since 1945—of assisting vocational education by offering training in new types of specific skills. Some programs involve long and intensive apprenticeships; entrance to such programs is often controlled and regulated by powerful trade unions. The more common work/study programs support the student financially and give him or her a taste of the "world of work."

The most extensive effort to enlarge work/study was embodied in the Neighborhood Youth Corps, authorized by Congress in 1964 and started in 1965 as part of the "War against Poverty." It was organized as a paid

8. See Harold Lewack, "Requiem for a Dream: The Job Corps on Trial," in Ira Godenberg, ed., *The Helping Professions in the World of Action* (Lexington, Mass.: Lexington Books, 1973).

work experience for low-income 14–21-year-old youth. The corps had two major objectives: to increase the employability of youths, and to reduce school dropout rates. There were in-school, out-of-school, and summer programs. (In 1970, under the name Neighborhood Youth Corps 2, it came to focus more heavily on employment preparation via skills training, supportive services, and remedial education.) Almost 138,000 youths participated in the first year. Peak enrollment in 1967 reached 556,000, then dropped to 500,000 for several years. *The Neighborhood Youth Corps: A Review of Research*, published by the U.S. Department of Labor, presents a sampling of research on the agency's programs.[9] As expected, the "better" the student, the more likely he or she was to benefit from these programs. Minority group females oriented toward clerical positions were most likely to obtain employment after a work/study experience.

The 1964 Economic Opportunity Act, in addition to establishing the Neighborhood Youth Corps, authorized establishment of the Job Corps. The Job Corps had as its major goal improved employment prospects for severely disadvantaged youth. The participant population of the Job Corps was defined as 16–20 years old, requiring intensive remedial education in reading and arithmetic as well as vocational and skill training. Terms such as *support services* were used to deal with the interpersonal aspects of the program. Job Corps centers were not only designed to assist young people; they were viewed as demonstration centers to show how training for employment could best be achieved. The program was established with the specific intention of moving participants from their home environment to resident centers. Some Job Corps centers are of particular relevance for our analysis because of their intended parallel to the CCC, since they were originally established for natural resource conservation work.

The Job Corps, in its early years, had numerous problems and withstood much hostile publicity. Programs run by contract with business and industrial corporations did not live up to expectation. The objectives of the program were not always clear and the dropout rate was high. At the start, enrollment fluctuated. The program reached a peak of 42,000 participants in 1967, dropped to 21,000 in 1970, and remained at this level until 1978.

By 1977, performance had improved dramatically. Retention rates rose in good part because of more careful screening. The Job Corps learned to select applicants most likely to succeed—"the cream," so to speak. (The phrase *to cream* came to be used to describe the selection process by which "high risk" youth were avoided.) More important, the Job Corps worked

9. U.S. Department of Labor, Manpower Administration, *The Neighborhood Youth Corps: A Review of Research*, Manpower Research Monograph no. 13 (Washington, D.C.: U.S. Department of Labor, 1970), passim.

out cooperative arrangements with employers and unions which resulted in much improved placement services. Thus, for fiscal year 1977, the Job Corps national placement rate was close to 93 percent. This figure included those placed in jobs (64 percent), entering the military (6 percent), and returning to school (23 percent).[10] As a result, toward the end of the 1970s, Congress authorized doubling the size of the Job Corps. But retrenchment followed expansion in the recession years of the early 1980s.

Manpower experts have used the available documentary data and results of special studies to claim a relative effectiveness of the Job Corps program.[11] It has become fashionable to subject social experiments to "evaluation research" to assess their consequences. In commenting on early research findings, Sar A. Levitan and Benjamin H. Johnston, two of the strongest research-oriented supporters, point out that some of the noteworthy positive reports must be interpreted "in the light of some rather misleading bookkeeping."[12]

Because of a subsequent extensive research effort, we are no longer uninformed about the impact of the Job Corps. This research incorporates a longitudinal design following a sample of enrollees and a control group. It has been documented that former Job Corps enrollees make more money; are less likely to be unemployed; are less dependent on welfare assistance and other public transfers; are less often arrested on criminal charges; are more likely to receive a high school diploma; and are more likely to attend college than a comparable group of youngsters not enrolled in Job Corps. These positive impacts, translated into economic terms, represent an excess of program benefits over costs.[13]

On balance, my assessment is that there is a place for a Job Corps program based on residential skill training centers. Certain youngsters from deprived backgrounds respond favorably to the residential setting, which serves as an alternative for very difficult and frustrating home settings. However, from program reports and data collected it is clear that limitations of the Job Corps result from the studied neglect of participants'

10. Sherraden, "The Civilian Conservation Corps," p. 252.
11. Sar A. Levitan and Benjamin H. Johnston, *The Job Corps: A Social Experiment that Works* (Baltimore: Johns Hopkins University Press, 1975).
12. Levitan and Johnston, *The Job Corps*, p. 89.
13. "Findings from a comprehensive evaluation of the social benefits and costs of Job Corps suggest that public investment in Job Corps is economically efficient. Our benchmark estimate is that the value of benefits in fiscal year 1977 exceeded costs by almost $2,300 per corps member, or by approximately 45 percent. Furthermore, the program is found to be economically efficient under a wide range of alternative assumptions and estimates. Because more than 40,000 youths enrolled in Job Corps during fiscal year 1977, our benchmark estimate of the net social benefit for the entire program is approximately $90 million for that year." Mathematica Policy Research, Inc., *Evaluation of the Economic Impact of the Job Corps Program: Second Follow-Up Report* (Princeton, N.J.: Mathematica, 1980), pp. vi–vii.

social and cultural values and self-conceptions. The strategy was essentially to create some form of a "learning and placement machine." When issues of self-esteem and civic consciousness were dealt with, it was in terms of individual guidance rather than a group milieu.

One cannot operate a program such as the Job Corps on the assumption that the moral worth of the participant derives solely from his marketplace value—important as such measures are, especially among the socially deprived. The social deprivation of participants was to be compensated for by remedial programs, which implied at least some concern with strengthening not only their rights but their sense of civic obligation. Yet little interest was accorded these experiments from the point of view of civic education. During the first years, Job Corps centers were organized and reorganized in great haste, without sufficient administrative forethought. When an element of stability finally emerged, administrators were compelled to confront broader, more humanistic goals.

The length of training at a residential center in 1974, as reported by Levitan and Johnson, was 5.2 months, though even these figures may be inflated. "The median length of stay, for example, was only 3.1 months, with 27 percent of enrollees leaving within the first 30 days and 49 percent before three months were up. Only 36 percent remained longer than six months."[14] These periods (in contrast to the average ten-month experience of the CCC worker) were hardly enough to permit effective instruction or an enriching experience. The most frequently reported reason for leaving the Job Corps prematurely was "resignation" followed by AWOL or disciplinary charges.

The Job Corps centers gave high priority to intensified instruction in reading and arithmetic, as well as emphasizing "vocational skills." The experience with reading and mathematics was similar to that of inner-city school experimental programs, especially those which made use of tutors. Participants gained about 2.1 months in reading for each month of instruction, and 2.5 months of mathematic progress for each month of instruction. But whether the improvement endured is problematic, and there is no evidence that students increased their motivation to read either for self-advancement or for personal satisfaction. There is little reason to believe that their educational progress linked them more closely to the larger community to which they would return.

As the Job Corps improved its operation, systematic data was collected about the level of vocational skills developed and job placement. As we have seen, Job Corps placement nationally was 93 percent by 1977. The results were described as "encouraging," even though "placement" rate

14. Levitan and Johnston, *The Job Corps*, p. 87.

included one quarter who returned to school and some who went on to further training. It is important to note that only a relatively small proportion of Job Corps participants actually took jobs for which they were trained.[15] An important development was the linking of a few Job Corps programs to union-dominated apprenticeship programs. National political pressure apparently compensated for educational deficiencies in permitting greater access to certain employment.

As expected, the Job Corps initially included conservation work, reflecting the CCC. Many administrators, however, were unfamiliar with the CCC. Powerful group interests as well as important administrators in the War against Poverty believed that the model of the CCC, with its residential work camps, was not appropriate for the highly industrialized United States of the 1960s and 1970s. This is baffling, since the early performance of the conservation program clearly was as adequate as that of the vocational skill training centers. But opposition was persistent enough to force these residential centers to include educational and vocational training, which did not articulate well with the work-oriented strategy. In the end, the unique opportunity to reinstitute an updated version of the CCC was lost, at least temporarily. This failure has not been adequately investigated.

I have already spoken of the lack of thoughtful administration that characterized the organization and reorganization of various phases of the War against Poverty. These shifts were part of the effort to demonstrate rapid "results." Moreover, the second-generation CCC effort lacked the direct presidential oversight and public interest that assists any federal program. It was organized and administered with an overload of goals, especially "training" and "education" as opposed to the sharper focus of the CCC. Of equal if not greater importance was the difficulty of the Job Corps in obtaining effective, trained personnel to administer its residential centers. By contrast, the CCC could draw on a cadre of lieutenants and captains to direct its camps. These officers had some background appropriate for the task as well as a strong sense of loyalty to the success of the project. Another explanation is that the Job Corps center took the cream of the participants, while conservation centers got the least qualified.

Various programs of the Job Corps were directed by policy guidelines to recruit young people from exceedingly deprived social backgrounds. The unemployment rate among young high school dropouts, especially young blacks, was indeed high. Thus, among participants, the sense of

15. "Only one in seven corps members who enters a vocational training cluster ends up completing and being placed upon termination in a job in the same cluster." U.S. Department of Labor, *Assessments of the Job Corps Performance and Impact*, 2 vols. (Washington, D.C.: U.S. Government Printing Office, 1979), vol. 2, p. 2.

relative deprivation was greater than among CCC workers. Since there were large concentrations of blacks, many of whom had been touched by the social protest movements of the 1960s, they were much more oppositional in their outlook toward U.S. society than the typical participant of the CCC. Moreover, the Job Corps programs did not have the technical assistance which the CCC got from the Forest Service, the National Park Service, and other expert organizations.

From the standpoint of civic education, one can hypothesize that social heterogeneity enhances the effectiveness of enterprises such as the CCC, for it stimulates both informal and formal learning among the populations in the program. The selection criteria for the Job Corps programs produced more homogeneous participants.

The legislative origin of the Job Corps and especially the conservation element can be traced to the efforts of Senator Hubert H. Humphrey, who, in 1958, advanced a bill for a residential youth conservation corps. In 1959, the Senate passed an enabling act, but the bill was not acted on by the House of Representatives. Thus, it was not until the antipoverty legislation of President Lyndon B. Johnson was passed in 1964 that a Job Corps was authorized, to include (in its original form) 40 percent of participants in a residential conservation program. The bill that passed had no role for U.S. military personnel and thereby eliminated an important source of administrative assistance.

Despite a clear mandate from the U.S. Congress, the outdoor conservation work program encountered strong opposition from administrators of the Office of Economic Opportunity. The escalation of the Vietnam war reduced the budget of the Job Corps, especially the conservation element. These cuts resulted not in a smaller and more effective conservation program but in a disruptive struggle over which programs would be maintained and which eliminated. Females were dropped from the conservation program as early as 1965. (It remained for the all-volunteer U.S. military and not the Job Corps to open up female opportunity for training and employment in "unconventional" occupations; that is, manual or blue-collar jobs.) Moreover, when the Nixon administration reduced the budget for the Job Corps as part of its opposition to the projects of the War against Poverty, cuts in the conservation centers were disproportionate. In April 1969, fifty of the eighty-two conservation centers were scheduled to be closed. With the elimination of the superstructure of the Office of Economic Opportunity and the transfer of the Job Corps after 1973 to the Department of Labor, the conservation effort was further weakened. In due course, it was discontinued.

Levitan and Johnston have derided the conservation center idea as part "of a lingering American belief in the beneficial effects of the rugged outdoor life. Somehow it was hoped that the exposure to clean air and deep woods might help to cure the accumulated ills of childhoods spent in poverty and big city ghettos."[16] They point out, in fact, that the time spent on work at the expense of "education" resulted in charges that conservation centers were disguised labor camps. Such attitudes completely missed the rationale that a challenging work experience would be "educational" and would have civic educational elements as well.

The General Accounting Office and the Department of Labor singled out the conservation centers for attack, arguing that the participants were not being realistically prepared for employment. Yet the data indicate otherwise. For example, "in 1968 costs per man year were lower and average length of stay, reading and wage gains were greater for conservation center enrollees than for any other group."[17] Among other positive findings is the fact that, by 1974, "conservation centers led the starting average wage per hour for job placements."[18] Although these data should be taken with serious reservation, I estimate that the actual work experience was as good, if not better, than specially designed vocational instruction in assisting in the transition to adult life. Socially deprived young men and women, especially those from urban centers, have experienced defeat and failure in the "official" mass public school system, not once but repeatedly. They are in effect without a sense of citizenship. The defeat and failure has been precisely in the classroom setting. The conservation center has important advantages for such youth. It is a new setting in which they have not accumulated a record of failure. Without elaborate preparation, they can participate and succeed rapidly with a real sense of satisfaction. On such success more conventional classroom instruction can be built.

The failure of efforts of the War against Poverty to develop an effective youth conservation program based on residential centers did not extinguish Congress's interest in such institution building. The Neighborhood Youth Corps and vocational aspects of the Job Corps hardly satisfied the lingering attachment to the CCC. To the contrary, the enduring spirit of the CCC led to the establishment of the Youth Conservation Corps in 1970.

The Youth Conservation Corps began as a summer residential program with a major goal of contributing to conservation work in national forests and parks. It was also conceived of as offering gainful employment to teenagers and increased knowledge and appreciation of the natural environment. Following the format of the CCC, job training and placement were not seen as primary objectives. Sherraden describes the program as

16. Levitan and Johnston, *The Job Corps*, p. 39.
17. Ibid., pp. 41–42.
18. Ibid., p. 43.

popular and generally successful.[19] The program is limited but has public acceptance and is, in effect, institutionalized. Despite its goals of broad recruitment, it has been criticized for not having recruited sufficient urban, black, and economically disadvantaged youths. Participant satisfaction is reported high, and, in terms of amount of work, accomplishments are impressive.

The closest parallel to the original Civilian Conservation Corps is the Youth Employment and Demonstration Projects Act of 1977, which created, among other programs, Young Adult Conservation Corps (YACC). YACC, like the older CCC, has the twin goals of conservation work and providing jobs. Job training, education, and job placement per se are not emphasized in the program. It is a year-round program, partly residential, limited in numbers, and oriented toward the recruitment of disadvantaged youths. The program had some problems initially with recruitment of participants from the desired backgrounds and faced difficulties in obtaining sufficient funds to support residential living and transportation costs. However, it is reported that participants have responded well, and popular support seems likely.

HUMAN CONSERVATION AS NATIONAL SERVICE

The record of the CCC and the Job Corps supply the background for discussion of a comprehensive system of national service—obligatory or voluntary. The debate about national service has a long tradition, which has intensified since the ending of conscription.

From its early proposed formulations, national service was hardly seen as the domain of the "underclass." Nor were conservation programs envisaged. National service was thought of as a form of citizen work designed to develop civic discipline for a democratic society. The "toughness" of a society should not have to depend on preparation for war or war itself. Military service could find a substitute in universal work programs which would be broad in terms of those who participated and in jobs to be performed. National service in these original terms was designed to help various segments of society, especially the more privileged strata, learn about the realities of society and thereby develop civic consciousness.

In the 1930s, Mrs. Eleanor Roosevelt emerged as a spokesman for national service. In the years that followed, advocates of national service sought to make more precise the type of work which would be undertaken. Advocates spoke of the duality of national service: on one hand, improvement of the quality of life of an advanced industrial society, especially to make more effective the human services the welfare state was seeking to

19. Sherraden, "The Civilian Conservation Corps," p. 252.

achieve; on the other hand, growth and maturity of the participants in national service, who would gain a deeper understanding of the realities and problems of their society. From this perspective, national service was a device for development of personal maturity which would serve as a realistic form of civic education.

As the Vietnam war came to an end, spokesmen for national service were particularly concerned to present themselves as realistic about both the attainable goals and the resources required. Public leaders of national service and associated specialists drew up detailed plans and feasibility studies. Three such efforts are worth mention. First, the comprehensive University of Chicago conference on conscription held 4–7 December 1966 contained extensive materials on alternative forms of national service, including the linkages between national service and military manpower problems.[20] Second, in 1979, with the support of the Ford Foundation and other foundation groups, a review of basic issues and a set of alternative blueprints appeared under the title "Youth and the Needs of the Nation: Report of the Committee for the Study of National Service."[21] This effort was under the leadership of two educational administrators, Jacqueline Grennan Wexler and Harris Wofford. Third, the most comprehensive analysis of alternative approaches to national service was presented in a volume entitled, *National Service: Social, Economic and Military Impacts*, edited by Michael W. Sherraden and Donald J. Eberly.[22] The importance of this third work was its attempt to relate national service to the complex and difficult problems of manpower for an expanded all-volunteer military.

Before 1970, the idea of national service was embodied by the outdoor conservation work of the CCC; a limited range of small, urban, social-service experiments; and the Peace Corps. After the Vietnam war, national service became an elaborate plan with ambitious goals for an urbanized and industrialized society. Conservation work was defined to include ecological programs in urban metropolitan centers. The range of human service programs was extensive. It is understandable that emphasis was placed on the role of national service in dealing with deprived minority youth. As a result, plans for national service included conservation work and work training such as those organized by the Job Corps. The goal was to reduce the discontent of youth who had failed to make an effective transition from high school to regular employment. These frustrated youth

20. Sol Tax, ed., *The Draft: A Handbook of Facts and Alternatives* (Chicago: University of Chicago Press, 1967).
21. The Potomac Institute, *Youth and the Needs of the Nation: Report of the Committee for the Study of National Service* (Washington, D.C.: The Potomac Institute, 1979).
22. Michael W. Sherraden and Donald J. Eberly, eds., *National Service: Social, Economic and Military Impacts* (New York: Pergamon, 1982).

are largely black, but include other dispossessed minorities. Their anti-social behavior is relatively enduring and destructive. Elijah Anderson, the black sociologist, speaks of their participation in an "underground economy in which deviant and semicriminal social definitions come to be significant elements of group life."[23] Although no single program or approach will serve the needs of these unemployed minority groups, manpower specialists believe that residential outdoor programs serve as appropriate agencies for a portion of this youth group. Such programs also interest better-situated young men and would therefore not become centers for the socially deprived but would parallel the social mixing that took place in the military under the draft.

Plans for national service after the Vietnam period included human services. In our contemporary society, human services are primarily in the hands of professionals or careerists, who frequently became routinized and even superficial in their performance. The vigor and enthusiasm of young people who serve only for a short period should provide an important human asset, which cannot be purchased in the marketplace. Already in 1967 I started to list the types of work and organizations which would be compatible with such a conception of national service, for example, a police cadet corps, a national teacher corps, a national health corps, a peace corps, and an equivalent domestic VISTA (Volunteers in Service to America) corps, as well as various job training programs.[24] By 1979, the national conference on national service was able to offer a much more refined list which included: public safety, facilities for recreation, community health, schools, transportation for the handicapped, and work opportunities in environment, child care, waste treatment and recycling, cleanup and pest/insect control, home services for the elderly and ill, recreation programs, energy conservation, paraprofessional assistance in schools, and art and cultural activities.[25] The total number of jobs to be filled annually was listed as more than 1,400,000. I would add to this estimate at least another 100,000–200,000 openings for residential conservation camps in the model of the CCC. Emphasis was on jobs not currently being performed adequately, which could be filled by persons with low skills or limited training.

Contemporary advocates of national service were also concerned with the sons and daughters of socially better-situated families. For this group,

23. Elijah Anderson, "Some Observations of Black Employment," in *Youth Employment and Public Policy,* ed. Bernard E. Anderson and Isabel V. Sawhill (Englewood Cliffs, N.J.: Prentice-Hall, 1980), pp. 64–87.
24. Morris Janowitz, "The Logic of the National Service," in Tax, ed., *The Draft,* pp. 73–90.
25. The Potomac Institute, *Youth and the Needs of the Nation,* p. 92.

national service was hardly an antipoverty program. Specialists engaged in drawing up blueprints for national service could point to the growing tendency of college students to take a year off from the "grind" of college to have a set of experiences and opportunities for increased maturity which could not be offered by institutions of higher education.

It is difficult to estimate the interest among young people for posts in a voluntary national service. I speak of effective interest as opposed to answers in opinion surveys. Opinion surveys, I believe, give positions and attitudes that are inflated. Clearly, available voluntary posts at the beginning of the 1980s were inadequate to meet the demand. If we exclude part-time job training programs under federal sponsorship and limit ourselves to meaningful national service programs, only a tiny number of youth was involved. The Peace Corps has enrolled about 6,000, with 60 percent under the age of twenty-six. VISTA numbered 4,000, with 40 percent under the age of twenty-six. In addition, there was a National Teacher Corps of 200 and a National Health Service Corps of 700. Plans being developed for the Young Adult Conservation Corps anticipated 22,500 participants. William James's aspirations were not being implemented even on a token basis.

Actual numbers enrolled are hardly meaningful indicators of the interest of youth in such enterprises. These programs are conducted in a low key, with little publicity. No doubt there are more qualified applicants than actual recruits. The number of available positions in the Peace Corps is oversubscribed eight to ten times. On the other hand, the number with "realistic" interests should not be inferred from the findings of "rough and ready"—that is, superficial—public opinion polls. While surveys indicate considerable popular support for the idea of national service—one year, for example—it is my assessment that only a minority of eligible youth have attitudes in strong support, while the bulk are relatively indifferent. Of course, an important segment of the indifferent might be mobilized if demonstration projects were successfully executed. Over the last thirty years, I have informally interviewed hundreds of college students about their attitudes toward participation in national service. Those interviews have helped me assess contemporary youth attitudes.

Various public opinion polls indicate that adults, especially adults over fifty years of age, are strongly in support of national service. But they are not the persons who would be involved. Expressed levels of support depend on the wording of the question—whether respondents are being asked about one year, eighteen months, or even two years. The longer the period, the less the support. There is a clear element of negativism in certain groups toward compulsory inclusion of females. While older persons are strongly in support—in fact, up to 70 or 80 percent—attitudes of younger people are more balanced, with strong concentrations of young people in the "don't know" category.

The issue of voluntary versus obligatory service complicates the answers given. On the one hand, there are those whose support of national service is based on a voluntary decision to make the enterprise compatible with their conception of a democratic society. On the other hand, many support national service only if it is presented as obligatory—that is, based on equality of obligation.

The careful observer of the potential of national service needs to keep in mind that each year hundreds of thousands of college students become bored, restless, and unclear about their academic and personal goals, and take a year off school. Most of the time off is spent in routine work. Although these students often report that much of the time was spent in boring work, the experience sometimes had a good effect on their academic work, and sharpened their career goals. More and more students are taking such breaks, and only in part for economic reasons. These interruptions could be articulated into effective national service assignments.

It has been my experience that, while a minority—perhaps as many as 20 or 25 percent of college students—is attracted to the idea of national service, the bulk of the student body has profound reservations, regardless of the extent to which they offer appropriate verbal support. National service is certainly not limited to college-bound students, but they are very important if it is to be a success.

The barrier to national service is that most college students have the very attitudes William James sought to avoid—self-interest and narrow concern with their own careers. Only if reluctant participants think the experience would be good for their careers—for example, increase their maturity—is a more favorable outlook expressed. In short, the "monetarization" of careers is powerful, as is the struggle to perform effectively in the academic setting. The language of economics has penetrated the rhetoric and overt consciousness of the modal college student. Some even describe national service as a special form of conscription which represents a hidden and unjustified form of taxation. They speak the language of Milton Friedman. The thought that such a tax might be justified is frequently dismissed out of hand.

If we probe more deeply, we find that economic self-interest covers a different set of negative and hostile attitudes toward national service. An important segment of young men and women who would be eligible to serve believe that national service would be too authoritarian—too rigid, too formalized, and too much of an invasion of privacy. In particular, the large-scale character of national service would interfere with the personal search for pleasure. The spread of sexual freedom before marriage also reduces the attractiveness of enterprises such as military and national service. Young people often equate the pattern of life in the military with that which they expect to encounter in national service.

Thus, negative attitudes toward national service reflect the resistance of young people to large-scale organizations—to the inefficiencies and arbitrariness of such institutions, especially remote federal agencies, and to the mistrust that bureaucracies develop. Advocates of national service are well aware of this issue and have sought defensive strategies. If one examines literature prepared after 1975 on forms of national service, one finds the phrase *community service* given strong emphasis, and for two important reasons. First, it needs to be recognized that particular projects can be organized and monitored by private sector groups, in particular by not-for-profit organizations. Second, national service programs can be community oriented rather than organized on a national basis, and as a result can be of small scale and limited scope. Both dimensions are designed to overcome the resistance of young people to participation in massive projects.

Resistance is reinforced by the reluctance of many professionals and administrators who see national service—and various forms of community service—as a threat to their own organization's fiscal support and operating mandate. The development of national service would alter the organization of education, social welfare, and health service, as well as environment and conservation practices. Paradoxically, public school personnel are often highly reluctant to see experimental national service programs implemented, and college and university officials are often indifferent or even opposed. Change is generally resisted in agencies that would need to be articulated with national service. Trade union organizations, in particular sectors, are also resistant to involving personnel in national service schemes.

However, agitation for national service is persistent. The form most often pressed is voluntary national service to be introduced on a step-by-step basis. A handful of congressional leaders are strongly in favor. Others have favorable attitudes but are unwilling to express them openly.

In the post-Vietnam period, with the introduction of the all-volunteer force officially on 30 June 1973, the debate on national service was broadened to include military service. The all-volunteer military, hard-pressed to recruit adequate numbers and quality, has prompted markedly different policy positions on the issue of military and national service. A small but vocal group of national leaders believe in the need for a return to conscription, which would in effect be obligatory national service. They recommend a form of universal obligatory service, with the option of selecting either military or civilian service. Would such a system generate adequate military recruits?

A second approach is that of *voluntary* national service, again with the option of selecting military or civilian service. It would add volunteer civilian national service to the volunteer military recruiting system already in effect. Military manpower planners have been doubtful whether such an arrangement would assist the military, especially in the combat arms. These two alternatives are offered as fundamentally at variance, and compromise is not seen as very feasible. As a result, efforts to link national service to military manpower requirements have not served to increase the prospects of national service in any form. Rather, the debate over national service, like so many fundamental legislative issues, fails to highlight the areas of agreement.

In the next chapter I shall explore the convergence of obligatory and voluntary national service. I shall seek to explore national service as an aspect of citizenship, with the logistical and organizational issues in their proper setting.

Eight

Toward the Reconstruction of Patriotism

CIVIC CONSCIOUSNESS AND CITIZENSHIP

During the last two hundred years, the apparatus for civic education in the United States has grown into a complicated enterprise. But it has not become more effective or sensitive. To the contrary, the machinery of civic education as it expanded has produced less real consequences than earlier efforts.

From the American Revolution to the outbreak of World War II, the relative success of civic education in the United States resulted from two central efforts. First, a simple and rudimentary civic education was pursued in the schools. Second, the American armed forces followed to a considerable extent the pattern of the "citizen soldier" which came into being during the American Revolution. The United States is one of the very few nation-states where a revolution ultimately strengthened, rather than weakened, internal democracy. The citizen soldier concept helped both to win wars and to institutionalize democratic practices.

Until the outbreak of World War II, primary and secondary schools served as agencies of acculturation for immigrants. Although the constitution guaranteed separation of church and state, the impact of civic education rested in part on an uncomplicated religious ritual in the schools. The decline in religious orientation weakened the school system as a device for spreading a sense of nationalism. Civic education did not develop a model of the new American but, rather, generated cultural pluralism, which until the years of the Great Depression can be considered relatively successful. The growth of the media, especially television, became a powerful factor after 1945 in shaping images of citizenship.

After World War II, there was considerable discussion of the need for new forms of civic education. It was claimed that "real" life training in the form of political obligation was needed. To what extent and in what form could national service, or aspects of national service, assist the struggle for more effective civic education?

The school system and forms of military service contributed to a balance between individual rights and civic obligations. Civic education in the past implied that each ablebodied male had a series of military and non-military tasks to perform on behalf of the nation-state. It is for that reason that I stress the American Revolution as a form of civic education. In the conduct of that war, officers and enlisted personnel learned that sheer destruction of the "enemy" was less important than winning them over politically to the goals of the Revolution. They developed a strategy which stressed the need for restraining the use of military force. (Unfortunately, such a strategy did not dominate the Vietnam intervention.) The principle of civilian supremacy was established, together with a locally based national guard.

The relative balance between federal forces and local militia was beneficial to democratic forms of control of the military. Political pluralism was strengthened by the interplay of federal forces, which represented aspirations for a national state; on the other hand, pluralism was strengthened by the vitality of national guard units which represented local aspirations.

It is my observation that this dual system, even as it began to decline, continued to contribute to patriotism. Cross-national surveys show Americans very much more likely than citizens of other Western industrialized countries to report patriotic sentiments. Surveys conducted in the middle and later 1970s contain the question "What nation in the world do you have the most respect for?" ("None" was a possible response.) The percentages naming their own countries were: United States, 59; Canada, 35; United Kingdom, 33; France, 26; Italy, 15; and West Germany, 12 (*Public Opinion* 4 [June-July 1981]: 27).

Yet Americans are suspicious of insitutional programs of civic education, especially those with overtones of manipulation. Wide segments of the American people would like to see stronger patriotic sentiment and greater emphasis on civic obligation. But Americans are skeptical about the ability of present-day public schools and agencies to mold civic consciousness.

Military service still contributes to a sense of patriotism, but the meaning of patriotism has become less and less clear. The public is resistant to any form of civic education that gives the impression of partisanship. Nevertheless, in the period after 1945, the need for more civic education became apparent, although there is little agreement about the form, content, and locus of efforts to strengthen patriotic attachment. The Korean war increased demands by public leaders for increased efforts in civic education to strengthen patriotism. The Vietnam war produced renewed debate about the strengths and weaknesses of patriotism in the United States.

The result of my research effort has been to reinforce my belief that a simple-minded program of increasing civic education to reinforce patriotism is of little import. Old-fashioned, uncritical patriotism is not effective in the current interdependent world. The more relevant term *civic consciousness* implies the persistence of love or attachment to a country—a territorially based political system. Civic education becomes a pressing issue when we realize that immigration into the United States is and will continue to be immense. Most immigrants are non-English-speakers. Moreover, the processes of acculturation have become more complex. In particular, for the broad range of Spanish-speaking immigrants, there is a powerful attachment to the home country which operates against the acculturation of immigrants into the larger society.

Democratic states are not particularly effective in civic education. However, at the risk of being misunderstood, I assert that civic education and youth socialization are more important in a multiparty state than in a single-party state. Single-party states make greater use of coercion; they operate with low conceptions of the importance of persuasion.

Civic education means exposing students to central and political traditions of the nation, teaching essential knowledge about the organization and operation of modern governmental institutions, and fashioning the identification and moral sentiments required for performance as effective citizens. It is clear that civic education remains deeply intertwined with patriotism and nationalism. To teach "civics" without encouraging students to explore their sense of nationalism is to render the subject tepid.

Patriotism, as attachment and love of one's country, leads to various forms of belief and behavior. While patriotism can result in performance which enhances the moral worth of a nation-state, it can also be a narrow-minded xenophobia. Given the extensive interdependence of the world community, an "update" in the form and content of patriotism is required to contribute both to national goals and to a more orderly world. As we analyze patriotism we repeatedly encounter the question whether some form of national service can operate to strengthen democratic practices and attitudes. In my view, there can be no reconstruction of patriotism without a system of national service.

I have sought to use a sociopolitical definition of citizenship. The result has been to highlight the conclusion that by legislation and judicial action the difference between citizen and noncitizen has lessened. The inherent advantages of citizenship are either not obvious or increasingly limited in consequence. These advantages in a democratic polity require repeated emphasis. As a result, classroom instruction in citizenship has grown even more important and, with increasing communalism and bilingualism, even more difficult. Some educators hold that the minimum cultural unity for democratic citizen rule in the United States has been eroded and has lost its self-generated effectiveness. I reject that view if only because of the potentials of the existing education system.

Education in the United States, despite weaknesses, produces a youth population with a high level of achievement, especially among its very numerous college graduates. College- and professional-level education remains impressive, even if cultural achievements are not effectively translated into a sounder set of political practices.

Moreover, the system of post–high school education touches an immense number of students who attend junior and community colleges. This junior college population includes large numbers of minority members who come from families with limited academic backgrounds.[1] Economic goals are very important to these students. Whether the essential balance between cultural pluralism and minimum common understandings can be achieved in the United States depends as much on the civic education of community college students as on the regular college graduate.

But it is clear to me that classroom instruction as presently organized is incapable of teaching the meaning of political obligations associated with citizenship. Economic goals appear paramount. Political obligation, especially in recent years, appears to be heavily derivative. Such an observation is incomplete for the United States. A tradition of political obligation is carried on by participation in voluntary organizations, many of which include various economic groups. Since classroom teaching is insufficient for civic education, the interesting question is whether the particular educational experience of national service with real-life content will strengthen popular understanding of civic obligations. Various types of national service are offered as a way of "teaching" citizens to perform the tasks which are part of civic obligation. National service should operate to balance the pursuit of economic self-interest against collective civic obligation and thus should have long-term positive effects on the individual involved.

For more than thirty-five years, I have advocated various forms of national service in order to improve and clarify one's sense of civic obligation. The early years of the 1980s have seen an intensification of the debate over the positive and negative consequences of national service. Can we think of national service as an institution that has a concern with the nation as a whole? Or must we plan for a disparate set of specialized agencies? I face an unsolved dilemma. The closer I examine the problems that must

1. A considerable number of young men and women learned their "trade" at private vocational and trade schools. These schools are important institutions in the U.S. economic system, but they hardly offer any civic education.

be solved in order to organize a meaningful national service, the more complex those problems become. I have not abandoned the desirability of some form of national service. But I shall argue that the forms of national service are likely to be different from those currently recommended. We do not now know how to administer a system of national service, and learning to administer it by a series of experimental programs is likely to alter its scope and content.

National service includes a military element, but of necessity the military and civic components will be separate. Moreover, it is doubtful if various social and community elements could be extensively integrated. The outcome may be voluntary national service composed of decentralized units and diverse programs. Even the term *decentralized* remains too bureaucratic: we are probably headed for a series of localized agencies.[2]

THE MILITARY DIMENSIONS OF NATIONAL SERVICE

Young men and women who have enlisted in the all-volunteer army reveal strong patriotic motives as contributing to their decision to enlist. In data collected by military recruitment stations, patriotic reasons were given by 20 percent of new recruits as either the first or second reason for joining. Attitudes manifested in these data reflect a much higher patriotic orientation among enlisted personnel than reported by the mass media. In fact, among new recruits 80 percent included service to country as a reason for enlisting during the years 1971, 1977, 1979, and 1980. Other data demonstrate the stability of such attitudes. For the period 1974–1980, active duty personnel were asked whether "everyone should have to serve his or her country in some way." About 55 percent of career personnel agreed. In essence, self-selection into the military and the impact of military environment were at work. By contrast, first-termers revealed a discernible rejection of the proposition that everyone should have to serve his or her country in some way. This negativism gradually dropped from 27 to 7 percent. Clearly, without formal instruction or indoctrination, first-termers were internalizing values of the career armed forces. The character of patriotism expressed remains to be studied.

The social composition of ground combat arms and debate about performance of the all-volunteer military set the stage for proposals for linking active duty force to a contemporary military option within national service. Under a national service military option, the armed forces might be able, if properly organized, to recruit between 100,000 and 150,000 persons

2. There is an extensive body of writing on national service. For an overview see The Potomac Institute, *Youth and the Needs of the Nation*. See also, especially, Sherraden and Eberly, eds., *National Service*.

annually. The rest would be recruited by present procedures, improved as feasible. The military option is designed to increase the social representativeness of the armed forces and to increase the educational qualifications of recruits. One obvious goal is to include more white middle-class Americans in the enlisted ranks. It is a program designed to increase the outlet for patriotic motives and, in turn, to strengthen the civic education of new generations.

Let us examine a hypothetical set of proposals for the military option of national service. The term of service would be two years; national service personnel would be expected to have above average academic achievement qualifications. They would be responding to national goals and values as well as to economic incentives. They would not be assigned to specialized training programs but to run-of-the-mill assignments, especially those combat assignments that could be learned in a few weeks. A central element of such a program is that aside from nominal subsistence allocations and very limited cash payments, compensation would not come through monetary reward. Instead, educational benefits would be used. We would be dealing not with a mass GI education proposal but, rather, with a more limited program. Experimental programs of this variety have attracted superior personnel. For each year of military service, two years of college benefits (tuition plus a modest cost-of-living stipend, for a maximum of four years) would be offered. Such a program could solve the manpower needs of the second half of the 1980s. The cost would be equal to or less than the current cash bonus. The program would restore to the enlisted ranks important components of college-bound personnel, who would enrich educationally, technically, and morally the climate of units to which they were assigned. Their presence would be a contribution to restoring the effectiveness and self-esteem of military units. A unit composed of all or most recruits with limited educational background cannot have the morale and clarity of purpose of a unit with mixed educational achievement. Soldiers with heterogeneous backgrounds supply broader linkage between the military and larger society. I would even offer the observation that mixed educational units will have higher standards of morality and personal conduct.

THE FRONTIERS OF NATIONAL SERVICE

There is a sharp difference between national service organized to supply military personnel and one oriented to civilian tasks. This distinction will persist and become greater if national service develops in the United States.

197

There is no shortage of plans for organizing a civilian component of national service. The list of tasks to be performed continues to grow. While national service could, in theory, be either volunteer or obligatory, it is my view that obligatory national service in the years ahead is not feasible. The political support for an obligatory program does not now exist and is unlikely to develop in the next decade. Advocates of a comprehensive national service can aspire, over the short run, to the development of a series of experimental exercises. But in time, for example, a decade of effort could lead to a gradually growing number of participants that would involve at least half of the eligible youth—male and female.

Obligatory national service would mobilize a very small minority who are in blind opposition based on personal deviance or criminal-like personality. I would estimate that at least 5 percent of youth would fall into this category. Neither the armed forces nor the civilian component would want to act as a reformatory for delinquents. It does not take many deviants to wreck or severely strain a program. Administrative leaders would have to maintain a system of rules which would allow for easy withdrawal of those who had an oppositionist mentality. In fact, most current planning for national service is based on voluntary involvement. Milton Friedman's view that national service is a tax is widely accepted; the central issue is the size of the segment of society who are willing to pay the tax voluntarily.

Even limited experimental programs of national service with civilian options are difficult to organize. Advocates of voluntary national service are sensitive to the complex administrative and organizational tasks. Many proposals for national service envisage a national, central organization. This reflects, in part, the ideology of energetic leaders concerned with social integration.

In my view, organization on a state-by-state basis or even by metropolitan centers would simplify administration. Many plans have called for national service to be run by public, nonprofit national agencies. The effort is to separate the agency from the governmental structure. In fact, plans generally call for a national agency to direct the operation and a series of operating subagencies to oversee specific programs. I am not impressed with the potential of such decentralization efforts.

Plans for national service that point to a single agency to oversee specific operational programs are attempting to make up for existing institutional confusion. Such a direction does not excite me. Planners of national service are seeking to make up for defects in civilian society. I am more inclined toward a "loose" plan. To be effective, national service would have to be more of a youth movement than a youth organization. The youth movement would seek to fill in gaps and to be fluid in its approach and organizational structure.

A voluntary national service must develop a widely based strategy of recruitment. There has been considerable debate on this point. We are looking for a strong element of diversity in the youth groups recruited. At stake is the question, why are the work features of national service likely to produce more effective citizens? First, national service is committed to a heterogeneous population. The mixing and social interaction is designed to enhance the self-awareness of those who participate. Second, the work program of national service should increase awareness of socioeconomic realities. Third, and most important, cooperative endeavors should serve as forms of education that produce positive responses for a democratic society and lasting positive consequences for participants.

I am likely to be misunderstood when I emphasize that prospects for broad-scale national service opportunities are indeed limited and likely to remain so. The political support for a system of national service does not exist despite verbal support for particular programs. Private groups can organize equivalent programs, but they have failed to do so to any great extent.

My research leads me to the conclusion that national service can be defined as working at subsistence level after high school or later on one of the broad range of tasks such as conservation, health, or old age problems in order to participate in learning about the civic institutions of society. It is a device for teaching the student to balance rights against obligations. One cannot, of course, overlook the importance of prior classroom study in civic education. Because of routinized patterns of education one can afford to give a very broad content to national service. The goal is not the reinforcement of traditional patriotism but rather the development of an understanding of the tasks which must be performed in a democratic society.

We are a statistically minded nation; therefore, the suggestion has been made that we should tabulate annually the young people engaged in some form of national service. I am convinced that, even without governmental support, participation in some type of private national service is certain to grow year by year. Such an observation, however, fails to confront the central issue of developing a national service program—governmental or private sector—which will not be limited to the graduates of elite colleges but will include a broad pattern of participants. No national service system fills its objectives unless it includes all segments of the population.

Over the past fifty years, a variety of service programs open to young people have been created and abandoned, a process which reflects an unstable commitment to service opportunities. During the Great Depression, hundreds of thousands of young people participated each year in the programs of the Civilian Conservation Corps and the National Youth

Administration. No federal programs existed from World War II through the 1950s, though small, CCC-like programs were organized at the state level. In the modern era of youth service programs, the Peace Corps began in 1961 and VISTA in 1964. The 1970s brought the revival of the conservation corps idea in the Youth Conservation Corps (1970–83) and the Young Adult Conservation Corps (1978–82). Major demonstrations of national service in urban areas occurred in Seattle (1973–74) and in Syracuse (1978–80).

However, as of 1982, the nation witnessed the decline of several youth service programs and abolition of several others. Among those eliminated as part of budgetary restrictions and retrenchment were the National Teacher Corps, the Youth Conservation Corps, and the University Year of Action. Estimates for total numbers of participants in the remaining programs for 1983 are as follows: At the federal level, the Peace Corps numbers approximately 6,000, VISTA about 3,000, and the National Health Service Corps about 3,000. Of Peace Corps volunteers, about one-half are aged 18–24, the other half 25 and older. The size of VISTA remains uncertain. In 1982 it entered a phase-out schedule, although Congress has been resisting its elimination. Altogether, one could say that federally sponsored service opportunities for teenagers and young adults in 1983 are estimated at approximately 10,000 (estimates from National Service Secretariat, Washington, D.C.).

At the state level, the conservation corps idea has been taken up by several states—most notably California, with about 1,900 year-round participants in the California Conservation Corps in 1982. Much smaller programs in Ohio and Minnesota add 300 more slots. Part-year and part-time programs in Illinois, Iowa, Kansas, Maine, and other states might add an additional 1,000 positions, for a total of about 3,200 (estimates from Human Environment Center, Washington, D.C.). Other service programs may exist at the local government level, but these are few and far between and are not systematically tracked.

In addition, there are many purely voluntary efforts in which young people participate in health, education, recreation, social welfare, religious, political, and other volunteer work. In a nationwide survey of volunteer service in 1974, 22 percent of 14–17-year-olds and 18 percent of 18–24-year-olds were engaged in part-time volunteer work of one kind or another.[3]

3. Donald J. Eberly, in "Patterns of Volunteer Service by Young People: 1965 and 1974," *Volunteer Administration* 4 (Winter 1976): 20–27, cites data from surveys by the Census Bureau.

In plans developed or implemented in the United States, most recent national service programs involve adding one year to public school schooling. I prefer and am prepared to see the sixteen years required for a college degree gradually and selectively reduced to fifteen years. The "freedom" year would be devoted to some form of national service. Advance placement of high school students into college courses is an essential movement in this direction. The advantages of such a pattern would be immense; especially the financial saving in expenditures for education. I expect a gradual, long-term expansion in productivity of the U.S. economy. The current surplus of youthful labor will give way to increased shortage, especially of trained young workers. Given that shortage, the additional labor supply should in the decade ahead be of vital importance to the U.S. economy.

There is support for national service among both liberal and conservative political leaders. Various bills have been introduced, but the drive for either extensive programs or even small experimental ones does not command wide political support in part because of restraints on the U.S. federal budget.

Public opinion findings must be carefully assessed. An overwhelming majority of American parents want their children to receive civic education. Only a very small portion have specific ideas. Moreover, there is a revival of concern with a "sound" education program in selected local communities. A "sound" local school program means an attack on liberal trends and parental rejection of programs they believe excessively permissive. Such agitations receive extensive media coverage, but do not generate actual widespread parental participation. Nevertheless, it is striking that the bulk of U.S. parents—to judge by national surveys—support the idea that young people should give one year of national service. There is a view that a year of service would "be good" for their children. To some extent such a reply is fashionable; but the replies also represent patriotic feelings and the belief that national service will make their children more aware of their obligations as citizens.

The fundamental barrier to national service (including local programs of community service) is the attitude of American youth. Again, public opinion surveys need to be read with great care. In the abstract, there is considerable support among young people for the idea of national service; almost one-half of youth in the early 1980s expressed favorable attitudes and interest in serving. But many responses represented conventional expressions of what were considered appropriate attitudes. I do not doubt that there is considerable genuine desire among college students and selected young workers to demonstrate that they are "good citizens." I cannot make an effective estimate of the real support. Young people are caught in a bind generated by parents and the school system. They are attracted to the adventure and moral value of national service, but also feel obliged to get on with their careers. Many people believe—incorrectly in my view—that the economy will get worse. There is therefore considerable pressure to get on with education and the world of work. In addition, for some students, national service is no more than a possible alternative to service in the infantry and ground combat arms.

Nonetheless, there is clearly enough interest in, and need for, national service for a range of programs to be launched. Priority should be accorded to conservation work and to meeting the needs of neglected senior citizens. Programs for the elderly could be locally managed and organized, while resource conservation could be linked to national and state governmental agencies.

It is fortunate that the United States is not about to launch a large-scale national service program including both military and civilian options. Existing restraints mean that when programs are developed, they will be small and thus likely to develop slowly and adequately. We may be thus spared the typical American pattern of policy implementation which is one of shifting from extreme restraint to overexpansion. As the nation moves gradually to new forms of national service, the resultant programs could be organizationally sound.

Most important, the forms of national or community service must be seen not as welfare programs but as expressions of civic duty by those who actively participate. Those very conditions which can work to re-socialize poverty youth away from a dead-end existence depend upon national service not being defined as an employer of last resort, a definition that is hard to escape unless participation is relatively representative of all American youth. National service must be structured as part of a citizen's obligation.

One idea that has received lively discussion is to make federal aid to college students dependent on national service. This formulation, initially advanced by Charles C. Moskos,[4] has attracted the attention of several political leaders. Most government loan and scholarship programs have helped young people avoid military service through college deferments. In effect, we have created a GI bill without the GI. It is not politically possible to require *military* service as a condition for a government loan. But a program requiring some community service for particular forms of governmental assistance to attend college is feasible and will most likely be introduced as legislation. Although this format does not encompass what I believe are the worthiest elements of national service, it does make

4. See, for example, Charles Moskos, "Making the All-Volunteer Force Work: A National Service Approach," *Foreign Affairs* 60 (Fall 1981): 27–34.

sense today. It is fully compatible with the previously discussed program of education benefits in exchange for military service.

Linking government-guaranteed loans for higher education to service in the student's local community is a modified version of the old work/study idea. It involves national, political incentives as well as economic ones. The nation appears increasingly prepared to accept such a work/study program. As of 1982, more than six billion dollars annually are spent for student loans. A work/study program would add little to those expenditures. To the contrary, by making a loan dependent on community service, federal costs would be reduced by the value of the work completed.

The vitality of democratic citizenship cannot be maintained by the existing range of political forms, such as voting and political participation. Historically, citizenship and patriotism have included various forms of local self-help currently associated with the idea of community or national service. Participation in these activities gives the idea of obligation concrete meaning. The need to make use of this tradition has grown, ironically, with the growth of the welfare state. The first step to make is voluntary national service available to all young men and women. But there is no reason why voluntary national service should not ultimately involve older people too, as they retire from regular work.

Acknowledgments

I wish to acknowledge the generous support of the Spencer Foundation which made this study possible. Those who have worked with the Spencer Foundation, and especially its president, H. Thomas James, know that it is the near perfect foundation.

In the course of preparing this study, I had the opportunity to talk with and receive assistance from many, many persons. I could not possibly acknowledge the names of all these persons and the valuable help they extended to me. But I can thank them collectively for their contributions to this study.

I do wish to acknowledge those colleagues of mine who spent many hours in reading, commenting on, and criticizing the early drafts. In particular, I wish to mention Charles Bidwell, Edward O. Laumann, Edward Shils, Gerald Suttles, and William Julius Wilson. These colleagues, in effect, by their detailed efforts, transformed the manuscript and helped give it some boundaries, for the subject is indeed vast.

In addition, a number of colleagues reviewed the manuscript, concentrating on their areas of expertise. They included Bernard Barber, Donald J. Eberly, John Faris, Don Higginbotham, Ruth Horowitz, James Jacobs, Peter Kleinbard, Michael W. Sherraden, and Mayer Zald. Their critical comments were invaluable.

James Lewis did a great deal of searching and checking of references and citations. And I am particularly appreciative of the endless number of drafts that Bernice Johnson typed in the course of the preparation of the book.

Given the extensive scope of the subject, I could easily say that my goal was no more than to stimulate realistic research on citizenship and civic consciousness. But I believe that the basic issues are too important and too pressing to hide behind such a limited goal. I have sought to offer a sociopolitical conception of citizenship relevant to the central issue of "national service." National service is a public issue which must be debated and resolved one way or another in the next decade. The real danger is that the nation will not face the basic issues and instead will drift rather than act on the very difficult problems which need to be acted on and decided in one form or another.

Author Index

Abbott, Grace, 87
Abrahamsson, Bengt, 71n
Addams, Jane, 87, 90, 91, 141
Aiken, Wilford M., 104n
Anderson, Elijah, 187
Aristotle, 2, 4, 12, 30

Bachman, Jerald G., 71–72
Badillo, Gilbert, 61n, 127n
Bailyn, Bernard, 33n, 34–35
Barker, Ernest, 2n
Barnard, Henry, 83n
Beard, Charles, 95
Beard, Mary, 95
Bell, Derrick, 116n
Berelson, Bernard, 149n
Bettelheim, Bruno, 117–18
Biderman, Albert D., 61–62
Binkin, Martin, 66n
Blair, John D., 71–72
Bogart, Leo, 126n
Bracey, John H., 112n, 113n
Bridges, Claude, 71n
Brinkman, Carl, 151n
Broger, John C., 62
Browning, Harley L., 137n
Buehler, Marilyn H., 135n

Cabbone, Peter F., 101n
Callahan, Raymond, 93n

Callcott, George H., 83n, 84
Campbell, Angus, 149
Campbell, Donald T., 70n
Carter, Jimmy, 139
Clinton, Sir Henry, 38
Cremin, Lawrence A., 78n, 90n
Curry, G. David, 61n, 66n, 127n
Curti, Merle, 83

Dahrendorf, Ralf, 24
Dennis, Jack, 168n
DePauw, Linda Grant, 34, 36–37
Dewey, John, 87, 90, 100, 163–64

Easton, David, 151n, 168n
Eberly, Donald J., 186, 200n
Eckland, Bruce K., 167–68
Edwards, Lyford P., 107n
Elkins, Stanley, 33n
Epps, Edgar G., 118n

Fanon, Frantz, 119
Fechner, Robert, 175
Fitzgerald, Frances, 84n
Flacks, Richard, 65
Fligstein, Neil D., 60n
Follett, Mary, 91
Foner, Jack D., 124n
Forbes, Jack D., 129–30
Fox, David J., 118n

Analytic and Subject Index